MW00830477

THE BIDEN CRIME FAMILY

THE BIDEN CRIME FAMILY

THE BLUEPRINT FOR THEIR PROSECUTION

RUDY GIULIANI

Foreword by Stephen K. Bannon

Skyhorse Publishing

War Room Books may be purchased in bulk at special discounts for sales promotion, corporate gifts, fund-raising, or educational purposes. Special editions can also be created to specifications. For details, contact the Special Sales Department, Skyhorse Publishing, 307 West 36th Street, 11th Floor, New York, NY 10018 or info@skyhorsepublishing.com.

War Room Books® is a registered trademark of WarRoom, LLC.

Skyhorse Publishing® is a registered trademark of Skyhorse Publishing, Inc.®, a Delaware corporation.

Visit our website at www.skyhorsepublishing.com.
Please follow our publisher Tony Lyons on Instagram @tonylyonsisuncertain.

10 9 8 7 6 5 4 3 2 1

Library of Congress Cataloging-in-Publication Data is available on file.

Cover design by Brian Peterson
Cover photo by Getty Images

Hardcover ISBN: 978-1-64821-034-1
eBook ISBN: 978-1-64821-035-8

Printed in the United States of America

CONTENTS

FOREWORD BY
STEPHEN K. BANNON

It was the early 1980s, and five crime families ruled much of New York City services and goods. Names such as Bonanno, Columbo, Gambino, Genovese, and Lucchese, the so-called "Commission" controlled the construction industry, the garment industry, narcotics trafficking, the prostitution business, as well as many city services. If it was illegal, the mob had a piece of it. And with too many Democrat politicians controlling city government . . . the mob ruled.

Until Rudy Giuliani came along. As United States attorney in New York, Rudy indicted eleven organized crime figures under the RICO Act, the Racketeer Influenced and Corrupt Organizations Act. The famous "Mafia Commission Trial" last from February 1985 until November 1986. Eight of the mobsters were convicted, and most were sentenced to 100 years in prison in 1987. One other died of cancer during the trial and one was murdered.

It was later revealed that that Gambino family boss John Gotti backed a plan to kill prosecutor Rudy Giuliani, but the rest of the Commission objected. Too much heat.

Rudy ran for New York Mayor in 1993, and he won, holding office through December 2001. Any American alive on September 11, 2001, remembers the power of Rudy's historic leadership after the terrorist bombing of the World Trade Center in New York that day.

America's Mayor turns his prosecutorial expertise and insightful eye on Joe Biden and his entire family in this extraordinary book. He does so not just as a brilliant lawyer, but as a patriotic American citizen who is revolted by the corruption of President Joe Biden and his family. He details the fifty-plus years of influence peddling that has allowed the Biden family to trade access to Joe's position as US Senator, Vice President, and now President. He details income to the Bidens from Russian and Romanian oligarchs to the highest members of the Chinese Communist Party.

It will be clear to any American, after reading this book, that the Biden family . . . and even non-blood-related close allies—are a threat to the United States.

INTRODUCTION

RUDY GIULIANI, THE PROSECUTOR, THE MOB, AND HIS FIGHT AGAINST CORRUPTION

Much of this book was written before the summer of 2024 controversy about President Joseph Robinette Biden Jr.'s mental health and his fitness to serve as President of the United States. Now, as we sit here at the end of the most consequential election cycle in our lifetime—with Donald Trump and Kamala Harris battling it out to lead America's future—it's tempting to paint Joe Biden as irrelevant. That would be a mistake. He may be kicked to the curb by the Democrat party that he has served since 1973, but he is still POTUS and, nominally, the leader of the free world, until January 20, 2025. In that time, he still has the power to do a lot. How he uses it remains to be seen.

There's also the issue of Joe Biden's legacy. He should not be remembered as Nancy Pelosi—widely viewed as the Brutus who struck the final knife in his bid for a second presidential term[1]—characterized him, as "one of the most consequential Presidents in American history."[2] Rather, he should be remembered as the Godfather of the Biden Crime Family, and I'll argue that case in this book. Further, the corrupt system of influence peddling and crony capitalism that allowed the Bidens to conduct their fifty-year personal enrichment schemes under the noses of the public, other possibly complicit politicians, and a complacent media is still in place. Somebody needs to be held accountable for that.

But of all the misdeeds that the Biden Crime Family and their collaborators—including Harris, the vice president, who always wanted to be the "last person in the room"[3] on decisions—have committed in Joe's fifty years in office, the most egregious may be the cover-up of his mental and physical condition. To paraphrase Senator Howard Baker's (D-TN) famous question from the Watergate era, "What did the Bidens know and when did they know it?" Hunter Biden's so-called "Laptop from Hell," which I had a hand in exposing, holds the possible answer. When fully revealed, it may be the smoking gun that convicts the Biden Crime Family of their most atrocious offense yet. Before that, though, we've got five decades of wrongdoing to talk about.

So let's start with the obvious. Why the hell am I writing a book about the Biden Crime Family? I'm not a young man. I've had a fantastic life as a lawyer, was hailed as a hero by everyone for successfully prosecuting the Mafia in New York in 1985, sending eight brutal Mafia leaders to prison for hundreds of years. I took on the five Mafia families that controlled major industries in New York City, from trash collection to the enormous Fulton Fish Market, the Teamsters Union and Las Vegas. I served as Mayor of the greatest city on Earth, helping New York survive and endure a terrorist attack that killed nearly three thousand people on September 11, 2001. Twenty-three years on, more than five thousand have died from 9/11-related illnesses and over forty-five thousand have contracted cancer from the horrors inflicted that day.[4] A great actor—James Woods—portrayed me in a movie called *Rudy: The Rudy Giuliani Story*. And today, I am closest to people who love me unconditionally.

So why have I not retired to Florida, stayed out of this messy political fray, avoided the lawfare that threatens to bankrupt me and take my homes, and just enjoyed life on the golf course?

Listen, these are good questions—and ones I sometimes ask myself!

But I have a simple and truthful answer: I love this country. And I hate corruption.

My paternal grandfather, Rodolfo Giuliani, for whom I am named, left the small town of Montecatini Terme in Tuscany, Italy, in the

1880s, arriving in America with just twenty dollars in his pocket. Sadly, he died before I was five years old. My maternal grandmother, Adelina Stanchi at the time—my Nana—I knew very well. She, too, left a culturally divided country in the 1880s, only her hometown was Gesualdo in Avellino, near Naples. Life for all four of my Italian (legally) immigrant grandparents was not easy. And I also have some criminal issues in my family background. At least ten years before I was born, my father was convicted of robbery and served a year and four months in Sing Sing State Prison. My uncle was a loan shark. His son, my cousin, turned out to be the head of an auto-theft ring and died in a shootout with the FBI.

The Brooklyn neighborhood of Flatbush was home for my first seven years. First settled as a Dutch village over 350 years ago, by the time I came along it was very much an ethnic mix of Italians, Irish, and Jews. Some of my contemporaries (although I didn't know them growing up) were Barbra Streisand, Neil Diamond, and Bernie Sanders. Also in the neighborhood, just a mile or so away from our apartment, was Ebbets Field, home to the Brooklyn Dodgers. However, I was a Yankees fan (still am!), so having the Dodgers so close led to some, shall we say, not so pleasant standoffs during my childhood.

The Dodgers left Flatbush in 1958, but six years earlier, my parents had made the decision to move to a house in the Long Island town of Garden City South—in part, I believe, to keep me from hanging out with the "wrong kids." I went to Catholic school and even con-templated becoming a priest, but instead decided my calling was law. I studied at New York University School of Law and graduated cum laude in 1968.

My first job in the legal profession was clerking for Lloyd Francis McMahon, eventually the chief judge of the Southern District of New York. He was my mentor, advisor, and "second father." From him, I heard stories of how he prosecuted Luciano mob boss Frank Costello for tax evasion and presided over the drug-trafficking trial of Bonanno head Carmine Galante. Early on I learned how to spot a criminal enterprise. I mastered the "tells."

So when I read Joseph Bonanno's 1983 biography, *A Man of Honor*, I knew I had a blueprint for how to prosecute the Mafia in New York. But let's backtrack just a little to fully set the scene. That was the year I became a US Attorney in the Southern District of New York. At the time, the Mob had its tentacles in nearly every aspect of New York City. Author Selwyn Raab perfectly described its influence in his 2005 bestseller, *Five Families: The Rise, Decline, and Resurgence of America's Most Powerful Mafia Families*. "The Mafia, aka the Cosa Nostra and the Mob, generated a toxic effect on the lives of all New Yorkers and untold millions of Americans from coast to coast."[5]

The self-titled Five Families had set themselves up in businesses both legitimate and illegitimate. For the most part, they weren't publicly squabbling over who got which proceeds. But their pathological homicidal behavior often became apparent with messy executions that generated gruesome front-page photos and colorful headlines like "Mafia Rubout"[6] when Paul Castellano was shot to death in 1985 entering Sparks Steak House in Manhattan, or "Crazy Joe Gallo Eats His Last Clam,"[7] when he was killed while trying to run out the front door of Umberto's Clam House in Little Italy. (Fun side fact: That very famous 1979 death photo of Carmine Galante on the front page of the *New York Daily News*, with one eye shot out, a lit cigar still clamped in his jaw after being gunned down at Joe and Mary's Restaurant in Brooklyn? It was partially staged. Galante was nicknamed "The Cigar" because he was rarely seen without one in his mouth. He didn't actually die like that though. For his final photo, photographers shoved a stogie in his mouth for greater effect. True story.)

By 1985, I knew my first major prosecutions would be the Mob. There had been many—successful—attempts to curb parts of this organization, including the ones involving my former boss Lloyd McMahon, Robert F. Kennedy, Estes Kefauver, Tom Dewey, and, of course, the legendary Elliot Ness. But nothing truly stopped this criminal enterprise. There was even a disagreement among top law enforcement officials in the United States as to whether or not the Mafia actually existed. J. Edgar Hoover, head of the FBI, for example, denied for many years that there was such a thing as organized crime.

But even when lawmakers recognized its existence, the problem was how to dismantle the organization. When you put individual family heads like Lucky Luciano or Frank Costello in jail, they either ran their crew from a comfortable cell or someone else stepped up to take their place.

Book III of Bonanno's *A Man of Honor* is titled "The Commission." It starts out, "In the beginning was the Father. Without him nothing can be done. A Family of friends coalesces around the Father, from whom flows all authority. . . . The Family should be viewed as an organism, a living tissue of binding personal relationships."[8] The then retired seventy-eight-year-old former "Father" of the Bonanno family (who was frank about being called "a gangster, a racketeer, a mobster . . . [and] the 'boss of all bosses' . . . whatever that means"[9]), Bonanno then kindly gave a detailed description of the elements and actions of a crime family. He put it in a book and gave it to me personally during the time I visited him in Tucson, Arizona. That was more than enough to prove the longstanding existence of the Commission of the Mafia as a RICO enterprise.

(As an aside, we also have Bonanno to thank for filling us in on origins of the word "Mafia." His story takes place in 1282, when Sicily was ruled by the French. Wrote Joe, "while the people of Palermo were making their way to evening worship (vespers), agents of the treasury waited outside the churches to apprehend tax debtors . . . As it happened, a young lady of rare beauty, who was soon to be married, was going to church with her mother when a French soldier by the name of Droetto, under the pretext of helping the tax agents, manhandled the young lady. Then he dragged her behind the church and raped her. The terrified mother ran through the streets, crying,—Ma fia, ma fia! This means 'My daughter, my daughter' in Sicilian. . . . The mother's cry, repeated by others, rang out through the streets, throughout Palermo and throughout Sicily. Ma fia soon became the rallying cry of the resistance movement, which adopted the phrase as an acronym for Morte alla Francia, Italia anela—'Death to France, Italy cries out.'" Joe goes on to say that the story may or may not be true, "but so what? The important element of the story is not its factual veracity, but the Sicilian spirit which it exemplifies."[10])

Here's how Wikipedia sums up the Mafia Commission Trial, which lasted from February 25, 1985, until November 19, 1986. "Using evidence obtained by the Federal Bureau of Investigation, 11 organized crime figures, including the heads of New York City's 'Five Families', were indicted by United States Attorney Rudolph Giuliani under the Racketeer Influenced and Corrupt Organizations Act (RICO) on charges including extortion, labor racketeering, and murder. Eight of them were convicted under RICO, and most were sentenced to 100 years in prison on January 13, 1987, the maximum possible sentence under that law."[11]

Understandably, the Mafia Commission Trial generated a lot of headlines that year. So did another case I prosecuted, that of Stanley M. Friedman. Friedman was the very powerful—and very corrupt—boss of the Democratic party in New York's Bronx borough. He was a lobbyist who got people hired, then used that influence to get what he wanted. At the time, he wielded a great deal of power within New York Mayor Ed Koch's city hall government. The *New York Times* described the case like this: "A complicated, sometimes interlocking set of corruption investigations that began more than a year ago has implicated New York City, state and Federal officials, toppled political leaders and shaken the administration of Mayor Koch. These cases are not all directly related, but together they provide a view of a government where influence was routinely traded, and political allies became involved in secret business deals to reap profits at the taxpayers' expense.

"[Re the] Parking Violations Bureau [charges], The United States Attorney in Manhattan, Rudolph W. Giuliani, said in this case that the New York City Parking Violations Bureau 'was turned into an enterprise for illegal profit.' Stanley M. Friedman, Convicted Former Bronx Democratic leader, a major stockholder in Citisource Inc., which won a $22.7 million contract for city traffic agents' hand-held computers . . . Prosecutors say he helped the company get the contract without disclosing his holdings. . . . Convicted Nov. 25 by a Federal jury in New Haven . . . Sentenced to twelve years in prison . . . Also found guilty of paying $60,000 to two other officials to help obtain a contract for Datacom, a computer-service company."[12]

Friedman, who served four years of his sentence and went on to run a hotel in Staten Island, was convicted under the RICO statute as well. Note my statement to the *New York Times*, where a corrupt politician used his position to turn a government office into "an enterprise for illegal profit." When I started to look into Joe Biden's activities, the similarities became glaringly clear.

There are few things I abhor more than a corrupt politician. Our democracy, a representative democracy, depends on the intelligence of the electorate and the integrity of public officials. I used to say, when the drug dealers ran neighborhoods in New York, the people there might as well be living in East Germany. They did not have any freedom. And the same thing is true in a corrupt government. A corrupt government is a totalitarian government because they control your behavior and you must submit to bribery to vindicate your God given rights.

Which is why what is happening to America on Joe Biden's watch is so disturbing. America is not just any other nation. America is an ideal and a beacon of freedom for the world.

But there are ways to stop this now pervasive corruption of our country. It's the same RICO act I used against the Mafia Commission and Stanley M. Friedman. (I used it to convict Ivan Boesky of racketeering and securities fraud back in 1989 as well, just to keep the record straight.)

The RICO act is very simple. Per the Department of Justice, the "RICO statute expressly states that it is unlawful for any person to conspire to violate any of the subsections of 18 U.S.C.A. § 1962."[13] (That's the statute on Prohibited Activities.[14]) "The government need not prove that the defendant agreed with every other conspirator, knew all of the other conspirators, or had full knowledge of all the details of the conspiracy. . . . All that must be shown is: (1) that the defendant agreed to commit the substantive racketeering offense through agreeing to participate in two racketeering acts; (2) that he knew the general status of the conspiracy; and (3) that he knew the conspiracy extended beyond his individual role."[15]

As we will report in the coming chapters, there is overwhelming evidence—video, audio, personal records, and even admissions and confessions—to prove that the Biden family's activities meets the burden of proof on these counts. One important corroborating piece of evidence comes from Hunter Biden himself. On January 3, 2019, Hunter texts his oldest daughter Naomi, "I Hope you all can do what I did and pay for everything for this entire family Fro 30 years. It's really hard. But don't worry unlike Pop I won't make you give me half your salary."[16] And even though Hunter may disavow that text, claiming he was drunk, high on crack or didn't mean it (those were his explanations for other incriminating emails and texts when he testified before the House Oversight Committee on February 8, 2024), the text is still evidence of the commission of a lifetime of crime, that there was a family business that made money and, most important, that Joe Biden knew about it and profited from it.

Now I've crossed paths with Joe Biden too many times to count over the fifty some years we've both been in public life. Most of those encounters—at least up until about five years ago—have been cordial. His niece, Missy Owens,[17] even worked for me when I was Mayor of New York. I was introduced to Joe in 1981 by his law school classmate, who was my chief of staff when I was an associate attorney general. He said, "you guys should develop a good relationship." At the time, my job was to get US attorneys and US marshals confirmed. I had 116 of them that would have to go through the Senate Judiciary Committee, where Joe was the ranking minority member, so the advice was sound. My chief of staff went on to preface the introduction by saying, "Don't get impatient because I know you don't suffer fools gladly. He's a really nice guy, you're really gonna like him. But he's really dumb. He was the dumbest guy in my law class."

But I was shocked at what I discovered in 2018 when I was tipped off to look into Joe Biden's activities in Ukraine. I bought the whole Delaware/Amtrak/Middle Class Joe from Scranton persona. Even when newspapers started reporting stories about him, his brother

James, his son Hunter, and the family being a lot too cozy with MBNA Bank in Delaware in the 1990s, I thought at most, like too many members of Congress, he might be a small time crook. After all, as Biden proudly pointed out to special counsel Robert Hur during his 2023 interview in conjunction with unlawfully taking and keeping classified documents, "for 36 years I was listed as the poorest man in Congress."[18] But a big time crook whose family raked in tens, maybe hundreds of millions from our foreign adversaries? That never occurred to me.

The evidence came to me when I got involved with Donald Trump's defense during the Robert Mueller investigation into "Russian collusion" on Trump's 2016 presidential campaign. I spent twenty-four hours a day traveling the country with the candidate during those final months. If there had ever been "Russian collusion," I would know it. I knew there wasn't, so I volunteered to join the legal team for my friend of thirty-five years, helping him defend himself against such fraudulent and false allegations.

One day, I got a call from my former chief of the criminal division in the US Attorney's office, who is now the president of one of the larger investigatory firms in the world, and he said, "I have a source that can provide witnesses that will blow open the Russian collusion allegations." I said, "What do you mean?" He went on to explain that he had a source he wanted me to interview. This source, he said, had information that the so-called "black ledger"—the one that supposedly revealed Paul Manafort, Trump's 2016 campaign manager, got $12.7 million under the table from Ukraine's pro-Russian Party of Regions political party[19]—was a forgery. Furthermore, he said that the infamous "Steele dossier" (now debunked by even so hostile an outlet as CNN[20]) was created not in Russia but in Ukraine, and was also false. There's no way I could pass on talking with someone who had that kind of information! I met with the source and after about forty-five minutes, he suggested, "You should look into the Bidens' corruption in Ukraine." I asked what that meant. He replied, "Have you seen this?" and showed me a YouTube clip.

In the clip, Joe Biden is part of a three-person panel discussing an article he co-wrote for *Foreign Affairs* magazine titled "How to Stand Up to the Kremlin: Defending Democracy Against Its Enemies." As usual, it is an embellished version, but this time—and very unusually—it's mostly accurate and a full admission of bribery. The date is January 2018. The audience is comprised of members of the Council on Foreign Relations. The talk turns to Ukraine, and Biden relates an incident from two years earlier when, as vice president, he had been Obama's "point man," tasked with handing out money and clamping down on corruption in that country to supposedly rebuild a nation that was trying to regain its feet after a revolution and being looted by its former president and other officials.

"I went over for the 12th, 13th time [and] I was supposed to announce that there is another billion dollar loan guarantee. And I had gotten a commitment from [Ukraine's president Petro] Poroshenko and from [prime minister Arseniy] Yatsenyuk that they would take action against the state prosecutor and they didn't. So they're walking out to the press conference and I said we're not going to give you the billion dollars. . . . I said I'm leaving in six hours. If the prosecutor is not fired you're not getting the money. Well son of a bitch. He got fired!"[21]

I couldn't believe what I'd seen. "Play it again," I directed. After he did, I said, "That sounds like a bribe to me!" After all these years of being a prosecutor, I know the elements of bribery: offering something of value in exchange for an official action. In this case, Joe was offering a billion dollars (the "something of value") in exchange for firing the prosecutor (the "official action".) What was missing was the real motive. Why would he do something so stupid? When I took my source's advice and started investigating the Bidens and Ukraine, I found the motive—and much more. That led to a seventy-five-page presentation that I (along with my attorney, Robert (Bob) Costello) gave to a group of US Attorneys and FBI agents in Pittsburgh two years later.

The case that Bob and I took to Pittsburgh was developed solely from our investigative efforts in Ukraine. It would be many months later that Hunter Biden's so-called "Laptop from Hell" fell into our laps. That happened when John Paul Mac Isaac, owner of a computer repair shop in Wilmington, Delaware, filled out the "Contact" form on my Giuliani Security and Safety website. Frustrated after almost a year of trying to get somebody in authority to pay attention to the fact that Hunter Biden—son of a former vice president who was now the Democrat candidate running for president of the United States—had left a damaged computer in his office to fix that was filled with porn and detailed financial improprieties with America's enemies. Having gotten nowhere with government officials, Mac Isaac turned to us.

In this book we will build on that initial Pittsburgh presentation and outline our blueprint for a RICO case against the Biden Crime Family. Our principal defendants are Joe Biden, Hunter Biden, and James Biden. The most heinous crimes had to do with their activities in Ukraine, China, Russia, and Iraq. However, since this criminal enterprise has been ongoing for nearly fifty years, we will show the trail of corruption and destruction caused by these defendants—aided by other family members and trusted associates that were treated like family—that has put less well-connected individuals in jail, left companies bankrupt, people injured (or, in at least one instance, dead) and that now threatens to destroy the America we all love.

The next few chapters detail the many instances where we posit that the Bidens crossed the line from being mere "grifters,"[22] as law professor Jonathan Turley called them, to being the Biden Crime Family. You will be the judge in this case. And at the end, after hearing the evidence and the arguments, you will render your verdict. Now it's time to meet the defendants.

CHAPTER 1

MEET THE DEFENDANTS:

AN INTRODUCTION TO THE
BIDEN CRIME FAMILY

In *A Man of Honor*, Joe Bonanno lays out the structure of a Mafia crime family. "In the beginning was the Father. Without him nothing can be done. A Family of friends coalesces around the Father, from whom flows all authority. The Family which a Father holds together embodies an ancient way of life . . . It is a way of life that gives primary allegiance to the Family state, to the tribe, to the clan."[23]

Those are the Mafia family values. One particular family value— maybe a little different, but a family value nonetheless—was drilled into Joe, Valerie, James, and Frank Biden almost literally at their mother's knee. Jean Biden often repeated this mantra to her four children. "No one is closer. . . . You're blood. You're closer to one another than you are to your dad and me. You have the same blood."[24]

That meant the Bidens stuck together, no matter what. They also kept the family secrets inside the family walls, no matter what. Joe recounted the story of the time he was in Catholic grade school and the nuns gave him a blue badge, appointing him to the safety patrol, in charge of reporting kids who acted up on the bus. When his sister Valerie did just that, he agonized over what to do—turn her in or not turn her in. At dinner that night, Joe Sr. pointed his son towards the answer, saying, "Well, Joey, you know that's not your only option."[25] Jr. handed in his blue badge.

The Mafia has a word for that—*omertà*. That's the "the code of silence that forbade the slightest cooperation with law enforcement, or more ominously, informing, ratting on anyone."[26]

Talk about a Crime Family . . .

Defendant #1 in our indictment: Joseph Robinette Biden Jr. (b. 1942) a.k.a. Joe, Joey, Celtic, Peter Henderson, Robert L. Peters, JRB Ware, & Robin Ware.

To go back to another Joe for a minute—Joe Bonanno, that is— the mob boss has perhaps a more precise definition of the Biden crime family structure and Joe's position in it. "Some Fathers . . . attain greater influence and are consulted more than others. In Sicily we would refer to such a man . . . as a *capo consigliere*—a head counselor, a chief advisor. . . . [He] is not an executive or administrator. He is a figurehead whose influence . . . derives . . . from their willing coopera- tion with him. More than anything, the role he plays stems from a willingness in men to congregate around a greater man."[27]

Funny how that sounds so much like how the Bidens operate. In that family, Joe acts as the Father. It is from his political positions, first as a senator, then vice president, and now president that all things flow.

Joe has always liked to present himself as Middle Class Joe Biden from Scranton whose family went through some hardscrabble times when his pop was out of work, but yet they fought through that tough period to prosperity. That's not exactly true. Yes his dad, Joseph Robinette Biden Sr., didn't work for a period of time. But before his brief descent to the middle class, Joe Sr. was a high-flying, horse rid- ing, free spender. He was employed in Boston by his wealthy uncle, Bill Sheene[28] Sr., who manufactured armor plate for ships during WW2 and made a fortune doing it. But the war ended. After failing at a crop dusting business in Long Island with his lush of a cousin, Bill Sheene Jr., Joe Sr., his wife Jean, and their two (soon to be four) little ones sped off to live with her family, the Finnegans, in Scranton,

Pennsylvania. When that didn't work out so well, Joe Sr.'s brother invited him to Wilmington, Delaware where, after jobs cleaning boilers and selling tchotchkes at weekend farmers markets, he landed at a car dealership. Selling used autos may not have been Papa Joe's favorite profession, but it paid well enough for the family to be comfortable, for young Joe to go to the elite Archmere Academy and then to the University of Delaware, where he spent a season on the football team and the rest of the time reportedly chasing girls.

Long before that, as a youngster, Joe was writing papers that his teachers, the nuns, produced showing he wanted to be president of the United States.[29] (He did succeed in being elected president of his junior and senior classes in at Archmere.) But the self-admitted "arrogant and sloppy"[30] student almost didn't make it out of law school.

"Syracuse University Law School initially failed him for plagiarizing, without citation, five pages from a published law review. The law review in question was Tortious Acts as a Basis for Jurisdiction in Products Liability Cases, which was published in the Fordham Law Review of May 1965. . . . Biden only included one footnote to that article in his paper. [He] said his 'mistake' at law school was neither intentional nor 'malevolent'. He said it was due to ignorance, and that he simply misunderstood the need to carefully cite sources."[31] In his own defense, he wrote, "My intent was not to deceive anyone. For if it were, I would not have been so blatant. If I had intended to cheat, would I have been so stupid?"[32] (Maybe.) Anyway, he was allowed to repeat the course, and in 1968, graduated 76th out of a class of eighty at Syracuse University Law School.[33] He subsequently managed to pass the bar and get his law license.

Friends who knew him back then said he always had some kind of plan to hit the jackpot either in motion or in development. Perhaps spurred on by memories of his earliest years in luxury's lap, thanks to his dad's halcyon days and subsequent entrepreneurial attempts, the ambitious fast talker (despite his childhood stutter) bought and sold real estate, sketched out a daycare center (this was in 1968) and a dozen other propositions, when he wasn't pursuing his legal career. But, to quote Richard Ben Cramer in *What It Takes: The Way to the*

White House, "Thing was, the get-rich-quick schemes never did make him rich. Something fell through, or Joe changed his mind. . . . If they worked, Joe had the money spent six ways before it hit his hand. The sonofabitch could do a deal. Thing was, he couldn't not do a deal."[34]

And then Joe discovered the most lucrative deal-making profession of all—politics. After a mere two years on the New Castle County Council, he was drafted by local Democrats to run for Senate against a veteran politician.

How he won the election has become a bit of a legend. The neophyte politician offered youthful enthusiasm, popular stances on issues like the Vietnam war, civil rights, and not a whole lot more as a Senatorial candidate in 1972. Biden had virtually no name recognition and only a few pennies in his campaign war chest to go up against J. Caleb Boggs, a two-term sitting Republican senator and former Delaware governor. Despite his deficits (and with help from the immensely popular Massachusetts senator Teddy Kennedy, who showed up to campaign for him), as election day drew near, Biden had built some momentum. For his part, after initially ignoring the challenge, figuring that this no-name had a snowball's chance, as they say, Boggs finally realized he had to fight back. His campaign created a newspaper insert designed to crush the upstart opponent, saying that the only thing Biden hadn't promised voters was the kitchen sink.[35] The insert was supposed to run in the Delaware papers the weekend before election day. Only . . . the Thursday before, union drivers who distributed the papers went on strike. Readers/voters (who were influenced by newspaper ads in those days) never saw the inserts. On November 7, 1972, Joe Biden was elected the youngest senator ever.

A few short weeks later, on December 18, Joe's wife Nelia was out shopping for a Christmas tree with their three children. She was hit by a tractor-trailer and killed, along with their one-year-old daughter, Naomi. Their two sons, Joseph Biden III (known as Beau) and Robert Hunter, survived but were badly injured. The accident created the image of Joe as a tragic young man, a man to be pitied, coddled, helped—and above all, a guy who should get a special pass because, well, after all, look what he and his family had suffered. That persona took Joseph R. Biden Jr. a long, long way. Later incidents (two brain aneurisms and the death of Beau Biden from cancer, to be precise) just added to his image as a tragic figure. But we're getting ahead of ourselves.

Defendant #2 in our indictment: Robert Hunter Biden. (b. 1970) a.k.a. Hunter, "temujin01," droidhunter88@gmail.com.

By all accounts, Hunter was a troubled child. With his birth mother and sister dead in the accident that landed him in the hospital with a skull fracture and possible brain damage, his brother in traction with broken limbs and hips, and his father spending long stretches of time 111 miles away in Washington, DC, he came to think of his aunt Valerie and uncle James as surrogate parents. Whatever his accomplishments, they were always overshadowed by those of his brother Beau, reportedly the favored, golden son. He admits he was only eight years old when he took his first drink (it was champagne.)[36] That was the first step on a downward drink/drug/sex spiral that is still being discussed in national (and international) media today, most graphically and intimately detailed on his abandoned "Laptop from Hell." There are plenty of potential sex and drug charges that could be developed from the material on that computer, but let's leave those for another prosecutor. As Steve Bannon says, "come for the porn, stay for the corruption." We'll just focus on the corruption.

Like his father, Hunter barely made it through college (he went to Georgetown University), had strings pulled to get him into Yale Law school, and somehow was able to pass the (legal) bar. When he was just out of law school, MBNA—the banking and credit card giant, a powerhouse business in Delaware—gave this son of a Senate Banking Committee member a "mystery job."[37] In 2001, after Hunter left the bank and set up a lobbying firm, MBNA continued to pay Hunter $100,000/year for five years as a "consultant"[38] for "Internet and privacy law."[39] His other jobs—in the US Department of Commerce, as a lobbyist,[40] a lawyer at the firm of Oldaker, Biden & Belair, and others that we will see later—also grifted off his father's political ascendance. In several of those ventures, Hunter partnered with his uncle, James Biden.

Before his descent into depravity, in 1993 Hunter married Kathleen Ann Buhle (b. 1968) and fathered three children: Naomi King (b. 1993), Finnegan James (b. 1998), and Roberta Mabel "Maisy" (b. 2000). The girls show up in one way or another in this narrative: Naomi in texts, Finnegan exiting a plane in China with her father and grandfather, Maisy as the conduit to Lunden Roberts (b. 1991), her basketball "mentor."[41] Roberts and Hunter began an affair in 2017. In 2018, Navy Joan Roberts was born. Mom Lunden had to drag the little girl's wayward dad to court in 2020 and force him to take a paternity test before he acknowledged his child. Even Grandpa Joe refused to publicly admit that he had a seventh grandchild.[42] There was no such distancing when it came to Hunter's youngest child, Beau Biden (b. 2020.) Hunter married his mother, Melissa Cohen (b. 1986), ten days after meeting her, and now says that meeting "rescued" him from his crack and alcohol addiction.[43]

Defendant #3 in our indictment: James Brian Biden. (b. 1949) a.k.a. Jim, Jimmy.

Back in that initial 1972 senate campaign, Joe's whole family got involved. Fundraising fell to his younger brother, James. Six and a half years younger, with no profession to speak of, James proved to be really good at finding money. Then, as now, James flirted with the edges of right and wrong.

Joe even told this story in his biography:

"Jimmy, who was in his last year at the University of Delaware, took on the toughest job: He had to raise money. . . . A few weeks before Labor Day, Jimmy said he had some good news from the international machinists union. . . ."[44] The union boss had some money but he also had a demand. 'I'm gonna give you $5000 but I want to meet your brother.' James tried to demur but set up the meeting, and continued the tale. "We walk into his office . . . and he's bigger than life and smoking a

cigar . . . He says, 'Listen Joe . . . [l]et me give you a hypotheti-
cal . . . How do you vote?'. . . Joe looks at me like he could put
a dagger in my chest . . . and literally says, 'If you're asking me
how I'm gonna vote on a particular issue, you can take that
check and stick it."[45]

In the book, Joe gets up, walks out, is dragged back by his brother to
make nice but still won't sully his hands by accepting the $5000. This
story is supposed to illustrate Joe's integrity. It falls to his college aged
brother to run back and snag the check.

Having discovered at this early age that he needed no professional
knowledge or experience to extract money from people who wanted
to rub up against a potentially powerful politician (just like those
mobsters who wanted to congregate around a greater man), James
continued to utilize that "winning" formula to enrich himself and his
family. His first venture was owning a disco called Seasons Change.
When it failed four years later,[46] it nearly took down two banks and
ended up in court. No matter. There were always more rich investors or organizations eager to jump into business with a Biden. James
would engage, make promises, cash a hefty paycheck, fail to deliver on
those promises, and walk away as the enterprise crumbled into debt
and lawsuits.

Defendant #4 in our indictment: Francis William Biden. (b. 1953). a.k.a. Frank, Frankie.

This youngest of the Biden siblings (born eleven years after Joe)
wasn't perhaps as grand a grifter as his big brother James or his nephew
Hunter, but he did generate his share of hustles. Before that though,
according to Biden lore (and Joe's biography,) Frank's biggest contribution to his eldest brother's legacy is that he was responsible for
setting Joe up on a blind date with the woman who came to be his
second wife. The official story goes, Frank knew Jill Jacobs Stevenson
from college and secured her phone number for his big brother.

That's not how Jill's first husband, Bill Stevenson, remembers it.
Bill, who owned a popular Wilmington rock club called the Stone

Balloon, told *Inside Edition* he first met Joe during his New Castle county council days, when the bar owner asked the politician for help getting a liquor license.[47] Stevenson vividly recalls sitting in Joe and Nelia's Delaware kitchen with Jill. "We worked on his campaign. I gave $10,900 to his first campaign—in cash."[48] He claims Jill and Joe started having an affair, which he discovered when someone confronted him at the Stone Balloon. A guy walked in and asked Bill if he owned a brown Corvette that had apparently crunched his car five months earlier. The Corvette's occupants—plural—had asked the crumpled car's driver to get a repair estimate. But when he tried to contact them, he never got a reply. "I said: 'Wait a minute. Who is they?' And he said: 'Funnily enough, Senator Biden was driving',"[49] Stevenson recounted.

Surmising that his marriage was kaput, Bill asked Jill to leave their home. That earned him a visit from Joe's youngest sibling. "Frankie Biden of the Biden crime family comes up to me and he goes, 'Give her the house or you're going to have serious problems,'" Stevenson told the *Daily Mail*. "I looked at Frankie and I said, 'Are you threatening me?' and needless to say, about two months later, my brother and I were indicted for that tax charge for $8,200."[50]

Whatever the origin of the Joe/Jill romance and Frank's part in it, what isn't in doubt is Biden's role in a deadly car crash. After college, Frank married (a Delaware journalist, Janine Jaquet, b. 1960), had a child (Alana, b.1989),[51] divorced, drifted through jobs in real estate, printing, and government in San Francisco, Washington DC, and Florida. "In 1999, aged forty-six, he moved to California for a fresh start and rented an apartment in San Diego, apparently without a source of income, and with a girlfriend whose name is unknown."[52] Frank also brought something else with him—a drinking problem.

The following are excerpts from the State of California's Traffic Collision Report 99051616-E dated August 14, 1999, describing a fatal collision that occurred in Encinitas. "At about 2325 hours the Sheriff's Communications Center received a 911 call from an unknown person at The Kraken Bar . . . in regards to a vehicle vs. pedestrian . . . Vehicle #2 is a 1999 Jaguar, XK8 . . . P-1 is a Hispanic

adult male. He was identified . . . as Michael Albano . . . Paramedics . .
. pronounced Albano as deceased"[53] at the scene.

The traffic report goes on to list the driver as Jason Turton. At
the time, he was a twenty-five-year-old part-time college student who
worked at Wholesale Foods. Among the passengers in the car was
one Frank Biden. Turns out Frank had rented the Jaguar from Budget
Rent-A-Car (despite having a suspended driver's license), and then . . .
well, let's let the *Daily Mail* tell the story:

At 10.15 pm [Biden] picked up Turton at Whole Foods (sic),
and gave the younger man the keys to 'test drive' the Jaguar,
apparently keen to 'impress' him.

They went first to the Belly Up Tavern beside Turton's
house in Cardiff-on-Sea, where they bought concert tickets and
Turton drank a beer and two tequila shots.

Then they went to Turton's house, meeting two women—
Charity Johnson, then 23, and Heather Pavlick, then 25, and
another man, David Russell, 32.

They planned to go together back to the Belly Up just a
block away; the group was drinking at the house, although
Johnson said that Biden was not.

It was a warm, dry Saturday night. Instead of going directly
to the Belly Up, they left at 11.15pm, and drove north on 101,
the Coast Highway, then turned back.

Just before 11.25pm, the car stopped at a traffic signal on
Chesterfield Drive to turn back onto 101.

Biden, riding shotgun, leaned over and put the stick into
manual, selecting second gear, a police report said.

After the signal turned green and the car pulled away,
Turton recalled Biden telling him to put the car in third gear
and saying: "Punch it."

Turton then put the car into fourth gear; sheriff's deputies
calculated that by that point the car was traveling at 76 mph,
according to court papers.[54]

The Jaguar plowed into Albano, flinging the helpless pedestrian into the air. On his way down his body hit the car's headlight, windshield, and backseat passenger Pavlick in the face before smashing into the pavement. "In the car, according to witness testimony, both the women said that they heard Biden say: 'Keep driving.'"[55] Turton didn't. He stopped the car but left the accident scene, returning about two hours later. His blood alcohol registered 0.10, which was still above the legal limit. When police interviewed him and wanted to know why he initially ran away, "Turton said he 'asked Biden what he should do.' The report says: 'He [Turton] said someone told him to just leave.'"[56]

At the time, Albano was a single father raising his two teenaged daughters, Lorraina and Nicole. They filed a wrongful death lawsuit in 2000 against Turton and Budget, which expanded the following year to include Biden, who fled California to avoid the case. It was settled in 2002, with the girls winning a judgment against Frank. He was ordered to pay $275,000 (with interest) to each of Albano's daughters. However, since he never showed up in the courtroom, the judgment was entered in default.

Frank quickly skedaddled out of California for Florida, where he ultimately found another partner, Melinda "Mindy" Leigh Rose Ward (b. 1972), a former American Airlines flight attendant and Hooters waitress. They settled in a $600,000, four-bedroom, four-bathroom house in an Atlantis, Florida gated community, bought black and white $40,000 Range Rovers, and Frank found jobs that traded on his brother's name. He also racked up at least one DUI in 2003 and another in 2004, again driving on a suspended driver's license. There was also his arrest for petty theft, occasioned by a bizarre attempt to steal two DVDs (*Rabbit-Proof Fence* and *They*) from a Pompano Beach Blockbuster store, by stuffing them down his pants.[57]

That's what he did do. What he didn't do was pay anything to the Albano sisters, who tried many times and many ways to enforce the judgement. They hired a private detective, who somehow failed to find Frank, despite his quasi-public profile. Figuring that Joe might be sympathetic to their cause (having lost his first wife and young daughter to an alleged drunk driver; an investigation later revealed he was sober[58]) in September 2008, they had their lawyer write the Senator a letter. The reply came from not from Joe, but from his chief of staff, Luis Navarro, who expressed his boss's "sympathy," then went on to say that "the Senator would certainly encourage his brother to pay the judgment if his personal financial circumstances made that at all possible. As you are aware, however, Frank has no assets with which to satisfy the judgment."[59] Mere months later, following Joe's promotion from senator to vice president, Frank would be rolling in assets from a deal in Costa Rica, some of them from the very government his brother oversaw (see Chapter 5). Still, no money went to the Albanos.

They were able to serve Frank with more court papers and even attempted to garnish his wages when they found companies that employed him. At one point they managed to attach his bank account—but the lawyers found only $29.16 in it.[60] It wasn't until the *Daily Mail* did several articles exposing his misdeeds that the scofflaw finally agreed to pay some of the nearly $1 million he owed. That was in 2020—more than two decades after Michael Albano was killed by a drunk driver egged on by Frank Biden.

Aiders, Abettors and Possible Co-Conspirators

Jill Biden. (b. 1951)–a.k.a. Dr. Jill Tracy Jacobs Stevenson Biden. Joe Biden's second wife.

Whatever the true story is about how their relationship started (see her ex-husband's version above), Jill Biden has been glued to Joe's side for forty-seven years. In that time, she's been his cheerleader, defender, stand-in and, if whispers are to be believed, today she's his nursemaid-in-chief, propping him up for the few public functions he can muster enough energy or lucidity to show up for. Joe has praised her as having saved his life on numerous occasions, including during his 2017 speech[61] when he was surprised with the Medal of Freedom by Barack Obama. Despite Joe's touching story in his biography about little Hunter and Beau barging into the bathroom while he was shaving and insisting that "we should marry Jill,"[62] Hunter disagreed with his father's Medal of Freedom speech. In a January 14, 2017 note to his father, he wrote, "every time over the last 30 years you say 'she saved OUR lives' with aunt Val standing right next and never mention her, I feel like grabbing the mic and saying she may have saved his life but beau and I were pretty happy with Mom mom and Aunt Val."[63]

So the family did not always enjoy a group hug behind closed doors. In public though, the former English teacher has rarely put a foot amiss. She did screw up once, letting the cat out of the bag to Oprah when she blurted out that Obama had considered Joe for two offices—Vice President, which he got, and Secretary of State, which went to Hillary Clinton. Jill made the decision for him. On the Oprah Winfrey show taped at the Kennedy Center, Jill reportedly told him, "If you're secretary of state, you'll be away, we'll never see you, you know . . . I'll see you at a state dinner once and awhile. But I said, if you are vice president, the entire family, because they worked so hard for the election, they can be involved."[64] I'm not sure Jill knew at the time just how prophetic her words were to be.

Joseph Robinette Biden III. (1969-2015) – a.k.a. Beau.

Joe's eldest child, Hunter's big brother, was, by all accounts, the good son. He "bore a sense of responsibility beyond his years. His childhood nickname was the Sheriff."[65] "It really is no secret that Beau was Joe's favorite son. He had most closely followed in his father's footsteps into a career in politics, serving as the attorney general of Delaware, and, at the time of his death, preparing a run for governor. Unlike his brother, Hunter, Beau lived a fairly scandal-free life."[66]

Yet Beau was not a complete saint. As attorney general (a job that he got despite having failed the Delaware Bar Exam three times[67]), he allowed a forty-eight-year-old DuPont heir, which is as close to royalty as you can find in Delaware, to avoid jail time, despite the fact that he admitted raping his young daughter from the ages of three to five.[68] One of Beau's fundraisers—Chris Tigani[69]—pled guilty and served jail time for campaign finance violations. And before he became Delaware's chief law enforcement officer, Beau partnered with his brother and uncle James in the 2006 takeover of a troubled investment fund called Paradigm Global Advisors, one of the Biden Crime Family's earlier grifts.

In 2002, Beau and Hallie Olivere (b. 1973) married and had two children, Natalie Paige (b. 2004) and Robert Hunter II (b. 2006.) The year before his daughter was born, Beau joined the Delaware National Guard, deploying to Iraq in 2008. His father thinks the toxins he encountered in a burning waste dump there led to the brain cancer that killed him in 2015.[70] Following Beau's death, his widow and his brother initiated a relationship that included crack cocaine binges, expensive gifts, a felony gun purchase, trips to rehab financed by Joe, and payments to Hallie that originated from a company co-owned by the CCP.[71]

It was suggestive photos of Beau and Hallie's underage daughter Natalie on the "Laptop from Hell" (including one from 2018 where the fourteen-year-old is lying on top of her uncle reclining on a couch) that prompted me to turn that hard drive over to the FBI so they could investigate Hunter for child pornography. Backing up the photos were rafts of texts between Hallie, Hunter, Natalie, James, Ashley, and even Joe talking about the sexual impropriety of the relationship. To the best of my knowledge, to date, there's been no investigation, let alone legal charges, generated by that material. And much of the activity depicted in the photos or discussed in those texts took place in a state (Delaware) where it's mandatory for those in certain professions—for example, social work (Ashley) or psychologists (Natalie and Hunter both had therapists)—to report suspected child abuse.[72]

Ashley Blazer Biden. (b.1981). Joe and Jill's daughter, their only child together.

Ashley seems to have taken more after her notorious stepbrother Hunter than the "sheriff," Beau. She had a few youthful scrapes (as a student at Tulane University she was arrested for marijuana possession in 1999; underage drinking two years later;[73] and obstructing a police officer outside a Chicago bar in 2002[74]). Most recently, like Hunter, she had a spell of forgetfulness that created some, shall we say, unsavory headlines. In January 2019, while attending a rehab facility in Florida, the thirty-eight-year-old started keeping a diary detailing her struggles with drug, alcohol, and sex addiction.

About a year and a half later, she departed Florida to join her dad's basement bunker presidential campaign, leaving the diary and several other belongings at a friend's house in Del Ray Beach. A woman named Aimee Harris moved into the room where Ashley had been staying. Finding the diary, Harris contacted another friend who allegedly texted that the two could "'make a s***ton of money' from selling [Ashley's] property."[75]

For context, this was in the late, heated, stages of the 2020 presidential campaign and Hunter Biden's "Laptop from Hell" with its sensational drug/alcohol/sex secrets had just been exposed in the national media. Harris and her friend pedaled the diary around. The *National File* website ended up publishing the diary which disclosed, among other things, that Ashley was "Hyper-sexualized @ a young age . . . was I molested. I think so . . . I remember . . . showers w/my dad (probably not appropriate)"[76] and more. Harris was ultimately arrested, pled guilty to "conspiring to commit interstate transportation of stolen property,"[77] and, on April 9, 2024, sentenced to a month in prison.[78] The entire saga took four years to play out. Every time there was another twist in the tale, the same salacious headlines would appear. Seems that the now forty-three-year-old social worker who claimed that she "never wanted to be in the public eye"[79] won't get her wish.

One fact that might get overlooked among all the slimy reportage is that Ashley has been married since 2012 to a head and neck surgeon named Dr. Howard Krein (b. 1966). He's also the chief medical officer of something called StartUp Health, which is a health-care venture capital firm. Like the rest of his in-laws, Krein isn't above using Joe to make money. Reportedly, he's advised his father-in-law on health-care issues over the years, even appearing in 2016 with Joe, standing at a podium carrying the vice presidential seal, while talking about the cancer moonshot initiative. More recently, it was Howard's involvement with StartUp Health[80] that raised eyebrows when it was asked by a company in which it had invested to introduce coronavirus vaccine software to government officials.[81] Mixing Joe Biden's relatives and government contracts? That's got a familiar sound.

Valerie Biden Owens (b. 1945) and **John "Jack" Thomas Owens** (b. 1943).

Joe's only sister, Valerie Biden Owens, was more than her brother's confidante and her nephews' surrogate mom. When Joe "had a debilitating stutter, she helped him overcome it. When he ran for high school class president, she directed the effort. And she has run Biden's campaigns ever since—for county councilman, US senator, and his first two bids for president."[82] In return, Valerie, too, has drunk from the money trough generated by Joe's political positions.

As far back as 2008, the Citizens for Responsibility and Ethics in Washington (CREW) issued a report that looked into "how members of Congress use their positions to financially benefit family members . . . . Although it is illegal for members of Congress to hire family members as employees on their official staff, it is not illegal for lawmakers to employ family members through campaign committees or PACs."[83] Valerie was one Biden family member who raked in the cash. "Senator Joseph Biden's principal campaign committee, Citizens for Biden, has paid salaries to his sister and his niece. The committee has also reimbursed his sister, his wife, two of his children, his brother and himself."[84] Valerie, along with her daughter Catherine "Casey" Eugenia Owens Castello (b. 1983) only took in $54,904.78 during that particular election cycle. Valerie's son, Cuffie Biden Owens (b. 1979), has helped fill her financial coffers (along with his own, no doubt), negotiating lucrative speaking engagements[85] and the contract for her 2021 book, *Growing Up Biden*.[86] Under Obama, Valerie secured a coveted appointment to the United National as Alternative Representative of the United States.[87] Plus, she's served as the vice chair of the Biden Institute at the University of Delaware, vice chair of the Biden Foundation and is on the advisory board of the Beau Biden Foundation for the Protection of Children.[88] Her maiden name has been very, very good to her.

It was Jack Owens, Valerie's second husband, who secured one of those loans for his brother-in-law, James, when he was running his nightclub, Seasons Change, into the ground. Jack, a lawyer, had been an aide to Pennsylvania governor Milton Shapp, and the dutiful brother-in-law prevailed on his former boss to recommend that First Pennsylvania Bank loan a twenty-six-year-old $500,000 to finance his disco. When James proved incapable of repaying that second loan, as well as the first, it got sold to a businessman who later sued the bank, claiming they tricked him into owning a dying club so news of the former Senate banking committee member's deadbeat brother wouldn't hit the papers.[89]

Valerie and Jack's offspring have done well in the family business too. Though she's now in the private sector, daughter Valerie "Missy" James Owens's (1976) "About" section on LinkedIn proudly starts out, "I have worked and lived in and around politics my entire life."[90] Currently at Starbucks, Casey was the US Treasury Department's Special Assistant to the Senior Coordinator for China from 2009-2001.[91] That, of course, was while her uncle was vice president. Cuffie followed his father into the legal profession, but as we noted, he negotiates lucrative deals for his mother, built around the Biden name.

Sara Catherine Jones Biden. (b. 1959) – James's second wife.

Married to James since 1995, the Kentucky native is a Duke University–educated lawyer who met her husband when she got a job on a committee for Senator Wendell Ford (D-KY). This sentence from *RealClearInvestigations* seems to be a perfect summation of their relationship: "Jimmy and Sara weren't just sweethearts; they were also business partners—with a taste for high living."[92]

Formed in 1997, their consulting firm, Lion Hall Group, was the vehicle through which they landed loans, purchased expensive real estate and pursued business opportunities that consistently straddled ethical lines. Some of their grifts are detailed in the following chapters. But Sara is now perhaps best known as the payer whose signature appears on the checks for $200,000 and $40,000 made out to Joe

Biden after James received his Americore payout as well as funds from Biden Crime Family dealings in China.

James and Sara had one son together—Nicholas "Nick" Coleman Biden (b. 1997). With his first wife, Michele (b. 1952; the two divorced in 1993), James had two children—James "Jamie" Brian Biden Jr. (b. 1982) and Caroline Nicole Biden (b. 1987). James's two sons seem to have avoided running afoul of the law.

Not Caroline. "In August 2019, Caroline Biden, thirty-three, a niece of former Vice President Biden, was busted in Lower Merion Township, Penn., for driving under the influence and without a license. . . . The Pennsylvania drunken-driving collar was the third run-in with the law for Caroline. . . . In September 2013, she was booked for allegedly hitting an NYPD officer during a full scale meltdown at her Tribeca apartment, following a dispute with a roommate over unpaid rent. The case was dismissed after Caroline agreed to anger management treatment. In 2017, she was busted for spending more than $110,000 on a stolen credit card. A felony conviction was later tossed, and she was allowed to re-plead to the lesser charge of petty larceny as part of a sweetheart deal negotiated by her attorneys. She avoided jail time."[93]

Instead, the then thirty-two-year-old elected to serve her two year probation in California where her cousin Hunter whined about having to "babysit"[94] her. As part of that probation, Caroline was supposed to get a job. She was offered one by the Massimo Corporation (headed by Joe Kiani, who, between foundations, super PACS and personal donations, contributed over $4 million to various entities that benefited Joe Biden.[95]) for an $85,000 salary, a 10 percent bonus, and other benefits. Caroline's response to that offer? "I cannot take a job full time and relocate for 85,000[.] That's below minimum wage in California after taxes."[96] Clad in a skimpy bikini, Caroline appears in photographs with her also shirtless cousin on his abandoned hard drive. She offers to line up women for Hunter, texting him in one case, "Does she have to be smart or just a transitional sex company object."[97] Joe surely hit the nail on the head when he told the audience at the inaugural Salute to Heroes ball in 2013, "We have a lot of bad judgment in our family."[98]

Now that you've met the characters (or, if you prefer, the defendants and their accomplices) let's examine their activities, which span more than five decades, several continents, a head-spinning number of LLCs, bank accounts, and businesses. Along the way, the Bidens have lured a potpourri of associates into their grifting schemes, including everyone from heads of state to Mafia relatives to well-meaning business people to just simply guys with their hands out looking to make a big score, no matter what side of the law it's on. In later chapters we'll outline our case for prosecution. What follows are activities that may not always rise to the level of criminality. But they're relevant to the discussion because they demonstrate the length of time this illegal enterprise has been operating. Now onto the business of Biden businesses.

PART 1

THE CRIMES

In all the Mafia cases I ever prosecuted, crime families owned businesses that made them money. Some—like prostitution, illegal narcotics, bootlegging back in the days of Prohibition, running numbers, extortion, loan-sharking—were plainly against the law. (But not, apparently against the Cosa Nostra's code of ethics. Says Bonanno of bookmaking and numbers, "In our world, such enterprises are not considered wrong."[99])

And then there were the legitimate businesses that members of the Commission used as cover for their illicit activities. Bonanno, again, on his family's livelihood: "[I] became a stockholder in various companies . . . . I was a venture capitalist. This is how I made my money."[100] The Bonanno crime "family" provided laundry services and mozzarella cheese to restaurants. They also had a hand in the garment industry. So did the Luccheses, who had also their tentacles in New York's construction business. The Lucianos, who ran the Manhattan docks and the Fulton Fish Market, set up the first Las Vegas casino when their associate Bugsy Siegel built the Flamingo Hotel, while the Gambinos hid their felonious dealings behind trash removal trucks. And then there was Joe Profaci, of the Colombo family. "Famous in the grocery industry as 'the Olive Oil King,' he was the largest importer of olive oil and tomato paste in the country through the Mama-Mia Olive Oil Company."[101] It was suspected that those imports masked the drugs his family smuggled.

In all those Commission cases, though, any prosecutor—or casual observer, actually —could easily put a name to that particular crime family's enterprise. Not the Biden Crime Family. What business were they in? That's been one of the most difficult questions to answer in the many investigations into the Bidens. In fact, it led to a shouting match between two members of the House of Representatives in the middle of a congressional hearing. "What did the Bidens do? What business were they in?" demanded Rep. James Comer (R-KY) as he chaired a House Oversight Committee hearing on China on April 18, 2024. Rep. Jamie Raskin (D-MD) sputtered, trying to somehow spin the answer to smear Donald Trump. Ultimately, Raskin replied, "I'll tell you what Joe Biden did. He was a senator of the United States, then he wrote a book and he said he made the most money he ever made in his life."[102]

Well, that's one explanation, but it's far from the whole one—or even a truthful one. From the very beginning of Joe's political career, the Biden family has capitalized on the fact that Joe was a senator, a vice president, and now a president to make themselves at least tens, perhaps hundreds of millions of dollars. As former Biden business partner Tony Bobulinski put it in his interview before the House Committee on Oversight and Accountability, "Joe Biden was the brand being sold by the Biden family."[103]

Cashing in on the Biden name started way back in 1973, right after Joe took his Senate oath of office in the hospital room where his sons were recuperating after the auto accident that killed their mother and sister. While the Crime Family business raked in a few million over the years, it wasn't until President Barack Obama designated his vice president Joe Biden as the "point man" in places like Iraq, Latin America, Ukraine, and China that the big bucks started rolling in. Because it was their first big score, our case is going to start by delving into what the Bidens did in Ukraine. Much has been written and said about it, but here's what I found when I investigated.

CHAPTER 2

WHAT REALLY HAPPENED IN UKRAINE . . . THE WHOLE STORY

In the Introduction, I related Joe Biden's boast in front of the Council of Foreign Relations where he told the story of threatening to withhold billions if Ukraine's president didn't fire the equivalent of their attorney general. When Biden told that story, I'm sure he thought he was bragging about how tough he'd been on combatting corruption in Ukraine. In fact, it's arrogant. I see it as Joe Biden confessing to committing a crime. How Biden got there and why he was able to pull off such outrageous actions necessitates some context. Let me start by giving you a little background on modern Ukraine.

To say that the thirty-three years since Ukraine declared its independence, with the fall of the Soviet Union in 1991, have been tumultuous would be, well . . . to call it an understatement would be an understatement. They've had two internal revolutions, one government collapse, five presidents, multiple scandals (including one sparked by a beheaded journalist), one jailed opposition prime minister, one poisoned presidential candidate, one political leader who died in a suspicious car crash, one stolen election, and a major church schism. Ukrainian governments have seesawed between pro-Westerner heads who wanted (and tried) to join NATO and/or the European Union and those who sought closer ties with Russia.

Through all the turmoil though, one thing has remained consistent in Ukraine—corruption. Transparency International, an organization that tracks corruption around the globe, put Ukraine at number 33 out of 100 on their Corruption Perceptions Index in 2022,[104] the most recent year available for their rankings. (A 0 on that scale means the country is "highly corrupt," while 100 is "very clean.") That puts Ukraine in the bottom third of the list worldwide, and the second most corrupt nation in Europe[105] (behind Russia, ironically). In most everything written about the country, the word "corruption" appears. When a tourist guide book to Ukraine titles a section "Nukes & Crooks,"[106] and lists Mezhyhirya as its newest tourist attraction, an opulent, nearly 340 acre, multi-million dollar estate—complete with "a luxury car collection, an ostrich farm, and even a loaf of bread made of solid gold"[107]—seized from the ousted Ukrainian president after he had to flee the country, well, it's clear that there was/is something rotten that nation.

From the start of its independence, the former Soviet satellite was ripe for corruption. According to Ukrainian historian Serhii Plokhy, "between 1991 and 1997, Ukrainian industrial production fell by 48 percent, while the gross domestic product (GDP) lost a staggering 60 percent."[108] Plokhy goes on to explain, "The 1990s brought terrible hardship to Ukraine . . . [The country] needed new owners and a new class of managers to revive its economy. [It] got both in a group of young, ambitious, and ruthless businessmen . . . [k]nown as the oligarchs."[109]

Industries that had been state-owned under the Soviets (like metallurgy, banking, media, agriculture, and energy, for instance) passed into private hands, some of them with "criminal origins and connections," according to Plokhy. Despite that, "the 'oligarchization' of the Ukrainian economy coincided with the end of economic decline. Ukraine began the new millennium with a rapid economic recovery, and, for better or worse, the oligarchs were important figures in that new success story."[110]

Critical to that success was international economic aid, which began almost as soon as the Ukraine took its first independent steps. In 1994, the country surrendered the nuclear weapons it had acquired while a part of the USSR, becoming "the third-largest recipient of US foreign aid after Israel and Egypt."[111] Even though the domestic economy picked up between 2000 and 2008, Ukraine needed foreign cash. A 2012 report by the Carnegie Endowment for International Peace, which called Ukraine the "sick man of Europe, and perhaps even . . . a potentially failed state,"[112] noted that "Europe, the United States, and the Euro-Atlantic community will continue to engage with Ukraine." Even Russia contributed to the billions in loans, loan guarantees and direct aid that flooded into Ukraine's coffers. Some of that money went into the economy, but a good bit wound up in the pockets of the country's political leaders. Said *The Guardian*, "between 2010 and 2014, officials were stealing a fifth of the country's national output every year."[113]

The year 2014 was a pivotal one in Ukraine's short independent life. That February, demonstrators, fed up with President Viktor Yanukovych, staged the Euromaidan Protests, running the Moscow-sympathizer out of Kiev and back to Russia. With him, he took some $70 billion[114] that he had managed to squirrel away in the foreign bank accounts that he and his family owned.[115] (Yanukovych is the guy who abandoned Mezhyhirya, the palatial estate turned tourist attraction.) In March, Russia seized the Crimean peninsula and in April, they provoked an uprising in the eastern Donbas region, sparking a bloody separatist war that didn't see an uneasy truce until later that year.[116]

By May, Ukraine had a new president, Petro Poroshenko. Before embarking on a political career, Poroshenko had been one of the country's early oligarchs, making his billion(s) by owning, among other things, auto and bus factories, a shipyard, a television channel, and a confectionary factory, which earned him the nickname, "The Chocolate King."[117] Along with the war in the Donbas, Poroshenko inherited a fairly empty national treasury. (It's rumored that Yanukovych only left behind some $800,000 when he and his cronies fled after looting the country of billions.)

Losing Crimea, coupled with the war, further strained the Ukrainian pocketbook. Promising reforms, Poroshenko's government talked the EU into coughing up €14 billion. Japan kicked in another $1.5 billion, Canada $785 million, and the US $2.2 billion.[118] The money had some conditions attached though. The benefactors insisted on reforms, and chief among the reforms demanded was a crackdown on corruption.

In February 2015, a new Prosecutor General was appointed to do just that. Viktor Shokin assumed the office. There's no doubt that Shokin made enemies on all sides. Street protesters demanded his resignation. There was even an assassination attempt, but bulletproof glass defeated the would-be sniper who unsuccessfully tried to shoot through it. It took Joe Biden threatening to withhold $1 billion to pry Shokin from his office.

But when Biden told his story to the Council on Foreign Relations, he left out a good part of it. In fact, I'd say he left out the relevant part that had absolutely nothing to do with fighting corruption, the part that was completely personal. And that part of the story is what I'm going to tell you.

What Biden chose to ignore had to do with the Ukrainian gas and oil firm, Burisma Holdings Ltd. Founded in 2002 by Mykola Zlochevsky and his college classmate Mykola Lisin (who died suspiciously when his Lamborghini Diablo crashed in a 2011 traffic accident), by 2016 "Burisma was the second largest privately owned natural gas producer in Ukraine . . . accounting for 26 percent of all natural gas produced by privately owned companies and more than 5 percent of total gas production in Ukraine."[119] One of the reasons Burisma got to be so big—and so rich—was because when Zlochevsky was the Ukrainian minister of ecology and natural resources under Yanukovych, he used his office to transfer the most lucrative oil and gas leases to his own company, Burisma.[120]

Those moves did not go unnoticed. Since 2012, there have been many investigations into Burisma and Zlochevsky's financial affairs.

In fact, he had barely left his official position when the first review started, with a Ukrainian prosecutor general checking into allegations of money laundering, tax evasion, and corruption. "The National Anti-Corruption Bureau of Ukraine (NABU) said an investigation was ongoing into permits granted by officials at the Ministry of Ecology for the use of natural resources to a string of companies managed by Burisma. . . . [I]t said the period under investigation was 2010-2012."[121]

The trouble in his own country was bad enough, but things were about to get worse for the Burisma chief. Along with the rest of Yanukovych's associates—the so-called Yanukovych Mafia—after the Revolution of Dignity in February, Zlochevsky fled the country, ending up in Switzerland where he reportedly had stashed $5 billion in stolen Ukrainian government funds. Then he got in trouble with the British. "In March 2014, BNP Paribas reported Mr. Zlochevsky to U.K. authorities on suspicion of money laundering after his companies tried to move $23 million to Cyprus from their British account at the bank."[122] The next month the UK's Serious Fraud office froze that $23 million.

Now here's Zlochevsky, sitting in a foreign nation, basically in exile. A portion of his funds are locked in London. His formerly powerful friends are holed up in Russia, and he's being pursued for "unlawful self-enrichment"[123] in his home country where the new pro-Western oligarch president Poroshenko is coming after Burisma and its leader.[124] What to do?

Like any New York bodega owner who pays the Mafia to keep local thugs from destroying his business, Zlochevsky looked for some protection. In his case, though, it would cost him more than a couple hundred dollars a week. He decided to add some new, different, even more powerful friends to the Burisma board of directors, including former president of Poland Aleksander Kwaśniewski. Next, as I said on my podcast, *Rudy Giuliani's Common Sense* in 2020, "President Obama does Zlochevsky the favor of his life. He appoints Joe Biden the 'point man' for Ukraine. What that means is Joe is going to be in charge of handing out the billions and billions of dollars to rebuild the country and he's going to try to make the country less corrupt. . . . Zlochevsky is a smart man. He says, I gotta have somebody who's more powerful than Poroshenko to protect me in case they want to come after my company and my money. And my savior is Joe Biden."[125] And then Zlochevsky meets two guys with a company trolling around Eastern Europe, trying to profit on Joe Biden's vice-presidency.

The company was Rosemont Seneca Partners[126] and the two guys were Devon Archer[127] and Hunter Biden. Archer told the House Committee on Oversight and Accountability how it all went down.

"We were doing a large deal with an Eastern European bank to basically invest in . . . Rosemont Realty for Rosemont Real Estate Acquisition Fund Two. And that meeting happened to be . . . March 4th, 2014 . . . in Moscow, which was also the day that Putin invaded Crimea. So that deal fell through, as you can imagine. So that started this entire process. [Zlochevsky] . . . was in Moscow. We were like, okay, well, now we got to get back on the fundraising trip. And I met with him. . . . [B]asically, the next day they called . . . and said . . . 'I don't know if they're going to be interested in Rosemont Realty, but President Kwaśniewski wants to meet with you.' . . . [L]iterally within days, I flew to Warsaw for the day. And Kwaśniewski asked me, 'would you be interested in joining the board?' . . . That's how the Burisma relationship started."[128]

Archer joins the Burisma board in March 2014, and Hunter follows a month later. Although neither has any experience with natural gas, the biggest natural gas company in Ukraine starts paying each of them $1 million a year—$83,000 a month apiece—for their services.[129] Now Zlochevsky has two guys with "juice" in his corner—one with connections to the US Secretary of State and the other is the son of that country's sitting vice president—the vice president who has just been sent to Ukraine to root out corruption and control the money. As the *Wall Street Journal* stated, "Behind the relationship between Mr. Zlochevsky and Hunter Biden is an effort to anchor the future of a controversial Ukrainian company amid shifting political and economic tides."[130] To put it more accurately, to get someone to fix the case against Burisma and have it dismissed, if necessary.

Briefly, those tides start to turn in Zlochevsky's favor. In January 2015—even as the oligarch was declared a fugitive by his native country—a UK judge unfroze that $23 million, claiming he hadn't gotten the requested documentation from Ukraine that showed evidence of a crime. This incenses Geoffrey Pyatt, the US Ambassador to Ukraine, who gives a speech on September 24, suggesting that "the court unfroze the money not because of Mr. Zlochevsky's innocence, but rather because of the incompetence of Ukrainian authorities."[131]

In comes Viktor Shokin. Now, the story the collective "they" want you to believe, is that Shokin is no better than his predecessor. That he was incompetent, that he slow walked the investigation into Burisma and Zlochevsky's corruption, that he was corrupt himself. Couldn't be more untrue. I found that out myself when I started to investigate. That investigation took me (along with *Just The News* investigative journalist John Solomon) to Ukraine, to Washington DC, to New York, and eventually, to Pittsburgh. We interviewed key players like Shokin, his successor Yuriy Lutsenko, Ukrainian diplomat Andrii Telizhenko, and others, were given access to the Prosecutor General's files and uncovered even more evidence that my attorney Bob Costello and I compiled into a seventy-five-page Powerpoint presentation. At the direction of then Attorney General Bill Barr, we delivered that presentation to a group of twenty or so enthusiastic and engaged US attorneys and FBI agents in Pittsburgh, who spent five lively hours in a packed conference room reviewing our findings on a snowy January day in 2020.

Now, remember that the reason I started this journey in the first place was because the Muller investigation into "Russiagate" was going on and, as Donald Trump's lawyer, I was looking for information that would prove there was no collusion between the Trump campaign and Russia during the 2016 election. While doing that, I was given the facts and details of the Bidens' activities. So when Donald Trump, during his "perfect" phone call, asked the new Ukrainian president Volodymyr Zelenskyy to "find out what happened with this whole situation with Ukraine. . . . There's a lot of talk about Biden's son, that Biden stopped the prosecution and a lot of people want to find out about that,"[132] I had plenty of evidence to prove that Trump had probable cause to make that request. There was also, unbeknownst to me and him, a copy of Hunter Biden's hard drive in the possession of the FBI, proving all of this conclusively.

The presentation we gave those law enforcement officials includes much information about the involvement of the US embassy in Kiev, US ambassador to Ukraine Marie Yovanovitch, Assistant Secretary of State Victoria Nuland, George Soros-funded NGOs, the Democrat National Committee (DNC), and a host of others in creating the fraudulent "black ledger" that caused Paul Manafort to resign as Trump's 2016 campaign manager. That group also did their best to restrict our access to several Ukrainian witnesses who wanted to come to the US and tell their story, but were denied visas.

Here are some of the Powerpoint slides we presented to the Pittsburgh agents:

August 20, 2014
- Prosecutor General Viktor Shokin opens another criminal investigation of Burisma. He identifies Hunter Biden and Devon Archer as persons of interest in the investigation. (Source: Shokin's case file, as quoted by *Just The News*.[133])

January 2015
- Zlochevsky officially named a fugitive by Ukraine government. (Source: *Kyiv Post*.[134])
- Hunter Biden and Devon Archer remain on Board of this company despite the status of the notorious criminal paying them at least $2 million per year.
- This evidence convinces Ukrainian officials and people, who on this issue are not brainwashed that this money is being paid to protect Zlochevsky, not for the useless efforts of two unqualified Board members.

December 7, 2015
- VP Biden calls Poroshenko and an anonymous source says that apparently for the first time he tells Poroshenko that he must dismiss Prosecutor General Viktor Shokin, allegedly

for unspecified corruption. (Also on this day, Biden and Poroshenko conduct a bilateral meeting, during which the US VP says the Ukrainian president must make "hard decisions" to "completely root out the cancer of corruption."[135])

December 7, 2015 to January 2016 onward

- Poroshenko has 4 or 5 conversations with Shokin urging him to slow down investigation of Burisma. He says the Obama administration and particularly Biden are pressuring him. (Source: Viktor Shokin interview.)

December 8, 2015

- *NY Times*'s James Risen writes an article raising the conflict of an entirely unqualified Hunter Biden sitting on the Board of a crooked Ukrainian company, Burisma.
- He points out this is inconsistent, to the point of hypocritical, since his father the Vice President is the Point Man for Ukraine in charge of handing out billions and combatting corruption
- There is no media or law enforcement or Obama administration follow-up. (Source: *New York Times*.[136])

February 2016

This Is the Month It All Comes Together.

February 2, 2016

- Shokin obtains an order from Ukrainian Court to arrest Burisma. Assets are frozen. (Source: *Interfax Ukraine*.[137]) Biden continues to remain on board of corrupt company. President Poroshenko warns Prosecutor Shokin that he must slow down case or he must resign. (Source: Viktor Shokin interview.)
- This evidence demonstrates Bidens are lying when they say that Burisma case was dormant or that Shokin was not pursuing it.[138]

February 5, 2016*

- VP Biden strong arms/threatens Poroshenko with not approving a critical a $1 billion loan guarantee unless he fires the Prosecutor General. If the loan guarantee were not

executed Ukraine would go into loan default. Biden gives him six hours to decide or the loan guarantee will expire.
- President Poroshenko tells Shokin he will have to resign because of pressure from Joe Biden. He says Biden will not give Ukraine $1 billion loan guarantee unless Shokin is fired. (Source: Viktor Shokin interview.)
- *Approximate dates because the bribe/extortion was done over a number of months, not in "heroic" way Biden presented to the Council on Foreign Relations

February 16, 2016
- Poroshenko announces Shokin will be resigning. (Source: *InterFax-Ukraine*.[139])

February 18, 2016
- Records show payments to Burisma board members of approximately $14.6 million laundered as loans to a shell company in Latvia, then to another one in Cyprus and payouts from Cypriot bank to board members. (Source: Latvian money laundering records, John Solomon.[140])
- Devon Archer and Hunter Biden amounts are blank.

February 11, 18, 19, 2016
- VP Biden and Poroshenko talk on phone numerous times during this critical period. (Source: US Embassy call readouts.[141])

May 12, 2016
- Yuriy Lutsenko named as new Prosecutor General. Lutsenko was considered a hero of Ukraine for having spent 1½ years in prison during the pro-Russian Yanukovych government. However, he is not a lawyer and is very close to Poroshenko. (Source: *Radio Free Europe*.[142])
- VP Biden praises the appointment of Lutsenko. (Source: This was during Biden's famous speech before the Council on Foreign Affairs.[143])

June 15, 2016
- Ukrainian law enforcement agency announces it has uncovered a massive fraud scheme involving Biden's company

Burisma. (Source: Wikipedia, Ukraine's Anti-Corruption Action Centre.[144]) Remember Hunter Biden is still on Zlochevsky's payroll.

November 2, 2016.

- Just before the United States election, and less than four months after announcing a massive fraud scheme against Burisma, Prosecutor General's Office announces closing of Burisma case. (Source: Reuters.[145])

January 17-19, 2017

- VP Biden makes his last of nine to thirteen visits to Ukraine. (Source: US Embassy remarks.[146]) What's he doing there right before the inauguration?

Yes, what was Biden doing there? Why would a vice president, as he was leaving office, spend the last three or four days of his term in Ukraine? There was no government purpose to it. Personally, I always thought he was just cleaning up, making sure he had all the records, and that may well have been the case. But there's much, much more to this story,[147] some of which we were able to tell the US attorneys and FBI agents in Pittsburgh.

Key among the interviews I conducted to put together the presentation was the one with ousted Ukrainian Prosecutor General Viktor Shokin in January 2018 (note that this is long before Joe Biden decided to run for president). Part of that interview aired on my *Rudy Giuliani's Common Sense* podcast on January 31, 2020. Through a translator, I asked Shokin about the investigations into Burisma before he was appointed Prosecutor General.

> **Rudy Giuliani:** When you came into that office, there was already a case against Burisma. Is that correct?
> **Shokin Translator:** Yes.
> **Rudy Giuliani:** And the case involves money laundering abuse of power . . . there was five or six cases . . . it was not just one case.

Shokin Translator: Actually yes, there were quite a few particular separate investigative cases but they were all concerned in one company that's why they were combined into one.[148]

Viktor confirmed the timing of Joe Biden's appointment as Obama's "point man" and Hunter's Burisma board appointment. I also wanted him to confirm what he understood Joe was supposed to be doing as "point man."

Rudy Giuliani: Part of Vice President Biden's job was to grant loan guarantees to help with the terrible fiscal problem.
Shokin Translator: As far as I know, the competence of Biden included anything connected with Ukraine including the financial guarantees."[149]

We covered the fact that the Ukrainians knew Hunter had no qualifications for being on the board of a gas and oil company, in addition to the fact that the US Navy had just dismissed him from his job in the Naval Reserves because he failed a cocaine test. So here you have a guy with a drug habit and no qualifications for being on the board of this corrupt company, a company that's under investigation, whose owner is a fugitive, who is looking at losing his billion-dollar corporation. It's December 2015, and the worried company owner asks his board member—whose dad happens to be in charge of handing out billions of US aid money to a country starved for cash—for a little help. I'm going to break away from my own investigation here and let another witness to that interaction describe what he observed.

In July 2023, Devon Archer, Hunter's business partner, testified before the House Committee on Oversight and Accountability about a December 2015 Burisma board of director's meeting in Dubai. After dinner at the famous Burj Khalifa, the world's tallest building, Mykola Zlochevsky had coffee with his board members back at the Four Seasons Hotel. There he asked Hunter to "help" alleviate some of the "pressure from the Ukrainian government investigations into

Mykola," said Archer. Committee member Jim Jordan wanted to know who the oligarch expected Hunter to call for "help." "Basically the request is like, can D.C. help? . . . There weren't specific . . . can the big guy help?" And after that Archer was asked who Hunter called. "He called his dad,"[150] Archer stated under penalty of perjury.

I asked the man who was the instigator of that "pressure" what happened next. Let's go back to the Shokin interview—which, keep in mind, took place four years before Archer's House Committee appearance.

> **Rudy Giuliani:** Did President Poroshenko tell you that he was getting direct and intense pressure from the US administration and Joe Biden?
> **Shokin Translator:** I'm not sure about the embassy, but definitely Joe Biden that he conveyed to me."

Then we get to February 2, 2016. That's when a Ukrainian court ordered the arrest of Burisma and seizure of its assets.

> **Shokin Translator:** Within 3, 4 days I got a phone call from the president.
> **Rudy Giuliani:** When you say arrested Burisma what does that mean?
> **Shokin Translator:** It means that you can't dispose of it. It was arrest for Mr. Zlochevsky assets and Burisma company assets.
> **Rudy Giuliani:** So Mr. Zlochevsky would have been arrested. If he was in Ukraine.
> **Shokin Translator:** Yes.

In the middle of all this turmoil—the Burisma raid where Zlochevsky's four houses and personal Rolls-Royce Phantom were seized, Hunter Biden calling his dad, Joe Biden leaning on Poroshenko to fire the prosecutor who's harassing his kid's boss—Latvia drops a bombshell. The Office for Prevention of Laundering of Proceeds Derived from Criminal Activity (known as the Latvian FIU) in Riga sends a letter to their counterparts in Ukraine. In my *Rudy Giuliani's Common Sense* podcast on January 29, 2020, I read it aloud while viewers followed along.

> This pretty much definitively puts the lie to these Democrats who say there was no investigation [into Burisma. Remember, this was allegedly the excuse for getting rid of prosecutor Shokin.]
>
> This is a document from the prosecutor's office of the Republic of Latvia. It is dated the 18th of February 2016. And it says 'according to publicly available information Burisma Holding Limited and its director Hunter Biden are involved in corruption affair. The following transactions made to Burisma Holding Limited account in AS PrivatBank are known to the Latvian FIU.' Their Financial Investigation Unit.
>
> And what they describe is a transfer of $14.7 million dollars from Ukraine Wire Logic Technology as a payment for loans. It then goes to another company Digitex Organization, LLP. And eventually it goes from Ukraine, to Latvia, Latvia to Cyprus. And there it's dispersed to people like Alan Apter[151], Alexander Kwaśniewski, members of the board of Burisma. And two other people, Hunter Biden and his partner, Devon Archer. The only difference is the amounts of money that are sent to Alan Apter and Alexander Kwaśniewski are listed. The amount sent to Archer and Biden is not. From the records of their company, however, you find that they receive $3 million. This is an out and out money laundering case. So in addition to bribery, this is what you would call a smoking gun for a prosecutor.[152]

I've got it in English, I've got it in Latvian. This is all from the prosecutor's office—the prosecutor that supposedly wasn't investigating Burisma and Hunter Biden . . . except it's right in the file on February 18 of 2016 that they were investigating Hunter Biden. And so the heat on Shokin reaches a boiling point.

Rudy Giuliani: Before he got to the point where Mr. Poroshenko told you that you had you had to resign. How many times did he—the President Poroshenko—how many times would you say he complained to you?

Shokin Translator: 5, 6, 7. More than five definitely.

Rudy Giuliani: And then there came a time if I'm reading your affidavit correctly in the prior statement. "I was forced to leave office under direct and intense pressure from Joe Biden in the US administration, in my conversations with Poroshenko at the time, he was emphatic that I should cease my investigations regarding Burisma. When I did not he said that the US via Biden were refusing to release US Dollars 1 billion promise to Ukraine. He said he had no choice therefore, but to ask me to resign." Do you remember that conversation?

Shokin Translator: Almost the way it's written there, the fact I was put in a situation where I have to quit, so that my country gets that money. Mr. Shokin just adds that that conversation contain that you know that we are waging the war, we need the money. You just have to quit so that the country gets the money. . . . He didn't want to quit.

Rudy Giuliani: But the President made it clear to you that the real reason he wanted you to resign was because of the pressure from the US administration and Biden, because otherwise, they wouldn't get the $1 billion loan guarantee.

Shokin Translator: Literally Biden demands that you are dismissed.[153]

So Shokin is gone by April 2016. The new prosecutor, Yuriy Lutsenko, opens and closes his investigation into Burisma and Zlochevsky within four months, the oligarch is allowed to return without incident, and now it's Shokin who's accused of corruption. During our interview I also put a dagger through the heart of that allegation.

Rudy Giuliani: So this is a certificate [I'm holding it up] saying from the [Ukrainian] Minister of Interior that you've never been in court charged with anything. . . . So the claim that you're corrupt, Mr. Shokin is another lie.

Shokin Translator: Yes.[154]

Not only is this man fired, accused of corruption, his reputation smeared, he's denied a visa when he tries to come to the US to tell his story. On top of it all, he gets poisoned. That's right, poisoned. It happened in September 2019, after he testified under oath about his firing. He got very sick one night, went to a hospital in Kiev, and according to the medical report, almost died twice. We got him out of Ukraine, fearing that he'd be poisoned again, and we got him to the Rudolfinerhaus Privatklinik in Vienna, Austria where he received treatment from Dr. Nikolai Korpan, Professor of Medicine. (That's the same doctor and clinic that treated former Ukrainian president Viktor Yushchenko for dioxin poisoning during the 2004 presidential campaign.)

Shokin's primary diagnosis was mercury poisoning. The medical report goes on to describe how much mercury was in his system, which is about five times more than you can possibly tolerate. Like Yushchenko, Shokin survived. He went on to force a Ukrainian court to look into Biden's role in his firing[155], but the 2020 criminal probe was closed after nine months and little or no actual investigation.[156] And just last year, Shokin told Fox News that he thought both Bidens were being bribed. "I do not want to deal in unproven facts, but my firm personal conviction is that yes, this was the case. . . .They were being bribed. And the fact that Joe Biden gave away $1 billion in U.S. money in exchange for my dismissal, my firing—isn't that alone a case of corruption?"[157]

That, in a nutshell, pretty much sums up our case against the Bidens in Ukraine. Joe Biden, the vice president of the United States, the "point person" who is supposed to clean up corruption in this Eastern European country, instead exacerbated it. And has the nerve to brag about it! He offers something of value—in this case, a $1 billion loan guarantee—in exchange for an official action—the firing of Ukraine's prosecutor general. And now we know the motive—to keep that prosecutor general from investigating his son's business involvement with a corrupt oligarch and company. That, my friends, is the classic definition of bribery. Or extortion. Take your pick.

Regarding the outcome of our presentation to the US Attorneys and FBI agents in Pittsburgh, after their initial enthusiasm, for about three weeks they called Bob Costello just about every day, looking for more information, more details, witness contact information, things like that. We even offered to put them in contact with the woman who kept the books for Burisma who said she would give us access to the bank records that detailed payments she said the company sent to offshore bank accounts owned by the Bidens.[158] Then the calls petered out. I was busy at the time with Donald Trump's first impeachment over the "perfect" call to Zelenskyy, so it took me a while to realize that we'd been sidelined.

All of this happened about eight months before Apple repair shop owner John Paul Mac Isaac filled out our "contact" form and we ended up with Hunter Biden's laptop. Here's but a taste of the corroborating evidence we found there that shows just how much Joe and Hunter Biden were entwined in Ukraine:

- April 12, 2014: Hunter emails his Rosemont Seneca partner Devon Archer with "thoughts" on how to make themselves useful to Zlochevsky and Burisma. Among the 22 points in his plan are "The contract [with Burisma] should begin now—not after the upcoming visit of my guy. [Joe was due in Ukraine the following week.[159]] That should include a retainer in the range of 25k p/m w/additional fees where appropriate for more in depth work to go to BSF for our protection. Complete separate from our respective deals re board participation."[160]
- April 16, 2014: Burisma posts a photo of Devon Archer and Joe Biden on their website. The following month, Eric Schwerin (another Biden apparatchik) emails the board members to let them know that Joe's lawyer requested that the photo be removed because "legally they aren't comfortable

with the VP's picture being up on the site as what seems like an endorsement."[161]

- April 16, 2015: Joe attends dinner with Burisma top executive Vadym Pozharskyi and others at Café Milano in Washington, DC. The next day Pozharskyi emails Hunter to thank him "for inviting me to DC and giving an opportunity to meet your father and spent (sic) some time together."[162]

- March 19, 2017: Joe is not even out of the VP office for two months when Hunter's compensation for being on the Burisma board goes from $83k/month to $40k/month.[163]

Now there's new evidence that's come to light. It's evidence (specifically, memos included in a cache of 3.39 million documents) that the FBI has had since 2016. Reporter John Solomon was finally able to access it—after it was hidden for eight years –through the work being done by the House Committee on Oversight and Accountability and its impeachment investigation committee. "The memos state Hunter Biden was . . . supposed to serve on the board of [a] new company called Burnham Energy Security LLC, and it was going to be capitalized in 2015 by Burisma owner [Mykola] Zlochevsky, [who committed to contributing] '$120 Million over thirty-six (36) months to be invested in exploration and leasehold improvements.'"[164] Zlochevsky was supposed to put up the money, but Hunter and his proposed partners in the new firm, Devon Archer and Jason Galanis, did not have to contribute financially. "The Burnham partners would have a 25 percent interest, basically at no cost. . . . Instead, Burnham was putting up the relationship capital of the Biden name,"[165] Galanis testified before the committee on February 23, 2024.

Keep in mind the wider context in which this particular venture was proposed. Zlochevsky is on the run from his own government, wanted for fraud. A little of his fortune has been restored, and now that his bank funds are unfrozen in the UK, he has $120 million to burn. He wants to return to Ukraine, to be able to move freely there, and he wants to stop all investigations into Burisma.[166] He's amassed this board full of what he believes are powerful friends, especially Hunter

Biden and Devon Archer. Proving that Zlochevsky's got "juice," one of his top executives, Vadym Pozharskyi, has just rubbed elbows at a fancy, upscale Café Milano dinner in Washington, DC that included VP Biden. To an oligarch with billions at stake, dropping $120 million into a fund which may or may not make money, but which might cement his insurance policy against prosecution, is just the cost of doing business. He needs the appearance of Biden backing, if not the actual flexing of Biden muscle itself. In an email proposing the Burnham Energy Security LLC board of directors, Pozharskyi writes to Devon, "You mentioned to me that it's also you and HB [Hunter Biden] who will be the founders of the Llc in Delaware. Cliff mentioned only yourself. For credibility 'Ukrainian' purposes you both would be better."[167]

The scheme runs into some significant roadblocks though. First, Beau Biden dies on May 30, 2015. That stuns the entire Biden family and is reportedly the catalyst for Hunter's rapid spiral into an abyss of a serious drug/alcohol/sex addiction that lasts for several years. Then, on September 24, Jason Galanis is arrested for conspiring to sell fraudulent junk bonds issued by the Wakpamni Lake Community Corporation (WLCC) of the Oglala Sioux tribe in South Dakota.[168] (He's just the first to be caught by law enforcement. His father, John, a con man that I prosecuted—and secured a conviction for—back in the 1980s, was also snared in the roundup,[169] as was Devon Archer.)[170] And even though "his fingerprints were all over"[171] the case, Hunter was never charged. His lawyers played the "dad card." In response to Hunter's SEC subpoena, they wrote on April 20, 2016, "The confidential nature of this investigation is very important to our client and it would be unfair, not just to our client, but also to his father, the Vice President of the United States, if his involvement in an SEC investigation and parallel criminal probe were to become the subject of any media attention."[172] Talk about "get out of jail free."

The final nail in the coffin of Zlochevsky's $120 million plan for Burnham was the Geoffrey Pyatt speech on September 24, 2015, where he slammed Ukrainian prosecutors for not going after the Burisma head on corruption charges. Explains John Solomon, "The

Pyatt speech proved particularly troublesome for Biden, Archer and Burisma. . . . [It] unexpectedly kicked Ukrainian prosecutors into a more aggressive effort to investigate Zlochevsky in fall 2015, an effort that came to an abrupt halt when Vice President Joe Biden pressured Ukraine to fire the chief prosecutor Shokin, by threatening to withhold $1 billion in U.S. loan guarantees. Archer told Congress last year that Burisma wanted Hunter Biden to get help from 'D.C.' to deal with the pressure from the Shokin probe."[173]

So now you've heard the story, you've read the testimony, you've seen the documentation and been given details of the activities that took place in Ukraine. No question that the Biden Crime Family cashed in big time there. That was the first huge cash haul for the enterprise, but there were more scores—even bigger ones—to come.

CHAPTER 3

IT HAPPENED IN CHINA

The 2013 photo is iconic.[174] Three generations of Bidens—Joe, grand-daughter Finnegan, and son Hunter (Finnegan's dad) wave to the waiting crowd as they exit the plane, Air Force Two logo prominent in the background. It looks like just the usual American vice-presidential arrival for a state visit in China with family members in tow. Traveling with them was an NBC reporter named Josh Lederman, who later wrote, "What wasn't known then was that as he accompanied his father to China, Hunter Biden was forming a Chinese private equity fund that associates said at the time was planning to raise big money, including from China."[175]

That's just one tiny bit of what wasn't public knowledge in 2013. For starters, this trip was not Hunter's initial foray into doing business with China. In fact, the Biden Crime Family, which had mostly restricted their grifts to the United States before Joe became vice president, started their plans for global expansion almost as soon as he and Obama were elected on November 4, 2008. Between then and 2011, Hunter hitched himself to partners in no less than eight new corporate entities. Those entities, in turn, made deals with companies all over the globe. It reminded me of that old 1970s commercial on TV, the one where one woman liked her shampoo so much she told a friend, and they told two friends, and they told two friends, and so on and so on and so on. Pretty soon the television screen was filled with lookalike women, all ostensibly raving about their shampoo. That's kind of what Hunter Biden's corporations seemed like to me—too many to differentiate, each with their own bank accounts, and all devoted to one thing—raking in cash for the Biden Crime Family.

We've already reported on the income from Ukraine. But that was small potatoes compared to the haul from China. One account puts that total at $31 million.[176] It would not be surprising if the total exceeded $50 million. There are allegations of offshore accounts deliberately ignored for years by all the Biden regime investigatory agencies.

How was Hunter Biden, a middle-aged alcoholic, drug and sex addict on the precipice of a dizzying downward spiral, able to pull off such a scheme? For one thing—the main thing—he had the last name that magically opened doors in the Middle Kingdom.[177] "Doing business in China often entails having the right contacts and relationships. . . . Having the proper connections or family ties in China is so important there is a single word for it: *guanxi* (pronounced gwan-Che.) It is a word that describes the system of social networks that facilitate business in China. . . .While guanxi in business and personal matters may be a noble cultural practice, when it involves American politicians and their families . . . *guanxi* crosses the line into corruption."[178] I would amend the last sentence of that quote to say that guanxi may be acceptable in a system dominated by billionaire Chinese Communist oligarchs, but when American politicians and their families are involved, the corruption is blatant.

Before Hunter got to China, another Biden family member went to work there. That would be Casey Owens (now Casey Owens Costello)—Joe Biden's niece, Valerie Owens's daughter and Hunter Biden's cousin. Casey landed a job in China with the Treasury Department in 2009—just after the Obama/Biden administration assumed office—as "special assistant to the senior coordinator for China."[179] As such, she was privy to information about the China Investment Corporation (CIC), a state-owned Chinese wealth fund that her cousin Hunter very much wanted to do business with.

From the belly of the beast, Casey emailed her relative and his business partner Eric Schwerin several times, passing along intel about, among other topics, the target company's conference schedule, its financial prospects and more. Hunter and another associate, Devon Archer, met with CIC officials in April 2011.[180] Apparently no deals were made but Devon did get a nice letter from Joe after the two attended a lunch that January for China's president Hu Jintao.[181] (Remember how Joe was adamant about "never"[182] discussing his family's business?) And when Casey left the Treasury Department in 2011, she got a heartwarming shoutout from her uncle at a speech he made on May 9 to the US-China Strategic and Economic Dialogue meeting. "My niece who—excuse me, as we say in the Senate, a point of personal privilege—who graduated from Harvard not too long ago, works for Secretary Geithner, she did exactly what we hope another 100,000 [young Americans] will do: She studied Chinese and went and lived in China and is now devoted to making sure the relationship gets better and better and better."[183] Joe went on to proclaim, "That a rising China is a positive, positive development, not only for China but for America and the world writ large."[184] Seems like the whole Biden family tried very hard to work on that "rising China" aspect of the relationship.

For his part, Hunter not only had the right name but he also picked the right partners. His contacts in the China "rackets" ran the gamut from other wannabe get-rich-quick schemers with political connections, to American mobsters, to Chinese billionaires with ties to the highest levels of the People's Liberation Army (PLA), Chinese Communist Party (CCP), and the heads of its spy apparatus. This unsavory cast of characters coalesced to put together the two main deals from which millions in China money flowed.

The first deal emanated from a Rosemont Capital offspring. You may remember from Chapter 2 that Rosemont Capital was, as a Securities and Exchange Commission investigation revealed, "'a $2.4 billion private equity firm co-owned by Hunter Biden and Chris Heinz' with Devon Archer as 'Managing Partner.'"[185] One of the

Rosemonts—Rosemont Seneca Partners—hooked up with a Boston company called the Thornton Group. Its chairman is one James Bulger. While it's interesting to note that James's father, Billy Bulger, once headed the Massachusetts State Senate, what's more pertinent is that his more notorious uncle (for whom he was named) was better known as Whitey Bulger—a Mafia hit man, indicted for murdering nineteen people, leader of the Winter Hill Gang in Boston, fugitive for sixteen years, and once the second most wanted person on the FBI's Ten Most Wanted list right behind Osama Bin Laden.[186] The law caught up with Whitey in June 2011, a little more than a year after his nephew and Hunter Biden were photographed meeting with top financial executives in China "to explore the possibilities and opportunities of business cooperation."[187] Also on that trip was Thornton Group co-founder and CEO Michael Lin (sometimes identified as Lin Junliang),[188] who allegedly "has a good connection with both the Kuomintang (a political party in Taiwan) and the CCP in Beijing."[189]

While the three generations of Bidens roamed around Beijing on that 2013 state visit—Dad meeting with top government heads for official talks, then posing for heartwarming photographs, sipping tea and eating ice cream with Finnegan—Hunter was presumably putting the finishing touches on his own deals. He and Devon Archer, as Rosemont Seneca Partners, teamed with Bulger and Lin's Thornton Group and a Chinese firm called Bohai Harvest to form a new private equity fund—Bohai Harvest RST Equity Fund Management Co. LTD, a.k.a. BHR.[190] "The Chinese business license that brought the new fund into existence was issued by Shanghai authorities 10 days after the trip, with Hunter Biden a member of the board."[191] He also acquired a 10 percent equity interest in BHR, which he didn't sell until 2021.[192] This made Hunter and Devon partners with the Chinese Communist government, as well as a Mafia hitman's nephew.

BHR quickly set about making deals. The firm's CEO, Jonathan Li (to whom Hunter introduced his dad on that same 2013 trip in the lobby of the hotel they were staying in[193]) explained their strategy on the company website. "One element of our business model is that we go abroad with industrial players from China. . . . Meanwhile, Bohai itself has connections with large Chinese financial institutions."[194] One of those institutions was the Bank of China, "an enormously powerful financial institution. But the Bank of China is very different from the Bank of America. The Bank of China is government-owned, which means that its role as a bank blurs into its role as a tool of the government. . . . In short, the Chinese government was literally funding a business that it co-owned along with the sons of two of America's most powerful decision makers."[195]

Another Chinese national who helped facilitate the BHR deal was Che Feng, who Hunter referred to on his infamous laptop as the "Super Chairman." Here's the rundown on Che and his colleagues.

Che Feng's influential father-in-law was Dai Xianglong, the former governor of China's central bank, who also served as a government regulator, mayor of the city of Tianjin and then, "in 2008, he became head of the National Council for Social Security Fund. During much of his career, he developed close ties with senior Chinese leaders, including [then Chinese Prime Minister Wen Jiabao], who served with him on the powerful Central Financial Work Commission. The commission oversaw China's banking, securities and insurance regulators, and the biggest financial institutions."[196]

Both Che and Dai mysteriously disappeared in 2015 after being caught up in Xi Jinping's anti-corruption campaign.[197] (Another of Che's confederates was a Chinese billionaire named Xiao Jianhua, "a key money launderer for [former CCP leader Jiang Zemin]"[198] who also disappeared and then was reportedly held for investigation.) But before falling out with his own government, Che was Hunter's hero. "I don't believe in lottery tickets anymore but I do believe in the super chairman," he gushed to Devon Archer in a 2011 email. "If you and me get around 7 percent of this fund [meaning BHR] it could be in many ways the end all and be all."[199]

Before we get to the "end all and be all" details, I want to give a little context to this particular company. At the time Hunter was putting together his deal, the Obama administration had declared its "Pivot to Asia." Rather than concentrate on the Middle East, as the Bush administration had done, Obama decided to focus on East Asia and specifically on the People's Republic of China. Cornerstones of the new policy included "strengthening bilateral security alliances; deepening our working relationships with emerging powers, including with China; engaging with regional multilateral institutions; expanding trade and investment; forging a broad-based military presence; and advancing democracy and human rights."[200] Initially, it was thought that the Obama official to oversee the "pivot" would be the author who penned that policy—then Secretary of State Hillary Clinton. But as it turned out, VP Biden "got" China in 2012.[201]

As the designated "point man," Biden failed miserably. He was supposed to curb China's military expansion. Instead, China created about three thousand acres of artificial islands in the South China Sea[202] and built military bases there.[203] He was also supposed to get China to agree to stop stealing US intellectual property.[204] That didn't work either.[205] As for "advancing . . . human rights"? In 2014, the Chinese Government launched the "Strike Hard Campaign Against Violent Terrorism"[206] in Xinjiang province, home of the ethnic Uyghurs. That led to internment camps (officially titled "vocational education and training centers") where the Muslim minority population was "subjected to torture, forced labor . . . even forced sterilization."[207] So much for Joe moving the needle in that arena.

What Biden did do, though, was get to know Xi Jinping. The two were equals—vice presidents of their respective countries—when they first met in 2011.[208] Xi was the heir apparent to Hu Jintao as the President of China and General Secretary of the Chinese Communist Party. He took over those positions in 2012. (Biden, of course, didn't assume the US presidency until 2021.) But in the early days, the aspiring #2s traveled and spent time together—lots of time. "I've spent more time with Xi Jinping than any leader in the world, over 90 hours alone with him since I've been Vice President,"[209] Joe declared to *Time* magazine.

So is the reason that President Biden is perceived as "soft"[210] on China due to his relationship with Xi? Or could it possibly be the result of something called "elite capture"? "Elite capture, as used by the CCP, is a form of political warfare that seeks to control the actions of political, academic, business, and cultural leaders outside of China to benefit the CCP. The means of control take a variety of forms including financial incentives, financial dependence or compromise, business entanglement, offers of access to opportunities within China, ideological appeal, and even blackmail. By incentivizing elites to act according to personal interests that have been aligned with those of the CCP rather than according to the interests of stakeholders in institutions which the elites represent, this strategy threatens to separate a country's elites from its citizens."[211] Surely the Biden Crime Family's financial entanglements with China fall into this definition.

Take, for example, some of the deals in which Hunter's BHR was involved. Keep in mind that all these transactions occurred *while Joe Biden was the sitting vice president of the United States*:

- It helped a financially struggling Australian coal mining firm, Yancoal, stay afloat by issuing bonds held by "two state-run Chinese banks and a subsidiary of a fledgling Chinese private-investment firm called Bohai Harvest, whose board roster includes Hunter Biden, son of U.S. Vice President Joe Biden."[212]
- BHR helped Chinese mining company China Molybdenum purchase a Congolese cobalt and copper mine—Tenke Fungurume—from a US company called Freeport-McMoRan for $2.65 billion. "As part of that deal, China Molybdenum sought a partner to buy out a minority stakeholder in the mine, Lundin Mining of Canada. That is when BHR became involved. Records in Hong Kong show that the $1.14 billion BHR, through subsidiaries, paid to buy out Lundin came entirely from Chinese state-backed companies."[213] (This is important because cobalt is essential to EV batteries.)[214]
- BHR was also an "anchor investor"[215] in a Chinese-owned nuclear energy company, China General Nuclear Power Company (CGN). One of their engineers—Allen Ho (though born in Taiwan, he later became a naturalized US citizen)—was sentenced to twenty-four months in prison after he pled guilty to "leaking [US] nuclear technology to China

over a 19-year period."[216] Ho, not so coincidentally, lived in
Delaware, not very far from Joe Biden's residence there.

- But perhaps the most egregious deal that BHR did—the
  one that was possibly the most damaging to US national
  security—was the one involving Henniges, an American firm
  that made anti-vibration technologies which had military, as
  well civilian uses. Senator Chuck Grassley (R-IA) outlined the
  problem in a 2019 letter to Secretary of the Treasury Steven
  Mnuchin. "The direct involvement of Mr. Hunter Biden
  and Mr. Heinz in the acquisition of Henniges by the Chinese
  government creates a potential conflict of interest. Both
  are directly related to high-ranking Obama administration
  officials. . . . The appearance of potential conflicts in this
  case is particularly troubling given Mr. Biden's and Mr.
  Heinz's history of investing in and collaborating with Chinese
  companies, including at least one posing significant national
  security concerns. . . . In September 2015, BHR joined
  with a subsidiary of the Aviation Industry Corporation of
  China (AVIC) to acquire Henniges for $600 million. AVIC
  acquired 51 percent of the company, and BHR acquired 49
  percent. According to reports, the acquisition of Henniges
  by BHR and AVIC was the 'biggest Chinese investment
  into US automotive manufacturing assets to date.' Because
  the acquisition gave Chinese companies direct control of
  Henniges' anti-vibration technologies, the transaction was
  reviewed by CFIUS [Committee on Foreign Investment in
  the United States]. CFIUS approved the transaction despite
  reports that in 2007, years before BHR teamed up with
  AVIC's subsidiary, AVIC was reportedly involved in stealing
  sensitive data regarding the Joint Strike Fighter program.
  AVIC later reportedly incorporated the stolen data into
  China's J-20 and J-31 aircraft."[217]

BHR was certainly lucrative for the Biden Crime Family (although I
don't have a final tally on the take), and the appearance of impropriety

raised eyebrows along with headlines. However bad those optics were, in 2015 when Hunter and co. started working with the China Energy Company Limited (CEFC), a Chinese energy company, it wasn't an *apparent* conflict of interest. The Biden Crime Family took money from the CCP—full stop.

The House Oversight Committee report on The Bidens' Influence Peddling Timeline pegs December 7, 2015 as the date Hunter Biden and CEFC Chairman Ye Jianming began communicating about a possible partnership.[218] The problem with that? "[S]peculation swirled that the company and its chairman, Ye Jianming, were connected to China's military . . . that Ye worked from 2003 to 2005 as deputy secretary-general of 'CAIFC,' the acronym for China Association for International Friendly Contact. That group is a political arm of the People's Liberation Army, according to a 2013 report by the Project 2049 Institute, an Arlington, Virginia-based researcher that focuses on Asia security issues."[219] Besides its military connections, "CAIFC has additional ties to the Ministries of State Security, Civil Affairs, and Foreign Affairs, and it is a platform for deploying undercover intelligence gatherers."[220]

Ye's CCP military and spy agency associations are one thing. But there's now evidence that he could have been connected to Mexico's premier drug cartel as well. The mysterious billionaire "was also business partners with the former leader of a Chinese triad called the United Bamboo Gang (UBG). His name is Zhang Anle, but he is more commonly known by the name 'White Wolf.' Ye and White Wolf set up the Shanghai Zhenrong Petroleum Company together. White Wolf's gang, UBG, also has a 'partnership' with Mexico's Sinaloa Cartel and helps them in the production and distribution of fentanyl in the United States."[221]

With more and more investigations into the Biden family's China dealings, more information about Ye and the CEFC has already come to light,[222] including the suggestion that Joe Biden himself considered joining the "board of a CCP-linked company."[223] But until these allegations can be proven beyond a reasonable doubt, for the purposes of this book, we'll stick to the evidence already documented.

Back to 2015 when Hunter and Ye were introduced. One account puts the intermediary as Biden family fixer/accountant/Rosemont Seneca Partners president Eric Schwerin, who fielded the approach from former Serbian foreign minister Vuk Jeremic, an acquaintance of Joe Biden from his VP days.[224] Another says it was a wealthy "consultant" and (relatively) small time Democratic donor named Scott Oh.[225] Whoever facilitated the introduction, Hunter and Ye hit it off. Over the next three years, the duo's initial meeting sparked a series of deals that—despite Hunter sinking to the darkest depths of his crack/alcohol/sex addictions[226]—netted the Biden Crime Family $6 million in just nine months, according to one account.[227] And that was just for starters.

Aiding, abetting, and (sometimes) sharing in the spoils was an overlapping spaghetti plate of characters, their associated corporations, and bank accounts. Among the main strands:

- Rob Walker—Hunter's friend and a partner in the Chinese venture. It was through the bank account of his company, Robinson Walker LLC, that the first of the CCP funds flowed. A former staff member of New York governor George Pataki's introduced Walker to James Gilliar.[228]
- James Gilliar—A mysterious Englishman, who, early on, sold advertising in rural England, was rumored to be a former MI6 agent, and also ran a company called European Energy and Infrastructure Group (EEIG). Gilliar is listed as an advisor to "Dr. Sheikh Sultan Bin Khalifa Bin Zayed Al Nahyan"[229] in the UAE. Gilliar also had dealings in the Czech Republic, where he is said to be based. He involved Ye and the CEFC in those dealings, which reportedly led to Ye's eventual downfall.[230] Interestingly, Gilliar did not have a fan in James Biden, who told the FBI in his September 20, 2022 interview that he was "unimpressed" with the Englishman who "was a big guy and wore a Superman T-shirt that supposedly cost $5-7000."[231]
- Anthony (Tony) Bobulinski—He was recruited by Gilliar, who gifted him on Christmas Eve, 2015 with a text

inviting him to participate in "a deal between one of the most prominent families from US and them constructed by me."[232] Through several different WhatsApp messages, Gilliar eventually let Bobulinski know the identities of his partners in the proposed "investment firm like Goldman Sachs,"[233] disclosing that one was the CEFC and another was the Bidens. "Joe . . . would be actively involved once he left office . . . Gilliar said."[234] An experienced financial executive, Bobulinski's job would be to manage the fund. Before accepting the role, the former naval officer voiced doubts about working with Hunter, due to his dismissal from the Navy reserves after testing positive for cocaine.[235] Gilliar tried to smooth over any apprehension, saying "'Money there, intent there . . . skill sets missing . . . We need to create the best deal platform in history and they haven't got a clue . . . . But he's super smart. . . . Has a few demons but u are used to those, right.'"[236]

- James and Sara Biden—James and Sara, through their Lion Hall Group, reaped over $1 million from this venture. After one cash infusion, Sara wrote a $40,000 check to Joe Biden for "loan repayment." Congressman Byron Donalds (R-FL) later traced the source of that money back to the CCP.

- Dr. Patrick Ho—Originally an ophthalmologist, Ho became Minister of Home Affairs in Hong Kong before teaming up with Ye and becoming the vice-chairman and secretary general of the CEFC.[237] His arrest in 2017 for bribing officials in Africa kicked off the company's eventual demise.

- Zang Jianjun—(a.k.a. Director Zhang.) Described as "an influential businessman in China . . . [Zang] is executive director of private Chinese conglomerate CEFC."[238] In that capacity, he oversaw the US company's daily operations.

- Zhao Runlong—(a.k.a. Raymond Zhao.) He was the interpreter for Zang, who spoke no English. Bobulinski described him as "sort of chief of staff for Director Zang."[239]

- Gongwen Dong—(a.k.a. Dongwen Gong, Kevin Dong.) Dong was Ye's representative in New York. Bobulinski described him as "sort of a deal guy who had signing authority for Chairman Ye."[240] Dong had his own company, Monochrome Capital Partners, LLC; the name shows up in some of the CEFC/Hudson West communications.
- Mervyn Yan—A friend and business associate of Kevin Dong's,[241] Yan described his role in the enterprise as an "on-the-ground person who execute and pretty much sourcing the infrastructure deals."[242] Yan also had his own separate LLC, Coldharbour Capital.

A number of excellent books and articles (not to mention government committees and the "Report on the Biden Laptop" on MarcoPolo501c3.org) have exhaustively chronicled the details of the CEFC/Biden partnership. A few of those sources are noted below.[243] We'll include some of that familiar information, but because we want to concentrate on material that could possibly be cited in our potential RICO case, what I'll focus on are the general timeline of the activities, the occasions where Joe Biden was present (both literally and, in one case, figuratively), emails/texts that document his involvement and, of course, the money trail.

There was business afoot with CEFC as early as February 23, 2016, according to an email from Gilliar to Walker and Hunter,[244] where the author advises them of a presentation he is planning on giving to the CEFC board the following week. "It has been made clear to me that CEFC wish to engage in further business relations with our group and we will present a few projects to them," he writes. But nobody gets paid for this work at the time. Joe's still VP. Money will have to wait.

Barely a month after Joe leaves political office on January 20, 2017 to resume being an ordinary citizen for the first time in over forty years, Hunter has a mid-February Miami dinner with Chairman Ye, and afterwards receives the gift of a diamond. (It weighs between 2.8

and 3.16 carats and is worth between $10,000 and $80,000, depending on which report you believe.[245])

At some point in the first quarter of 2017, Hunter, Rob Walker, Ye Jianming, and several other CEFC associates are having lunch in a private room at the Four Seasons Hotel in Washington, DC, when Joe Biden drops by. According to Walker, Joe stays about ten minutes, exchanges pleasantries, and leaves. "I don't think he even took a sip of water if there was water," Walker testified. The purpose of the encounter, according to Walker, was that "from time to time he [Joe] liked to lay eyes on his son who was in and out of sobriety."[246] Tony Bobulinski has a very different explanation for that drop-in at the end of this chapter.

About a month after the Miami meeting, State Energy HK Limited (Ye's company) wires $3 million into Walker's Robinson Walker LLC bank account,[247] proving, as noted in the November 18, 2020 report of Committee on Homeland Security and Governmental Affairs issued by Senators Chuck Grassley (R-IA) and Ron Johnson (R-WI), that "These transactions are a direct link between Walker and the communist Chinese government and, because of his close association with Hunter Biden, yet another tie between Hunter Biden's financial arrangements and the communist Chinese government."[248]

The cash doesn't stay in the Robinson Walker account for long. Between March 6 and May 18, $1,065,692 is dispersed to accounts associated with Hunter (Owasco P.C., RSTP II LLC), James Biden (JBBSR, INC), Hallie Biden, unknown "Biden" accounts and something called First Clearing LLC.[249]

With the first portion of cash safely banked, the Bidens and their associates set about formally setting up the new entity, which eventually emerges as SinoHawk Holdings LLC. Despite his misgivings about Hunter's dismissal from the Navy, on May 2, Bobulinski flies to Los Angeles for an in-person introduction to his new business partners. He meets Hunter, and spends an extensive amount of time with him on the patio of the Chateau Marmont Hotel, where the son "laughed off" Tony's concerns about the family being involved in ventures with the Chinese. "He was very emboldened, confident, that . . . he had access to his father whenever, wherever he wanted,"[250] Bobulinski told the House Oversight committee. According to journalist Miranda Divine's account of that meeting, Hunter also tells Tony that he "has his father's ear and can bypass his advisors."[251]

Next day, Tony, Hunter and James Biden gather in a nearly empty bar at the Beverly Hilton Hotel. That's where the Milken Institute's Global Conference was being held, with Joe Biden as one of the speakers. The plan was to introduce Bobulinski to the senior Biden via a late night private meet-and-greet. Tony continued, "What I thought was sort of slightly odd at the time is Hunter and Jim started coaching me about the meeting. . . . They sort of coached me to say, 'We're not going to go into a lot of detail [about CEFC.] . . . My dad will talk about what he sort of chooses to talk about."

Seeing Joe arrive and head towards the group, Hunter got up to brief his father before introducing the new business partner, a move that mystified Tony. "The only reason why I was there was because . . . I was a partner of the Biden family's in this operating business. There was no other reason for me to be, first, in that bar and meeting with him or him meeting with me." The conclave lasted for about forty-five minutes and focused mainly on Bobulinski's background. Next day, he was invited to be Biden's guest at the Milken conference, seated at the head table with Milken himself, to watch Joe's speech about the cancer Moonshot. Afterwards, the politician and the business CEO walked to Joe's car, where the interaction concluded, says Bobulinski, with an instruction to "look out for my brother and son."

Shortly thereafter (May 13, actually), Gilliar emailed the following proposal to his SinoHawk partners, titled "Expectations," laying out compensation and annual salaries. Hunter and Bobulinski are to each receive $850,000; Gilliar and Walker, $500,000 each; with an unknown salary for James Biden. But the real payout is in the percentage of the company each partner would hold. Gilliar writes, "At the moment there's a provisional agreement that the equity will be distributed as follows:

20 H

20 RW

20 JG

20 TB

10 Jim

10 held by H for the big guy ?"[252]

In his House Oversight Committee testimony on February 16, 2024—under oath—Bobulinski deciphered the partner shares. "This shows 20 percent for H. H is Hunter Biden; 20 percent for RW is Rob Walker; 20 percent for JG is James Gilliar; 20 percent for TB, that's me, Tony Bobulinski; and then it says 10 for Jim, and that's Jim Biden. And then it says, '10 held for H for the big guy.' The H in that message is Hunter Biden, and the big guy—100 percent—is Joe Biden."[253]

Bobulinski's unmasking of "the big guy's" identity has gotten a lot of pushback, not just from Joe's defenders, but also from two actual participants in the deal, namely Hunter and James Biden, who both denied Joe's involvement when they testified before Congress.[254] In his testimony, Rob Walker refused to confirm or deny Bobulinski's statement. When asked by Congressman Jim Jordan, "who is the big guy?" Walker replied, "You'll have to ask James [Gilliar.]"[255]

James's proposed deal structure did not meet with universal approval, as evidenced in these excerpts from the following text exchanges.[256] They also reveal the growing tension between Hunter and Bobulinski.

First Hunter says there's no way he can live on $850,000 a year, given his financial obligations (which include an expensive divorce, his three daughters' tuition in elite educational institutions like the Sidwell Friends School and the University of Pennsylvania, and his relationship with Hallie Biden, not to mention his drug and sex habits). Tony puts on his CEO hat to remind his free-spending partner that "we have to pay a team of people who will be working 100 hours a week." Infuriated, Hunter rebukes his colleagues, saying "Zhang" [meaning Director Zang] and the rest of the CEFC group is "coming to be MY partners with the Bidens. He [Zhang] has implied that the #1 [a reference to Xi Jinping] has made that clear."

Next day, Hunter attempts to lower the temperature with an apology, but clearly he's still not ready to totally make nice. "I'm the only one putting an entire family legacy on the line . . . and if you think it's reasonable that I turn the keys over to someone that I've spent less than 12 hours with than (sic) that makes me nervous."

Tony vents his concerns to Gilliar.[257] Bobulinski: "H [Hunter] brought in Jim [James Biden] simply to leverage getting more equity for himself and family in the final hour, that is evident." Gilliar: "I know why the [sic] wants the deal and what makes it enormous, it's the family name in reality, they could have asked for 51 per cent, maybe u would not be interested but many US moguls would have been." Gilliar then adds, "Ye wants."

The text dispute between Hunter and Tony spills over to yet another day. Hunter proposes meeting in person to resolve it. And he's not shy about raising the specter of his father as the 800 lb. gorilla to get his way. "In light of the fact we are at an impasse of sorts, and both James' lawyers and my Chairman gave an emphatic NO - I think we should all meet in Romania on Tuesday next week." Tony is unclear about the Chairman reference, but Joe's identity will be confirmed later. "[I] am not sure which Chairman you are referencing but they clearly don't understand the agreement as it is written," he tells Hunter. Then he tries to lighten the mood with a joke about his suggestion for breaking the logjam. "We could arm wrestle for it, play bingo, have your Chairman weigh in or something else that is fair and neutral to both sides."

With that, Hunter blows whatever cool he has left. "Well Tony it may just be the time of night or one too many drinks but you're [sic] trying to be funny is lost on me. . . . I care about one thing. My family. And your demands make me uncomfortable and you're [sic] insults remind me of [expletive deleted] the captain of the lacrosse team said to me in college about my dad right before I broke his [expletive deleted] jaw." Shot back Bobulinski, "That is exactly the point. I and all the partners around the table are trying to protect u and your family! Way more than you even obviously understand." Later, Tony drives home the point even more. "[I]f you are so worried about your family, you wouldn't be doing this because as u said, all of your dad's lawyers and any lawyer would advise you and Jim not to touch this with a 100 foot pole . . . so if you are willing to take risk so be it."

Rob Walker, who implored the two to cease their contentious group texts, explained Hunter's testiness to the new guy in the group. "When he said his chairman, he was talking about his dad and I think your dismissal of it maybe offended him a bit, but you didn't know what he was talking about. Let's let it go til the morning if we can."

That next morning, Gilliar is more explicit in his exchange with Bobulinski. Gilliar: "Don't mention Joe being involved, it's only when u are face to face, I know u know that but they are paranoid." Bobulinski: "You need to stress to H, does he want to be the reason or factor that blows up his dad's campaign." (Keep in mind this is almost two years before Joe actually declares his run for the presidency on April 25, 2019.[258])

Despite the infighting, the final SinoHawk deal is signed on May 24. There are two equal partners in the deal—Hudson West IV LLC, (controlled by Chairman Ye and Kevin Dong)[259] and Oneida Holdings LLC. Oneida is made up of five corporate entities[260]: GK Temujin (a holding company representing Hunter Biden); Sino Atlantic Solutions LLC (James Biden); Robinson Walker LLC (Rob Walker); 8 International Holdings Limited (James Gilliar); and Global Investment Ventures LLC (Tony Bobulinski). Each holding company has 20 percent. There is no 10 percent for "the big guy." But of course Joe Biden will be taken care of, as he has been for over thirty years, by getting 50 percent of his son's income.

Attention now turns to money. According to the terms of the agreement, the venture is to have a $10 million capitalization, with each of the 50-50 partners contributing equally. The CEFC, via Hudson West IV, will put up $5 million, period. Oneida's share comes in the form of a $5 million interest-free loan from the CEFC.

When the funds don't come right away, as they are supposed to, Tony sends a flowery introductory letter to Chairman Ye, on June 15, trying to get the ball rolling. Despite fuming privately to Gilliar about

Bobulinski,[261] Hunter follows up two days later with a cordial note touting Tony. He also sends his "best wishes from the entire Biden family," then explicitly asks that "$10 MMUSD" be wired "quickly so we can properly fund and operate Sinohawk [sic]."[262]

Ye took his time answering, as he was most likely busy working on finalizing CEFC's $9 billion purchase of a 14 percent share of Rosneft, Russia's 50 percent state owned oil giant (the acquisition was announced that September.[263]) He was also occupied with purchasing about $83 million in New York City real estate, including a four bedroom, 5278 square-foot penthouse at 15 Central Park West and another 4028 square-foot apartment on the 86th floor of 432 Park Avenue.[264] Still, Ye finds time on July 10, to reply to Hunter, promising that "Director Zang and Gongwen Dong [will] expedite the charter capital input to SinoHawk."[265]

That doesn't happen. Bobulinski continues to try to collect, but then gets an email on July 26 from Raymond Zhao (the interpreter), stating that Ye and Zang have a few qualms about the deal. Specifically, while "Chairman Ye and Director Zang fully support the framework of establishing the JV, based on their trust on BD [Biden] family . . . 5 million is lent to BD [the Biden] family in the 10 million charter capital. How will this 5 million be used (or the 10 million as a whole)? This 5 million loan to BD family is interest-free. But if the 5 M is used up, should CEFC keep lending more to the family? If CEFC lends more, they need to know the interest rate for the subsequent loan(s)."[266]

Though frustrated by his Chinese partners not carrying out their part of the agreement, Tony sticks with his CEO role and follows up with further businesslike communications. Hunter, though, has had it, and resorts to Mafia style extortion. On July 30, he sends this What's App message to Zhao: "I am sitting here with my father and we would like to understand why the commitment made has not been fulfilled. I'm very concerned that the chairman has either changed his mind or broken our deal without telling me or that he's unaware of the promises and assurances that have been made have not been kept. Tell the director that I would like to resolve this now before it gets out of hand, and now means tonight. And, Z, if I get a call or text from anyone involved in this other than you, Zhang, or the chairman, I will make certain that between the man sitting next to me and every person he knows and my ability to forever hold a grudge that you will regret not following my direction. I am sitting here waiting for the call with my father."[267] Zhao responds with, "Copy. I will call you on WhatsApp." A couple message exchanges later, Zhao reports, "Hi Hunter, Director did not answer my call, but he got the message you mentioned."[268]

When questioned by the House Oversight Committee, under oath, Hunter insisted that:

- He had no recollection of sending the message
- The Zhao he actually messaged was not Raymond Zhao, Zang's assistant, but a Henry Zhao[269]
- He was drunk or high when he sent the message
- Joe Biden was not with him[270]

(There was a question as to whether Hunter was in Delaware when he sent the message. Photos from his orphaned laptop, though, depict him on that same day with two nieces, sitting behind the wheel of Joe's beloved green 1967 Chevrolet Corvette Stingray convertible at Pop's 6850-square-foot primary residence in Greenville, Delaware.[271] So we may not be able to state beyond a reasonable doubt who was present when he typed out that message, if anyone, and who actually received the message, but we do know where Hunter was.)

We also know that the message uncorked a fast and furious flurry of events on August 2, starting with this email from Hunter to Gongwen Dong (Kevin Dong) and Mervyn Yan:

My Understanding is that the original agreement with the Director was for consulting fees based on introductions alone a rate of $10M per year for a three year guarantee total of $30M. The chairman changed that deal after we met in MIAMI TO A MUCH MORE LASTING AND LUCRATIVE

ARRANGEMENT to create a holding company 50 percent owned by ME and 50 percent owned by him. Consulting fees is one piece of our income stream but the reason this proposal by the chairman was so much more interesting to me and my family is that we would also be partners inn (sic) the equity and profits of the JV's investments. Hence I assumed the reason for our discussion today in which you made clear that the Chaireman (sic) would first get his investment capital returned in the profits would then be split 50/50. If you saying that is not the case then please return us to the original deal 10M per year a guaranteed 3 years plus bonus payments for any successful deal we introduce.[272]

More emails fly and by the end of the day an old Hudson West III LLC entity (it was set up in 2016 and has an EIN, which makes it convenient)[273] is amended with the revised partners becoming Hudson West V LLC (controlled by Dong and the CEFC group) and Owasco PC, the corporation solely owned by Hunter Biden (although his uncle James is also a manager.)[274] There's no James Gilliar. No Rob Walker. And no Tony Bobulinski.

In fact, Bobulinski did not discover that he'd been cut out of the deal until September 2020 when the Senate released their report, "Hunter Biden, Burisma, and Corruption: The Impact on U.S. Government Policy and Related Concerns."[275] "For years, I had no idea what transpired . . . in July and August of 2017," he testified before the House Oversight Committee in February 2024. "For the record, I was defrauded [in] July 2017 by the Biden family. . . . [T]hat Senate report was the first time that I found out that I had been defrauded by the Biden family—and subsequently learned that I was also being lied to by James Gilliar and Rob Walker."[276]

Evidence of the fraud, claimed Bobulinski, was located on the bottom left corner of both the Hudson West III and SinoHawk LLC operating agreements. "You'll see a serial number. It's a very long serial number," he said. "It appears to me to be exactly the same number on both documents."[277] He was right. The serial number

- 1829339.1 30168-0002-000—is identical.[278] "The reason for that is because the document is extensively the same document. They took the SinoHawk [H]olding . . . made some adjustments on exclusivity and payments, and then replaced the name of the [partners Oneida Holdings and Hudson West IV LLC] with Owasco and Hudson West V. And I'm not going out on a limb here—if they provided this LLC to a bank, it's called bank fraud and wire fraud. And I don't say that lightly," he concluded.[279]

Fraudulent or not, the financial gravy train started rolling. On August 3 there was a new Hudson West III bank account. August 4 saw CEFC Infrastructure (US) LLC wire $100,000 to Hunter's Owasco, PC account.

The next wire transfer was meticulously dissected years later, on March 20, 2024 when, in dramatic fashion, before a televised meeting of the House Oversight Committee looking into "Joe Biden's Abuse of Public Office," Congressman Byron Donalds (R-FL) laid out the money trail.[280] Brandishing copies of the corresponding bank records, he recounted:

On August 8th . . . $5 million is . . . transferred from the Northern International capital account . . . to Hudson West III. Hudson West III is a bank account controlled by Hunter Biden and Mr. Gongwen [Dong], a.k.a. Kevin Dong, who was a CEFC associate. That money comes from a Northern International capital bank account, a bank account that is tied to the CCP. . . . On August 8th . . . there is a wire transfer of $400,000 to Owasco PC from the Hudson West III bank account. . . .

On August 14 there is $150,000 that is transferred from Owasco PC, which is controlled by Hunter Biden, to Lion Hall Group, which is controlled by James Biden. . . . On August 28th . . . we have the withdrawal ticket from Lion Hall Group that is signed by Sara Biden, who is the wife of Jim Biden, for $50,000. . . . On August 28th . . . we have the deposit reference into Sara Jones Biden's account on the same day she withdrew it from Lion Hall. . . . Last document—on September

3rd 2007[281] from Sara Biden's own personal account there is a check that is written to Joseph Robinette Biden Jr., the president of the United States today, for $40,000, signed 'loan repayment'—a loan repayment, by the way, that Joe Biden's own personal accountant, Mr. Eric Schwerin, has no record for. . . . To the members of the committee, it is clear that the source of this money came from CEFC, and CEFC is a company that is directly linked to the CCP . . . and the chairman of the Chinese Communist Party, Chairman Xi Jinping.

The income didn't stop there. "[C]ontinuing through Sept. 25, 2018, Hudson West III sent frequent payments to Owasco, Hunter Biden's firm. These payments, which were described as consulting fees, reached $4,790,375.25 in just over a year. . . . [T]here is also evidence that Hunter Biden moved large sums of money from his firm, Owasco, to James Biden's consulting firm, the Lion Hall Group. Between Aug. 14, 2017 and Aug. 3, 2018, Owasco sent 20 wires totaling $1,398,999 to the Lion Hall Group."[282]

There's still more. On September 8, the same day the CEFC announced their Rosneft deal, "Hunter opened a line of credit with Gongwen under the name of his business, Hudson West III."[283] Hunter Biden, James, and Sara Biden were all "authorized users of credit cards associated with the account. The Bidens subsequently used the credit cards they opened to purchase $101,291.46 worth of extravagant items, including airline tickets and multiple items at Apple Inc. stores, pharmacies, hotels and restaurants. The cards were collateralized by transferring $99,000 from a Hudson West III account to a separate account, where the funds were held until the cards were closed."[284]

Later that month, The Biden Foundation (Joe's new entity) and Hudson West (CEFC US), were slated to share quarters at the exclusive House of Sweden office building in Washington, DC, where Hunter had already leased Suite 507 for Rosemont Seneca. Hunter directed House of Sweden executive Cecelia Browning to have keys made for Joe, Jill, Jim Biden, and Gongwen Dong, adding that the lease would remain under his company's name. Though the keys were cut, they were never retrieved, the group never moved in, and Hunter moved out the following year.[285]

Could the money train have rolled on indefinitely? Possibly. But then Dr. Patrick Ho got arrested. Ho, described as a Hong Kong ophthalmologist turned politician,[286] was vice-chairman of the CEFC and, as such, a close associate of Chairman Ye. Hunter called him "the f***ing spy chief of China."[287] And when the FBI came to arrest him for conspiracy, money laundering and attempting to bribe the president of Chad (to the tune of $2 million—in cash—handed over in a gift box) and Uganda's Minister of Foreign Affairs ($500,000 was the figure there), who he met at the United Nations in New York,[288] Ho's first call was to James Biden, who insisted he thought Ho was trying to reach Hunter.[289] After all, Ho had given Hunter $1 million in September for legal representation.[290]

Ho's arrest (and subsequent conviction a little over a year later[291]) was the start of the fall of the CEFC. In March 2018, Ye was detained in China, as part of what was described as a "crackdown . . . on private entrepreneurs and their freewheeling financing."[292] His detention was allegedly "ordered directly by the Chinese president Xi Jinping."[293] He disappeared into China and as of February 2023, his whereabouts were still unknown.[294] Control of the CEFC's daily operations passed to a Shanghai based portfolio and investment agency controlled by that city's government. It was left to Mervyn Yan to finally close down the CEFC's US operation in 2018.[295]

In December 2018, the *New York Times* wrote a wrap-up story on Ye Jianming, chronicling his rise, fall and ties to the Bidens.[296] After reading it, Joe called Hunter to talk about the article, reassuring him that there was probably not going to be any fallout. "I think you're clear," Joe said in a voicemail archived on Hunter's laptop.[297] This voicemail would conclusively prove that Joe was lying for years when he claimed he knew nothing about his family's activities. It would be a very powerful exculpatory statement when admitted into evidence. And a judge would instruct a jury that this alone would be intent commit a federal crime.

Tony Bobulinski perhaps best explained Joe's role in the Biden Crime Family's China enterprise. "[R]elationship development is business. Joe Biden walking into a room and shaking Chairman Ye's hand is business, in the world I live in. You don't have to take my word. Call . . . Jamie Dimon . . . the chairman of J.P. Morgan. He doesn't sit down at meetings and say, okay, I'm going to sit for this 2-hour meeting. He comes in and shakes three hands and walks out of the room. . . . [T]hat handshake is business.

"The fact that Joe Biden showed up—if he had spent 2 minutes and shook 3 businessmen's hand[s], the demonstration of that is power and business. . . . I've done it all over the world. I understand what it looks like. And doing business in Romania, Ukraine, mainland China, Hong Kong, Germany, and Russia is materially different than in New York City. So that is business. That is evidence of his involvement."[298]

Throughout this chapter I've been very detailed in showing the evidence of the Bidens' entanglement with the top echelon of the Chinese Communist Party—a government that seeks to replace America as the world's leader. "The East is rising, the West is declining,"[299] Xi Jinping is often quoted as declaring. His goal, he told the 19th Party Congress in October 2017, is to make China a "global leader in terms of composite national strength and international influence."[300]

I've described "elite capture," and how that works with top political leaders. The flow of money from CCP bank accounts through a web of shell corporations has been traced, showing how it ended up in Biden bank accounts. Despite an army of naysayers—including the man himself—declaring that Joe Biden was not involved in the family business, we've exposed his role. The schemes, the fraud former business partners allege, the money laundering and tax evasion the Senate and House investigative committees say took place, have all been documented with contemporaneous emails, texts, WhatsApp messages, phone transcripts, media coverage and more. I'm pointing all this out so you, the jury, can refer back to these facts and evidence when we get to the chapter on prosecuting the Biden Crime Family.

CHAPTER 4

TRAWLING FOR TREASURE IN EASTERN EUROPE AND CENTRAL ASIA

When the Senate Committee on Homeland Security and Governmental Affairs released its 2020 report on "Hunter Biden, Burisma, and Corruption: The Impact on U.S. Government Policy and Related Concerns," in addition to Ukraine and China, two particular foreign countries raised alarm for the Committee—Kazakhstan and Russia. "In addition to the over $4 million paid by Burisma for Hunter Biden's and Archer's board memberships, Hunter Biden, his family, and Archer received millions of dollars from foreign nationals with questionable backgrounds," they wrote. "Archer received $142,300 from Kenges [sic] Rakishev of Kazakhstan, purportedly for a car, the same day Vice President Joe Biden appeared with Ukrainian Prime Minister Arsemy Yasenyuk [sic] and addressed Ukrainian legislators in Kyiv regarding Russia's actions in Crimea. Hunter Biden received a $3.5 million wire transfer from Elena Baturina, the wife of the former mayor of Moscow."[301]

Here's why the Senate committee was so concerned.

When Rosemont Seneca principals Hunter Biden and Devon Archer ventured into Kazakhstan on behalf of Burisma, they attempted to strike a deal between Burisma, Zlochevsky's oil and gas company, and the China National Offshore Oil Corporation (CNOOC).[302] Why Kazakhstan? Dubbed a "net energy exporter," the country "is a major producer of oil, gas, and coal, as well as being the largest producer and exporter of uranium ore in the world."[303] "Until 2015, Kazakhstan was among the world's top ten fastest-growing economies, mainly owing to development of its rich oil, gas and coal resources and its export-oriented policies. The country is the largest oil producer in Central Asia, with the 12th-highest proven crude oil reserves in the world."[304] If an arrangement could be forged, the Rosemont Seneca partners just might make a fortune.

Pursuant to that goal, they enlisted the help of Kazakhstan's sitting Prime Minister, Karim Massimov, and the country's wealthiest oligarch, Kenes Rakishev. In 2014 and 2015, when these events occurred, Massimov was in his second term as his country's #2 leader. (Prime ministers are appointed by Kazakhstan's president. In both terms, Massimov was appointed by Nursultan Nazarbayev, who headed the country for nearly thirty years.[305]) Previously, Massimov held several other governmental posts, and when he stepped down as Prime Minister, he went on to spend six years as Chairman of the National Security Committee (KNB); in other words, he was the spy chief of Kazakhstan. Educated in Russia and China, Massimov studied international law at Wuhan University.[306] The institution was so proud of him that, when he was appointed Prime Minister for the second time, they marked his accomplishment with a congratulatory post on their website, commenting on his "close relation with China [and saying that he] has made a great contribution to the dialogue and exchange between two peoples and two countries."[307] In the course of the Kazakhstan affair, Massimov also became cozy with Hunter Biden, who described him as a "close friend."[308]

While Massimov, with his background in Russia and China, rose to political power in Kazakhstan, Kenes Rakishev pursued a business route, studying at the London Business School and at Oxford University in the UK. His dad, Khamit Rakishev, headed the Kazakhstan Chamber of Commerce and Industry. More important though, he had a powerful political ally in his father-in-law, Imangali Tasmagambetov,[309] who also served as Prime Minister and Kazakh ambassador to Russia. Like Massimov, Rakishev had close ties to Nazarbayev's government, ties which seem to have continued into the current regime, headed by Kassym-Jomart Tokayev.

These days, Rakishev tries to project the image of a modern successful international entrepreneur and philanthropist. His LinkedIn page (under Kenges Rakishev) lists him as "Kazakh Investor and Entrepreneur. President of the Fincraft Group" with 21 "Experiences," and 39 "Skills".[310] It also highlights the Saby Foundation,[311] a charitable organization he founded with his wife, Aselle Tasmagambetova[312] (the former prime minister's daughter.) He maintains a Twitter (now X) page, which notes his love of boxing and calls him a "Tech Enthusiast" and "Family Man."[313] Once a special envoy to the United States, Rakishev is heralded in his hometown newspaper[314] and the international media as "a reflection of the new Kazakhstan. Young, educated, worldly, and successful."[315] He even made *Forbes* Kazakhstan's "75 richest businessmen of Kazakhstan" list; with $435,000,000, he got the #19 spot as of May 2024, up one from 2023.[316]

There's another side to Rakishev, though. The British Parliament talked about it in 2022 when they called for sanctions against him (along with Massimov and about a dozen other "corrupt" Kazakhs) for belonging to "a kleptocratic elite that has grown rich off the back of money stolen from its people."[317] The *Daily Mail* wrote about it when leaked emails revealed that two companies that Rakishev owns "make mine-resistant armored vehicles which were seen driven by Chechen troops that invaded Ukraine."[318] The article goes on to quote the head of the Chechen Republic, Ramzan Kadyrov, as saying that "my dear brother" Rakishev "has always been a patron of our important projects"; there's even a photo of the two of them in military garb in the story.

So, back in the US, three years after the Senate first sounded the alarm, the House Committee on Oversight and Accountability also wanted to know the reason for the April 2014, $142,300 wire from Rakishev's company to Rosemont Seneca Bohai—sent just two months after he and Massimov met with Hunter Biden and Devon Archer. The "Third Bank Records Memorandum from the Oversight Committee's Investigation into the Biden Family's Influence Peddling and Business Schemes," dated August 2023, noted that sum was "the exact price of [Hunter] Biden's sportscar."[319]

The earlier Senate report had already traced the trail of the transaction. "On April 22, 2014 . . . Novatus Holding PTE. LTD. (Novatus Holding), a private holding company in Singapore, used a Latvian bank[320] to wire $142,300 to Archer's company, Rosemont Seneca Bohai. The currency transaction report states, 'For Rosemont Seneca Bohai LLC, . . . For a Car . . . It is unclear why a foreign company, Novatus Holding, would purchase a $142,300 car for Rosemont Seneca Bohai when the company does not deal in vehicles."[321]

The day after the funds landed in Rosemont Seneca Bohai's bank account, they were wired out to Schneider Nelson Motor Company in New Jersey. And on April 29, USAA insured a 2014 Porsche Panamera; the registered owner was Robert Hunter Biden.[322] A couple months after that, in July, Hunter started looking to trade in the car, a "2014 Porsche Panamera Executive 4S fully loaded blue w/cognac interior—sticker approx 135k—w/around 500 miles,"[323] along with another car he also owned (a BMW 740 Li xDrive), for an "Alpina B7 x drive w/all the bells and whistles—same color combination as [the] Porsche."[324]

So what did Massimov and Rakishev buy for their $142,300? For starters, they got two dinners with Joe Biden (other guests were present too) at the ritzy Café Milano in Washington, DC.—"where the world's most powerful people go."[325] One was in 2014 and the second on April 16, 2015. A photo of the two Kazakhs with Joe and Hunter appears on Hunter's laptop, as well as on several media sites.[326]

For another, the Kazakhstani Foreign Minister, Erlan Idrissov, got a trip to Washington in December 2014 and the chance to appear with Secretary of State John Kerry at the third meeting of the US—Kazakhstan Strategic Partnership Dialogue.[327] On Hunter's laptop, Devon Archer brags to two of his Burnham[328] associates, that he had a hand in introducing the two.[329] Keep in mind Archer's relationship with Kerry.[330] Also keep in mind that Archer's stated action—"I am coordinating the Sec State's [Kerry's] call with Foreign Minister Idrisov [sic] today in order for Idrisov [sic] to brief Pres[ident] Nazarbaz [sic]. I am going full Kazak."—is a violation of 18 U.S. Code § 951,[331] which says you have to notify the Attorney General before you are allowed to act as an agent of a foreign government. That is what Archer did. Without that notification, a person can be fined or go to jail for up to ten years. But not the Biden Crime Family members, who are in the Golden Circle of unaccountable, unprosecutable political criminals.

And finally, Massimov and Rakishev got Hunter and Devon's efforts to put together a $120 million deal designed to enrich a corrupt Ukrainian energy company (Burisma), a CCP-owned oil company (CNOOC), two Kazakhs with close ties to their "dictator" of a president, and the two Americans via one of their myriad LLCs (Bohai Harvest Rosemont). In the end, this particular iteration never came to fruition. Burisma did sign a deal with KazMunayGas (KMG), Kazakhstan's national oil and gas company in December 2014, to "conduct seismic and drilling operations for hydrocarbon exploration and production, as well as explore the possibility of building infrastructure in the territory of Kazakhstan."[332] Hunter merits a mention in the press release announcing the agreement. Massimov and Mykola Zlochevsky both promise more "joint projects." But the grand scheme of putting all those eggs in the same basket never happened.

CNOOC ended up being blacklisted by the Trump administration. Massimov lost his job as Kazakhstan's head spy, was arrested for treason, and sentenced to eighteen months in prison.[333] And Burisma—well, we covered that in another chapter. But the Kazakh politician and businessman did get to dine at Café Milano with Joe Biden, though.

So did another oligarch who was in business with Hunter Biden and Devon Archer. That would be Yelena Baturina, widow of Moscow's former mayor, Yury Luzhkov. Once the richest woman in Russia,[334] Baturina made her money with the plastics-turned-construction company Inteco, which she and her brother, Victor Baturin,[335] founded in 1991. Venturing into the hotel business in 2009, she developed a number of grand resorts and small luxury hotels in Austria, Ireland, the Czech Republic, and Russia. By 2014, she was buying US real estate. Specifically, Baturina's Inteco had invested "close to $120 million with us in Rosemont Realty,"[336] Devon Archer testified to the House Committee on Oversight and Accountability in 2023.

One of the reasons Baturina's financial entanglement with Biden and Archer alarmed the Senate in their 2020 Report, was that that her husband had been fired from his mayoral job for alleged corruption.[337] The Senate report states, "On Feb. 14, 2014, Baturina wired $3.5 million to a Rosemont Seneca Thornton LLC (Rosemont Seneca Thornton) bank account for a 'Consultancy Agreement DD12.02.2014'." Archer shed a little more light on the transaction. "On that particular wire, there was some commission element. . . . I don't know what the specifics of the wire were, but . . . quite frankly, it was not supposed to go there [to Rosemont Seneca Thornton], but that's where it went." James Mandolfo, the general counsel and chief of investigations for the Committee on Oversight and Accountability, followed up, saying, "We've also traced the money, the $3.5 million, that came from Yelena Baturina, and over $2 million of that travels into Rosemont Seneca Bohai. . . . Do you know why over $2 million of that was going to Rosemont Seneca Bohai, which was the same account also where Hunter Biden was receiving his money?"[338] (That's also the same account where Rakishev's $142,300 wire for Hunter's Porsche Panamera went.) Archer did not have an answer for Mandolfo's question.

London's *Daily Mail* dug further into the ties between Baturina and Hunter's companies. Regarding that $3.5 million wire transfer, Elena's brother Victor told the newspaper the funds were "a payment to enter the American market."[339] The paper also exposed more about Inteco's considerable investment in Rosemont Realty.

"In 2012 Hunter's firm had a $69.7million plan to invest in 2.15million sq ft of office space in seven US cities." They were Houston; Denver; Birmingham, AL; San Antonio, Albuquerque; Tulsa; and "Memphis, Alabama." (The prospectus quoted says Alabama, but the building referenced—White Station Tower—is actually in Tennessee.) The *Daily Mail* found the prospectus in a batch of leaked emails—communications from Archer to Rakishev in Kazakhstan, trying to lure him into the investment opportunity. "I knew you mentioned you were less interested in real estate," Archer writes, "but this is a deal we're closing next month and it's just too attractive not to share. Inteco, who I know you know, is taking a significant equity piece." The attached prospectus estimates that for an investment of $10 million, "the total income will be $20.7—$24.5 million" and shows that Inteco had already tossed $40 million into the pot.[340]

Archer also pitched Baturina on a plan to replace a two-story New York City parking garage with "a high end 12-story 57,000 sf residential condo building in the heart of Chelsea on 21st between 6th Ave and 7th Ave."[341] Yelena OK'd $41 million for that purchase as well. Whether or not either of those deals came to fruition is unknown. However, "in 2015 Baturina set up a US office to oversee her American investments and in 2016 she put $10 million in commercial buildings next to the Barclays Center in Brooklyn, New York."[342]

A final insight into the Biden-Baturina association came from Jason Galanis's interview with the House Oversight Committee in February 2024. The interview took place at the Federal Prison Camp in Montgomery, Alabama where Galanis is incarcerated for his part in that aforementioned scheme to defraud the Oglala Sioux tribe.[343] Here's what Galanis added to the Baturina story:

I was a business partner of Hunter Biden and Devon Archer, among others, during the years of 2012 to 2015. Our business included the acquisition of an 85-year-old Wall Street firm, Burnham and Company, the $1.5 billion surviving division of Drexel, Burnham, Lambert. (Michael Milken's old company.)

As a backdrop, in early 2014, when Russia invaded Crimea and the Burisma board appointments occurred, Archer had recently been told by Chris Heinz that Heinz would be exiting their Rosemont partnership, which included the $2 billion Rosemont Realty, the company funded by Mikail Shishkhanov and Yelena Baturina.

I . . . met Ms. Baturina in February 2014 when Devon Archer asked me to help open her a U.S. bank account. She had invested at least $105 million from Rosemont Realty by that time, which was a Devon Archer investment vehicle. She was having trouble opening a U.S. bank account based on reports of her ties to criminal figures in Russia and corruption allegations related to her politician husband. . . . Given the compliance red flags raised by various banks, I was unable to get her into the U.S. financial system, the access that she had wanted.

I was present when Hunter called his father on a cell phone and put the call on speaker. Present for the call were Yelena Baturina; . . . her husband Yuri, the former mayor of Moscow; and Devon Archer. This call took place on May 4, 2014, during a gathering hosted by Ukrainian associate of Ms. Baturina and a business partner of ours at Romanoff, a restaurant in Brooklyn, New York.

During the May 4th party, we were told to go to an area of the restaurant to gather because Hunter was going to call his father. Hunter called his father, said, 'Hello,' and 'Hold on, Pops,' then put the call on speaker phone and said, 'I'm here with our friends I told you were coming to town, and we wanted to say hello.' The Vice President said, 'Hello,' and some pleasantries, 'Hope you had safe travels,' and seemed like he wanted to bring the call to an end by saying, 'Okay, you be good to my boy.' Hunter responded by saying, 'Everything is good, and we're moving ahead.' The Vice President said something about being very helpful or being helpful, and Hunter ended the call by saying that he was going to call his father later.

I recall being stunned by this call, to actually hear the Vice President's voice on the phone. It was clear to me that this was a prearranged call with his father meant to impress the Russian investors that Hunter had access to his father and all the power and prestige of that position . . .

The entire value add of Hunter Biden to our business was his family name and his access to his father, Vice President Joe Biden. Because of this access, I agreed to contribute equity ownership to them, Hunter and Devon, for no out-of-pocket cost to them in exchange for their, quote, relationship capital. As part of the evolving and deepening partnership, Hunter served as vice chairman to Burnham and brought strategic relationships to the venture, including from Kazakhstan, Russia, and China. Burnham was the focal point for integrating a, quote, Biden family office into a large-scale financial company with international influence.[344]

OK, so here we have Hunter Biden pulling in huge sums of money from rich oligarchs with ties to organized crime, corrupt governments and Communist-leaning regimes. We also see Hunter making it a point to introduce his controversial foreign financial partners to his father, the vice president. "Every single person that wired the Bidens tens of millions of dollars from around the world had some type of communication with Joe Biden," House Chairman James Comer told *Just The News.* " Joe Biden is the brand, and his family was selling the brand."[345]

These transactions, which were large payments of money to purchase the influence of the second highest official in our government would be prosecutable as a broad ranging and lucrative conspiracy to commit bribery.

Here's an obvious instance where the Biden Crime Family did cross the legal line.

In Romania, where Joe Biden made one of his grand anti-corruption speeches,[346] Gabriel "Gabs" Popoviciu (a real estate oligarch, initially famous for introducing the Pizza Hut, Kentucky Fried

Chicken, and IKEA brands to his country, as well as for his marriage into "communist royalty,"[347]) got in trouble with his government over a commercial development in the Bucharest neighborhood of Băneasa.[348]

"The case against Popoviciu was set in motion in 2005 when a businessman lodged a criminal complaint against him and the rector of a Romanian university relating to the sale of a 550-acre plot of land near Bucharest, according to documents from the European Court of Human Rights. The businessman claimed Popoviciu had purchased the land for 'significantly less money than it was actually worth,' the documents say."[349] Following a 2016 conviction and sentence of seven years in prison, Popoviciu hired Hunter (and Boies Schiller Flexner LLP, the law firm where he was "of counsel.")

"It's unclear how much assistance Hunter Biden provided in Popoviciu's case. . . . Romanian police officers showed up at Popoviciu's home to take him into custody on Aug. 2, but he was nowhere to be found and soon declared a fugitive"[350] The businessman turned up in London where he was arrested, and then released on bail.[351]

As part of his "assistance," Hunter enlisted Mark Gitenstein, a Biden family friend, donor, and former ambassador to Romania, to see if the country's laws could be changed to reverse Popoviciu's conviction. When that didn't work, Hunter had Michael Gottlieb, one of the Boies Schiller partners, ask his friend, the sitting ambassador, Hans Klemm, to set up a meeting with the National Anticorruption Directorate (DNA), the authorities who brought the case against Popoviciu. "'I have reached out to Klemm and asked him to help us broker the meeting,' Gottlieb said in a May 17, 2016 email to Hunter Biden and other business partners. 'The Embassy has reached out to DNA to request the meeting. The first question we got back from DNA (within minutes) was whether this was about the Popoviciu case,' he wrote to them all again the next day."[352]

That didn't work either. The DNA refused a meeting, leading to Popoviciu's flight to the UK. When I last checked, in April 2024, he was victorious not only in getting his prison sentence overturned, but it looks like he'll also be able to do business in Băneasa again.[353]

To get back to our main point—and to be very clear—Hunter Biden's actions were not legal. Rep. Lisa McClain (R-MI) pointed that out at the House's Biden Impeachment Hearings on September 28, 2023. "In March 2016, Biden, who is not registered as a foreign agent under FARA [the Foreign Agents Registration Act] meets with the US Ambassador to Romania—red flag—then, coincidentally, over $1 million flows to the Bidens. I'm not much for coincidences, and I don't think the American people are either."[354]

Actually, Popoviciu "paid Hunter Biden and his business associates $3 million from 2015-17 through holding company Bladon Enterprises, a Cyprus-based LLC he used to conduct business, bank records released in May by the House Oversight Committee confirm. The payments were apparently sent to Hunter Biden's business associate Rob Walker's LLC and he allegedly wired more than $1 million to Biden family accounts, House Oversight discovered. Joe Biden served as vice president when 16 of Popoviciu's 17 payments to Walker were wired to Robinson Walker LLC."[355] Added Rep. McClain, "I think most Americans would find it suspicious that ironically, these payments ended shortly after Joe Biden left office. Another coincidence?"[356]

Unlikely, to say the least. And here's another "coincidence." On three separate occasions, Hunter Biden met with his father within hours or, at most, two days after meetings and calls concerning Popoviciu. The *New York Post* reports:

HUNTER'S CALENDAR
July 29, 2015

12 p.m. call with former FBI chief Louis Freeh, who is repping Popoviciu

Same day meeting with Joe Biden at his father's US Naval Observatory residence

March 29, 2016

Meeting with US Ambassador to Romania Hans Klemm in Washington D.C.

Meeting with Joe Biden at the US Naval Observatory

November 17, 2015
   Returns from trip to Romania
November 19, 2015
   'Breakfast with dad' at the US Naval Observatory[357]

The calendar dates, they note, are taken from Hunter's laptop. Hard to believe that Hunter's business dealings weren't discussed while dining with Dad. But you never know when it comes to the Biden Crime Family.

CHAPTER 5

BIDEN INC. – A.K.A., HOW TO WIN GOVERNMENT SUBSIDIES AND INFLUENCE BILLIONAIRES WHEN YOU'RE RELATED TO THE VICE PRESIDENT

The Biden family sure loved flying around the world on Air Force Two with Joe. Including his aforementioned trip to China, Hunter got a lift to at least fifteen countries.[358] There were family trips, like the one to Croatia and Italy for Thanksgiving in 2015, or the Serbia jaunt on August 17, 2016 where Hunter, his aunt Valerie Biden Owens, and Joe attended a ceremony naming a road in Kosovo after the deceased Beau Biden. And fun getaways like the one where Hunter and his dad took in a women's ice hockey game at the 2010 Winter Olympics in Vancouver, Canada.

And of course, there were the business trips. On one outing to Mexico in 2016, for example, Hunter boasted to a business associate that he would be meeting with the country's president alongside his dad the next day. That associate was Miguel Alemán Magnani,[359] CEO of Interjet airlines (and grandson of Miguel Alemán Valdés, one-time president of Mexico.) Hunter had been very helpful to Alemán Magnani, setting up two meetings for the wealthy airline head and the US Secretary of Transportation, Anthony Foxx, but made it clear that "I have no business with the company."[360]

Hunter did very much want to do business with one of one of Alemán Magnani's friends—Carlos Slim, who was #1 on Forbes' billionaires list from 2010-2013.[361] (He's slipped into the top 20 these days.[362]) In fact, the two Mexican moguls breakfasted with Joe, Hunter and Biden family friend/campaign contributor/business associate Jeff Cooper[363] at the VP's private residence, the US Naval Observatory, on November 19, 2015.[364] The moment is captured on Hunter's laptop, as are so many moments that belie Joe's continuing declaration that he had nothing to do with his family's business. It was one of several times Joe met Slim, meetings designed to impress upon the world's richest man Hunter's ready access to power.

Hunter (along with Cooper, Alemán Magnani, and even James Biden) tried to construct any number of deals with Slim, starting as far back as 2010 when the mega-billionaire was a guest at a White House state dinner for Mexican President Filipe Calderon.[365] At least one of the schemes, according to Cooper, was supposed to be "flippin' gigantic."[366] The goal, it seems, was for everybody to get a piece of the Mexican oil industry after the country's President, Enrique Peña Nieto, ended Petróleos Mexicanos' (Pemex, the state-owned oil company) monopoly on the market.[367]

There was an attempt to get Burisma involved too. "[I]n January 2015, Hunter laid out Burisma's plans in detail in an email to Cooper, [Devon] Archer and Magnani. He proposed the Ukrainian firm pay about $350,000 to access an oil 'data room' run by the Mexican Department of Energy, and laid out the structure of the proposed oil venture."[368] Hunter clearly envisioned a big payday for himself. "'I believe the current idea is that the Aleman Group will include a U.S. entity that is currently controlled by Jeff and Hunter. I (in full disclosure) will most likely be granted equity (commensurate with Devon) from the Burisma side. I am also currently 50 percent of the equity of the U.S. Entity that conceivably would partner with the Alemán group.'"[369] That idea fell apart though, when Alemán Magnani failed to smooth the way for Mykola Zlochevsky to get a Mexican visa, which meant the Ukrainian couldn't fly in and sign the agreement.[370]

James Biden tried to horn in too with this May 2015 email. "Have a very real deal with Pemex (Carlos slim) need financing literally for a few days to a week. Have the seller (refinery /slims) and buyer major being delivered from pipeline in (h/ USA) Nothing is simple but this comes very close. As always the devil is in the detail! . . . Need to know if there is any interest asap. Love you, u Jim.'"[371]

It doesn't appear that any of the oil deals or any other Carlos Slim pitches (like the ones for an online gaming firm or for Cooper's digital wallet firm ePlata[372]) were actually consummated. Alemán Magnani ended up with problems of his own, and had to flee Mexico for France[373] after his airline, Interjet, took a financial pounding from the COVID pandemic and declared bankruptcy in April 2021.[374]

All that, in spite of the help Hunter says he provided the CEO. In that 2016 email, Hunter writes, "'We have so many great things to do together and I want you at the plane when the the [sic] VP lands . . . and you completely ignore me. . . . You always say you will help but I haven't heard from you since I got you a mtg for Carlos and your Dad. We have been talking about business deals and partnerships for 7 years. And I really appreciate you letting me stay at your resort villa . . . but I have brought every single person you have ever asked me to bring to the F'ing WHite House and the Vice President's house and the inauguration and then you go completely silent."[375]

I include this, not to demonstrate how petulant the second son can be, but to point out that, since he's not registered as a foreign agent, Hunter admitted to being a serial violator of FARA.

But let's move on to another member of "Biden Inc," as *Politico*[376] termed the family. That would be James Biden. Never one to let a new assignment for Joe to go to waste, he sought out a potential pay-day when the Obama administration put the elder Biden in charge of rebuilding Iraq. James got himself hired as Executive Vice President by HillStone International LLC,[377] a subsidiary of the venerable construction firm, Hill International,[378] co-founded by Irv Richter. At the time, they were the 8th largest construction management firm in the United States, with 2,600 employees in 90 offices worldwide.[379]

Hill did a lot of business in the Middle East, as well as the US, but when the housing market bubble burst in 2008, causing the "Great Recession,"[380] Hill's construction portfolio took a hit. Enter HillStone International. The *New York Post* takes up the story:

"The president of HillStone International was Kevin Justice[381], who grew up in Delaware and was a longtime Biden family friend. On Nov. 4, 2010, according to White House visitors' logs, Justice visited the White House and met with Biden adviser Michele Smith in the Office of the Vice President. Less than three weeks later, HillStone announced that James Biden would be joining the firm as an executive vice president. James appeared to have little or no background in housing construction, but that did not seem to matter to HillStone. His bio on the company's website noted his '40 years of experience dealing with principals in business, political, legal and financial circles across the nation and internationally.'"[382]

What is not stated in that HillStone press release is that James had an ownership stake in the company.[383]

Within six months of James joining HillStone, the *New York Post* continues, "the firm announced a contract to build 100,000 homes. It was part of a $35 billion, 500,000-unit project deal won by TRAC Development, a South Korean company. HillStone also received a $22 million US federal government contract to manage a construction project for the State Department. . . . The Iraq project was massive, perhaps the single most lucrative project for the firm ever."[384]

Hill estimated that if it worked, the project would "generate $1.5 billion in revenues over the next three years."[385] But the company officials who made that projection did not add that "if the deal does happen, a chunk of that $1.5 billion will flow to the biggest connection

Hill has to government: James Biden. Hill International owns a 51 percent stake in HillStone; a group of minority partners, including Biden, hold the rest. That means that the minority partners would split roughly $735 million, pocketing millions of dollars even after expenses are paid."[386] No doubt, James was looking for a big payout, as was Hill International's head, Irv Richter. "There's plenty of money for everyone if this project goes through," he said.[387]

It didn't. The Iraq government was supposed to provide funding for the project. That didn't happen. Infighting between the partners erupted, leading to Justice's departure. Hill International "took a $1 million charge to terminate the operations of HillStone."[388] Two years later, after the final plug was pulled, Richter was singing a different tune. "I thought we had a good chance during a downturn in that market to become a player and I was wrong, so we closed it down,"[389] the Hill CEO told *Arabian Business*, citing three problems with the enterprise. "Number one we had a development partner that wasn't as experienced in housing as it needed to be. Secondly, we had a partner—the Government—that didn't have the money at the time . . . and thirdly we were inexperienced."

Irv's son, David, who boasted to investors that "It really helps to have the brother of the vice president as a partner"[390] when the project was originally announced, also changed *his* tune when he ran for office in 2020—as a Republican. The candidate for New Jersey's 3rd Congressional district said this about his ties to the Bidens: "'I have no ties to the Bidens. Jim Biden worked at a Hill subsidiary for a couple of years. That subsidiary did not report to me. I was not in favor of investing in that company,' Richter said. 'After several years of failure, it was shut down at my insistence, and I've never seen or heard from Jim Biden since.'"[391] (Richter won his primary that year but lost in the general election.[392])

Although the Iraq deal didn't work out, Hill International still found a use for James's talents—in Saudi Arabia. Seems that Hill had built desalination plants in the Kingdom back in the 1980s, but the Saudis hadn't paid up. Thirty-two years later, Hill sent James to be their bill collector because "KSA [the Kingdom of Saudi Arabia] would not dare stiff the brother of the Vice-President."[393] Even that assignment generated controversy. Besides Biden, Hill had hired three law firms to recover the funds. One of the firms—Lankford & Reed—claimed James's job was "to fix a back-door settlement for $100 million [thereby stiffing] the lawyers [of] their 40 percent cut after years of working on the case."[394]

When the lawyers decided to sue Hill for the double cross, they hired a former Treasury Department official named Thomas Sullivan to interview Biden about his role in the negotiations. In an affidavit filed in the case, Sullivan stated, "'I asked specifically if he [James Biden] had attended a meeting with the Saudi Ministry of Trade in mid-February 2012 to receive the final payment for the work Hill had performed. . . . He answered that, to the best of his memory, he had been at such a meeting, and that the reason he had attended was 'because of his position and relationship' with his brother."[395] Sara Biden supposedly backed up the claim, telling Sullivan that "her husband and Joe Biden were very close and 'told each other everything.'"[396]

Sullivan's affidavit goes on to quote James Biden as saying that the Saudi official attending the meeting knew "why I was there," that Hill "fully" expected to collect their payment, "which would be made both in cash and 'a very large amount' of new future contract work."[397] The Saudis made good on that promise, starting by awarding Hill two five-year contracts worth $34 million in October 2012 to design and construct medical facilities.[398] They're still doing business with KSA. In 2021, Hill was chosen to "manage two-thirds of Saudi Arabia's schools,"[399] and in 2023, to "provide Project Management Consultation (PMC) support for the new landmark city of Dahiyat Al-Fursan."[400] Looks like those Biden ties delivered after all.

James wasn't the only Biden brother to cash in on the VP's name. In late March 2009, during the first 100 days of the Obama administration, Joe Biden traveled to Costa Rica and met with president Oscar Arias and other Central American leaders[401] to discuss US aid to the area. In September 2009, just months after Joe's trip—and with no experience in international real estate development—Frank

Biden and Craig Williamson, his partner in the project, announced plans to "reform real estate in Latin America,"[402] via a $900 million venture in Costa Rica, the Guanacaste Country Club, a resort, hotel, casino, and country club with a Jack Nicklaus designed golf course.[403]

But before this remote corner of Costa Rica could be readied for a tourist influx, it would need electricity. Enter the Sun Costa Rica Initiative. That was a "massive solar energy plant [that would] not only power the Guanacaste Country Club but could also be expanded to meet the electricity needs of other communities in Costa Rica's driest region. . . . Sun Fund Americas is the holding company behind this Guanacaste Solar Park."[404] Guanacaste Country Club couldn't wait though. After five years of setbacks, the development's website ceased to function and Nicklaus's company announced that the project was "on hold."[405]

Sun Fund's endeavor plowed ahead, though. "In October 2016, the Costa Rican government signed a letter of intent with Sun Fund Americas to build a solar power facility in the country. The project, which involved a company called GoSolar, specifically earmarked more than $6.5 million in taxpayer-backed loans that had been approved in 2015 by the Obama administration's Overseas Private Investment Corporation (OPIC)."[406] OPIC approved another loan as well, this one for $47.5 million. "Around the same time that project was announced, Sun Fund Americas confirmed that [sic] signed a power 'purchase power purchase agreement to build a 20-megawatt solar facility in Jamaica.' In total, between 2009 and the end of the Obama administration, Frank Biden's Caribbean projects benefited from more than $54 million in U.S. taxpayer loans."[407]

And just to connect up all the dots, "The Obama administration had announced in June 2014 it was launching the Caribbean Energy Security Initiative (CESI) under the direction of Joe Biden."[408]

Proving that the Biden Crime Family isn't just a boys club, Joe and Jill's daughter Ashley Biden also enjoyed the Obama administration's largesse when the Delaware nonprofit outfit she was working for got a $166,000 federal grant. "In September 2014, the Delaware Center for Justice was selected for a competitive two-year grant by the US

Department of Justice through the federal Edward Byrne Memorial grant program. . . . Joe Biden was one of the top advocates for the Edward Byrne grant while in the Senate and helped steer $1.7 billion to the program as vice president. . . . The DOJ grant was a significant portion of the Delaware Center for Justice's revenue, according to its annual reports. The prior year, the group brought in a total of $768,305 in revenue. That increased to $1,517,854, according to the 2015 report, due to an uptick in both government funding and foundation grants."[409]

Ashley personally cashed in too. Two months after the grant, she was promoted from associate director to executive director. She also earned more than the previous executive director, who was paid $71,000 in 2013 and $69,000 in 2014. "Ashley Biden's starting salary was $82,000."[410]

Did Joe help steer these lucrative government contracts to his family members? I'm going to quote my good friend Steve Bannon, who always says, "There are NO conspiracies but there are NO coincidences." If Joe did, there's a federal statute that he violated. That would be 5 CFR § 2635.702, that says, "an employee [that would apply to a vice president or president] shall not use his public office for his own private gain, for the endorsement of any product, service or enterprise, or for the private gain of friends, *relatives*"[411] and a host of other people. Did Joe's relatives benefit? Undeniably. Was it "crony capitalism," defined by Merriam-Webster as "an economic system in which individuals and businesses with political connections and influence are favored (as through tax breaks, grants, and other forms of government assistance) in ways seen as suppressing open competition in a free market"?[412] Most likely. And while crony capitalism is not strictly illegal, were Joe's actions in these cases coincidence or corruption? It's my experience that, if the incontrovertible evidence of millions upon millions flowing to the select members of the Biden family for no other reason than the influence of Joe's public office were subjected to a federal grand jury investigation, it would result in far more evidence being uncovered. Then we'd have definitive answers.

CHAPTER 6

BIDEN INC. – DOMESTIC DIVISION

Before they went global, during Joe's years as a mere senator, the Biden Crime Family operated stateside. I've already talked about James's first failed venture as a nightclub owner, where he nearly took down two banks when he couldn't repay his loans. There was also Hunter's mostly no-show job at credit card giant MBNA in Delaware, the one where he drew down $100,000 a year til 2005, four years after he quit the bank. (Note that that Dad had been on the Senate Banking Committee, where he was nicknamed "Senator MBNA" because of his voting on bills critical to the credit card industry.[413]) There were other businesses too—businesses whose principals and partners may now rue the day they ever heard the name Biden.

The *Wall Street Journal* laid out the Biden Crime Family MO:

> During five decades in public office, Joe Biden built his political brand on his working-class roots. Over that time, members of his family capitalized on his political success by invoking the Biden name to bolster their business pursuits in deals worth millions of dollars. . . . [This] yearslong pattern of trading on the powerful name is at the center of an impeachment inquiry by House Republicans. . . . Lawmakers allege they unfairly

profited from the elder Biden's political clout. . . . on at least a few occasions before his presidency, Joe Biden was more present in his family's business dealings than he or they have acknowledged. . . . At times, business partners were ultimately disappointed when the Biden name failed to unlock access or markets, leaving a trail of legal proceedings and paperwork outlining the grievances of miffed former business associates. A number of the ventures failed, never got off the ground or landed in court.[414]

It was definitely a pattern the Bidens repeated. Not that Joe's relatives thought they needed any particular expertise or training to try to actually run the business they targeted for their next get-rich-quick scheme. In fact, James, who dabbled in a wide range of professions,[415] freely admitted his inexperience and ignorance. In his written statement to the House Oversight Committee on February 21, 2024 as part of their impeachment inquiry, James told them, "I do not have the necessary managerial experience to run most of the businesses for which I was acting as an adviser, consultant, or strategist. Those executive and operational responsibilities were the province of others with whom I was working."[416]

That proved to be unfortunate for a company called Paradigm Global Advisors, an investment firm specializing in hedge funds, started in 1991 by James Park, son-in-law of Sun Myung Moon (founder of the Unification Church—the "Moonies"). For a while, the fund was successful until "Park started binging on cocaine and . . . his company, suffered. . . . Park began hunting for a buyer friendly to his interests. As luck would have it, he found one in an unlikely quarter"[417]—the Bidens.

It was fortuitous timing for the Biden Crime Family, too. They were facing a dilemma. All of a sudden they had to find a new job for Hunter, who had traded in that cushy MBNA post and was now working as a lobbyist. That conflicted with Joe's plans.

"In early January 2006, James Biden called [Anthony] Lotito to inform him that his brother, Senator Joseph R. Biden, was concerned with the impact that Hunter's lobbying activities might have on his expected campaign for the 2008 Democratic presidential nomination. Biden told Lotito that, in light of these concerns, his brother had asked him to seek Lotito's assistance in finding employment for Hunter in a non-lobbying capacity. Lotito agreed to help."[418] That statement is taken from a lawsuit filed against Hunter and James (plus some corporate entities) by Anthony Lotito, a former New York City cop who was once James's friend, business associate, and partner in a security business called Americore International Security.[419] Lotito had worked with Paradigm and Park and figured this would be a perfect solution for the Bidens' predicament. He was right in one way and wrong in many others.

Lotito's Preliminary Statement continues, "Lotito contacted James Biden to propose that he, Lotito and Hunter Biden together purchase a controlling interest in Paradigm as part of an arrangement whereby Hunter would then assume a senior executive position with the company."[420] The group[421] formed LBB Holdings USA LLC, which was to "assume immediate managerial control over the Paradigm Companies as part of a merger in which it would pay $21.33 million and acquire a 54 percent interest in PCL, the parent to Paradigm's investment advisory and asset management companies."[422] James, Hunter, and Lotito were each supposed to own one-third of LBB.

All of which led to this account of the day the Bidens took over Paradigm Global Advisors in 2006, as told by the company's former chief compliance officer. The Biden family contingent consisted of Hunter, James, and Beau, who was in the midst of his campaign to become Delaware's attorney general. Lotito was there too, accompanied by burly Americore security guards. They were there to fire Paradigm's president, Stephane Farouze, and escort him out of the building.

According to the chief compliance officer, "Jim had a plan. 'Don't worry about investors,' he told the executive that day. 'We've got people all around the world who want to invest in Joe Biden.' In case the chief compliance officer did not get the picture, Jim painted it more vividly for him: 'We've got investors lined up in a line of 747s filled with cash ready to invest in this company.' . . . [Beau's] face turned red with anger, the executive recalled. 'This is not why we are making this investment,' Beau told his uncle. 'This can never leave this room. And if you ever say it again, I will have nothing to do with this.'"[423]

Shortly after that dramatic takeover scene, the trouble started. For starters, the hedge fund was managing nowhere near the $1.5 billion its marketing materials claimed it had on the books. The real figure was more like $200-300 million, and there were debts. Hunter had no experience in the financial industry; and he was making $1.2 million a year in this, his consolation job as Paradigm's CEO. To solve that problem, they needed to bring back James Park. But first they had to deal with his cocaine addiction. They sent him to rehab, but Hunter had his own drug problems, so putting the two of them in charge was not a good idea.[424] To make it even worse, one of the Biden financiers—a law firm named Simmons Cooper[425]—pulled out of the deal. The relationship between Lotito and the Bidens began "deteriorated rapidly."[426] Although the $21 million purchase price was supposed to be delivered within six months of the deal's close, the Bidens did not have the money. What to do?

Uncle and nephew went around Lotito and directly "approached Park, who was still in treatment, and cut a new deal: Instead of $21 million in cash, they would fork over an $8 million note."[427] Then the Bidens embarked on a campaign to excise Lotito once and for all.

"On July 17, 2006, Lotito was summoned to an afternoon meeting with James Biden at a Manhattan hotel. During the meeting, Biden demanded that Lotito renounce his interest in LBB on terms to be determined. Shortly thereafter, the Bidens offered to jointly purchase Lotito's one-third interest in LBB for $1 million. Believing the amount to be wholly inadequate, Lotito refused the offer.

"Angered by Lotito's refusal, the Bidens took steps to intimidate Lotito into disposing of his interest on-the-cheap. For example, when the Bidens found themselves embroiled in a dispute with LBB's corporate counsel over his bill, they seized on the dispute to gain the upper hand over Lotito. The Bidens refused to pay the bill, repeatedly citing their political connections and family status as a basis for disclaiming the obligation. When pressed further, the Bidens bizarrely claimed that Lotito had received 'kickbacks' from LBB's counsel, a charge which the Bidens knew to be untrue, but which they leveled in the hopes that it would force Lotito to sell his interest in LBB for far less than its true value.

"Ultimately, the Bidens threatened to use their alleged connections with a former United States Senator to retaliate against counsel for insisting that his bill be paid, claiming that the former senator was prepared to use his influence with a federal judge to disadvantage counsel in a proceeding then pending before that court. While the Bidens' claims about the former senator's intention to intervene in the case were, upon information and belief, untrue, their willingness to issue such outlandish threats demonstrated to Lotito the lengths to which the Bidens were willing to go to secure Lotito's exit from LBB."[428]

That exit was effected, with Lotito reportedly settling for $250,000.[429] Then the whole mess went to court, with Lotito filing a suit against the Bidens for fraud, the Bidens countersuing, blaming Lotito for, among other things, not letting them know about Park's coke problem. They also never told him about the side deal they had negotiated. In the end, "Weeks after Joe Biden was sworn into office as vice president, the law suit was settled on confidential terms, with the Bidens denying any wrongdoing."[430]

They were acting exactly like a group of would-be gangsters, a foreshadowing of the crime family that would make millions.

That was just the first of several visits to court for the Bidens during this affair. Stephane Farouze, that ousted Paradigm president, sued, claiming that "the controlling stake James Park sold to the Bidens was not in fact his to sell."[431] Hunter and James then approached a financial industry veteran, Charles Provini, to run the company. According to his contract, his starting salary was $15,000 a month (this was January 2007, after all), and if things worked out, by June the compensation was supposed to bump up to $40,000 a month.[432]

Politics were reportedly involved in Provini's recruitment. According to the *New York Post*, the uncle/nephew team said, "They wanted a non-Biden face atop the troubled firm. 'Joe Biden needs to distance himself from this,' they told him [Provini], 'Would you consider the job?'"[433]

The Bidens also assured their new executive that "'they had relationships with different unions and that they would anticipate being able to get union funding or union investments into the fund,' Provini said. . . . The pair said these relationships flowed from Joe Biden's political career, Provini said. Joe Biden would occasionally join business calls Provini had with James and Hunter Biden. 'I was a little star-struck at the time perhaps,' Provini said. 'I think most of the things that he was saying were just pleasantries . . . It might have been for credibility.'"[434]

But even a Wall Street veteran with a slew of credits[435] to his name couldn't save Paradigm. Before the whole thing slid south for good, Paradigm found itself snared in a Ponzi scheme.[436] And then the Securities and Exchange Commission (SEC) shut down one of the hedge funds Paradigm shared an address with—Ponte Negra—alleging fraud.[437]

When James Biden appeared before the House Oversight Committee in February 2024, he described Paradigm's eventual demise simply, saying, "In 2010, we decided to unwind and liquidate the fund and return the money to the investors."[438] Provini never did get his full salary. He sued Paradigm in 2008 for close to $1 million. But the suit was filed in New Jersey, where Provini lived, rather than New York, where Paradigm had offices, so the judge threw it out, claiming it lacked jurisdiction.[439]

The Paradigm debacle deterred neither Hunter nor James in their pursuit of big money. While Hunter went abroad in his search, James, in his perceived role as the Biden Crime Family rainmaker,[440] stayed stateside, looking for ways to fill the family coffers. Partnering with him was his wife, Sara. Married in 1995, the husband and wife team set up a consulting firm called the Lion Hall Group in 1997. As a licensed lawyer, Sara could do the legal work while James sought out opportunities.

In 1998, a juicy one was presented by a trial lawyer from Mississippi named Dickie Scruggs, once nicknamed the King of Torts. Here's how the *Washington Post* told the story:

> Scruggs "was tantalizingly close to a historic deal to force tobacco companies to pay billions of dollars—but there was one last hurdle. A divided Congress had to sign off. And Scruggs had identified one of the most skeptical senators, Joe Biden, as a key to winning the vote. Scruggs turned to Biden's younger brother James, an old acquaintance who ran a D.C. consulting firm with his wife, Sara. Scruggs paid the firm $100,000 in 1998 for advice on passing the bill, Scruggs said in an interview at his office here—the first time he has disclosed the amount. 'I probably wouldn't have hired him if he wasn't the senator's brother,' Scruggs said. Biden eventually backed the bill, which ultimately failed to pass Congress. 'Jim was never untoward about his influence,' Scruggs said. 'He didn't brag about it or talk about it. He didn't have to. He was the man's brother.'"[441]

The *Post* goes on to point out that initially, Joe was critical of the bill. But when it went to a vote in June, 1998, Joe was for it. That was two months after Lion Hall got its first $10,000 installment of the $100,000 payment. Did James's windfall have anything to do with Joe's change of heart? "Scruggs said he did not know whether James Biden had talked to his brother about his vote, 'but I hope he did.'"[442]

Through Scruggs (a donor to Joe Biden's political campaigns), James and Sara met two other Mississippi lawyers, Steve Patterson and Timothy Balducci (also Biden donors). There were talks about the duo teaming up with Sara to form a law firm.[443] "But the deal fell apart when Balducci and Patterson were indicted on federal bribery charges[444] in an investigation that also ensnared Scruggs. After all, three men went to federal prison, Joe was forced to return their donations."[445]

One of Scruggs's lawyers was a guy named Joey Langston. Like Scruggs, he was a Joe Biden campaign contributor and had hosted fundraisers for the senator. Also like Scruggs, he tried to bribe a judge, was caught, convicted and served jail time. Unlike Scruggs, he did go into business with James Biden. "Both showed up as managers in Earthcare Trina International, a marketing firm affiliated with a Sacramento, California, health care company called Trina Healthcare."[446] Trina had a novel way to deal with diabetes that utilized something called an "artificial pancreas treatment." It was so controversial that both Medicare and Medicaid refused to pay for the procedure. Still, Trina's founder, G. Ford Gilbert, thought he could get the Alabama Legislature to approve a bill requiring insurers to cover it. Bribery was the reason he thought he could get the bill passed. Like Langston, when caught, he pled guilty and saw prison time.[447]

Langston also was responsible for introducing James to Grant White, who was the principal behind a company called Americore.[448] Now, by the time James got to White, he had the Biden grift MO down perfectly. And with Joe out of public office for the moment, the timing was perfect. James could throw around the Biden "brand" without worrying about being scolded by government types or headlines implying bribery, fraud, extortion, influence peddling, and the like. If that was his intention, it backfired horribly.

What started out as a plan "to build a rural health care empire with the help of a Philadelphia-area consultant"[449] devolved into a complex mess that made the Chinese CEFC scheme look as clear as a cloudless blue sky. Included in the ultimate wreckage were bankruptcies, lawsuits, countersuits, investigations by the Securities and Exchange Commission, the Justice Department and the House Oversight Committee, fired employees, threats, bait-and-switch documents, Medicare fraud allegations, just plain garden variety fraud allegations, broken promises, mysterious Middle Eastern money that never materialized, visions of government contracts, a potential China tie-in, collapsed hospitals, at least one death—and a big payout for James and Sara Biden.

I won't attempt to completely untangle this web. These are some of the key points:

Founded in 2017, White's business model for Americore "was providing—or, revitalizing already distressed hospitals. Already, that's kind of a failing model. . . . The most profitable hospitals in our healthcare system are the ones that can achieve a balance between their Medicare and Medicaid patients and their commercial pay and private pay patients. So revitalizing these troubled hospitals without the requisite experience and maybe even an economies of scale was probably—in my opinion—[not] well thought out."[450] That was Carol Fox, the Chapter 11 trustee hired by the Department of Justice to oversee Americore's liquidation after it filed for bankruptcy in 2019. Before that, though, in the two years between its inception and its bankruptcy, Americore, under White, started buying up hospitals. One was in Pineville, Kentucky. Another was in western Pennsylvania's Ellwood City.

At the same time, Keaton Langston[451] was busy creating Fountain Health LLC, a company that provided lab testing services in Mississippi. (Keaton's dad was James's friend and colleague, Joey Langston.) The thought there was that insurance companies like Blue Shield, United Health Care, as well as Medicare and Medicaid would foot the bill for those medical tests, making the business very lucrative. Where the two companies came together was in Ellwood City, with Americore agreeing to use Fountain Health to conduct the tests, thereby providing a potential source of revenue for the company as it sought new ways to monetize financially ailing medical institutions.

James and Sara's Lion Hall Group was the "Philadelphia-based consultant." Just what that meant was open to interpretation. Carol Fox said she never found a contract that spelled out what services they were to provide. In fact, she never found any kind of contract—consulting, employment or otherwise—for James or Lion Hall. When asked, "Is it fair to say that you weren't able to identify any service that he provided to Americore," she answered, "Well that's why I sued him."[452] In his opening statement to the House on February 21, 2024, James disputed that characterization, saying he acted as "a strategic advisor in a variety of areas."[453] As one example of the services he provided to Americore, he offered that he and Kevin O'Connor

(Joe Biden's current White House doctor) had the idea of using the empty space in those rural hospitals to set up units that would treat post-traumatic stress disorder and alcoholism.[454]

He said he also "undertook to identify potential sources of investment capital to finance the acquisition, expansion, and renovation of those facilities. To that end, I had substantive discussions with more than a dozen investors . . . and I prepared investor presentations for these meetings.[455] I also enlisted my son Jamie to produce a video in support of investor presentations, and he was paid for his time."[456] (Jamie supposedly got $10,000 for his efforts. Carol Fox, in her House testimony, found a June 4, 2018 payment of $10,000 to "defendant's bank account [for] Consult and Marketing—2018."[457] Fox never did find any documentation explaining the reason for that payment, or for Jamie's production services.)

James went on to talk about the money Lion Hall received for its Americore involvement. "As part of that process, Amer Rustom introduced me to Michael Lewitt, who managed the Third Friday Fund and was interested in rural healthcare. Mr. Lewitt quickly committed that Third Friday Fund would provide Americore with $20 million.[458] At the same time, Americore began to pay me for my services, and I received $400,000 on January 12, 2018. . . . I then received an additional $200,000 for my services on March 1, 2018. At the time, I firmly understood that this money was compensation. Although I continued to seek investors, I grew increasingly frustrated with Mr. White because he was not providing necessary financial information to potential investors. In July 2019, I told Mr. White I would no longer work with him and Americore.

"Americore filed for bankruptcy on December 31, 2019. As part of the proceedings, bankruptcy trustee Carol Fox filed a complaint claiming that the $600,000 I received from Americore was a loan that needed to be repaid. That designation surprised me because I had performed substantial services for the company and no one had suggested to me before that the money was a loan. I later learned that the only reference to a 'loan' was a notation in the two wires, and I also learned that the company's financial statements did not carry it as a loan."[459] Rather than litigate—an expense James said he didn't want to incur—the first brother and the trustees settled the suit with James paying back $350,000.

Here's the final sentence of James' congressional statement on Americore: "Once again, my brother played no role, was not involved with, and received no benefits from my work with Americore."[460] There's a lot to dispute about that declaration. First, that $200,000 that James got on March 1? The very same day, Sara Biden wrote a check to Joseph R. Biden Jr. for $200,000—the identical amount— for "loan repayment." *Politico* points out that fact in their exhaustive investigation into Americore-gate, saying, "Joe Biden did benefit indirectly from his brother's work for the firm. . . . The White House has said the check was for repayment of a loan, but did not respond to questions about the circumstances of the loan."[461] Despite the questions surrounding the "loan," when asked, "So the money that Joe Biden received came from Americore?" James admitted, "It came from money that I earned at Americore."[462] That's one instance where James's original statement was, at best, a misstatement.

And then there was his insistence that he, at no time, either said or implied that Joe would join this merry Americore band. "Several former Americore executives said Joe Biden was central to Jim Biden's ambitions for the company. . . . In fact, Jim Biden told the executive, if Americore successfully demonstrated a model for revitalizing rural health care, Joe Biden could run on it in 2020. . . . Another former executive said that Jim Biden spoke of plans—which did not come to pass—to give Joe Biden equity in Americore."[463] None of it this happened. But it does provide an insight into how the Biden Crime Family operates. And it puts the lie to James's sworn testimony when he answered in the negative to these questions from the House Oversight Committee:

- Did you or anyone else at Americore discuss the possibility of Joe Biden receiving equity in Americore?...
- . . . And you or no one else, to your knowledge, discussed making Joe Biden a member of the board at Americore?...

- . . . Did you ever reference that Americore could assist Joe
  Biden's campaign if he were to run?[464] "Absolutely not" was
  James's response to the final query.

The rest of the story is, like the China deal, a tale of overlapping
LLCs, betrayals, and more lawsuits. In Americore's case, health care
at these rural hospitals declined to the extent that one poor soul in
Kentucky "died of cardiac arrest in late 2018 after receiving substan-
dard care."[465]

Here's the bottom line: In the Americore scheme, James used just
about every angle he'd ever employed in his previous scams. For all
this, James and Sara collected $610,000, $350,000 of which was paid
back. And $200,000 of that money went directly to Joseph Robinette
Biden—the head of the Crime Family.

Not to be left out of this story on the Biden Crime Family's
domestic grifts is the youngest brother, Francis "Frank" Biden. While
he may not have operated on such a grand scale as his brother James
or nephew Hunter, he, too, had a part in the family business. Like
James, Frank got involved in a scheme with supposedly lofty ideals run
by questionable characters. Frank's character in question was Mark
Rodberg, a real estate developer and restauranteur in Palm Beach,
Florida. With another education executive, Rodberg planned to build
a chain of charter schools where at-risk kids "would attend school but
take all of their courses online, using virtual technology that required
minimal maintenance. Classrooms could hold rows of cubicles with
computers where kids would sit elbow-to-elbow. There would be no
after-school sports teams, just 'cyber-athletics' with students . . . play-
ing Wii instead of shooting hoops."[466] Mind you, this is a decade or
so before COVID forced students to learn online—and we're just
beginning to find out how devastating that's been to their education.

In 2009, Frank was asked to become the president of Mavericks in
Education in Florida. His last name was key to the position. According
to former business associates, Frank was fond of dropping his eldest
brother's name in business settings.[467] He wasn't the first celebrity to
be the endeavor's spokesperson. His predecessor was NBA superstar

Dwayne Wade. At the time, there was just about nobody hotter in South Florida than the Miami Heat point guard—unless it was his teammate LeBron James. Rodberg transformed his existing restaurant chain, rebranding the properties as upscale sports bars called D Wade's Place. Part of Wade's involvement was to include "appearances on behalf of the schools."[468]

When that didn't work out (ending up in a lawsuit), Rodberg turned to Frank; the two struck up an acquaintance in a coffee shop. Frank seemed to enjoy his role in the spotlight, telling the *Miami New Times*, "'I'm a salesman. . . . I'm nothing but a P.T. Barnum for these kids.'"[469]

Frank also promised, "I give you my word of honor on my family name that this system is sustainable."[470] It wasn't. Five years later, there were allegations of overbilling, using fake checks to get reimbursed for expenses by the state, utilizing a curriculum that wouldn't allow students to graduate with legitimate high school diplomas, and all manner of misconduct. "The federal education department found 'questionable, possible fraudulent, activities occurred with regard to Free & Reduced-price applications'. . . . By April, the [Florida] Pinellas [County] schools had returned the money. One went out of business and the other reorganized under new management."[471] Once again, a Biden-involved business ended up going *out* of business, in litigation (this case was dismissed in 2015), with the Biden family member walking away with a comfortable paycheck.

There are a couple points I want to make before we move onto the next chapter. What we've covered here are some of the more elaborate grifts perpetrated by the Biden Crime Family. All of them have ended up in litigation of some sort or another, usually involving fraud. That's a key word to keep in mind when we get to the prosecution of this family and the RICO case we're building against them.

It's also important to know that what I've included is only what has been documented, either by my own individual investigations, the "Hard Drive From Hell," in the media, in documents filed during litigation, in bank statements, and/or in government testimony. The money banked by the Biden Crime Family is only what has been tracked. There is surely much more. We don't know, for example, how much Hunter and James might have made from a side deal in the Paradigm affair. We don't know if James had a percentage in one of the LLCs in the Americore web and if so, how much he pocketed from that. And we don't know if there are hidden LLCs that paid Frank during his time at Mavericks. Was he only the president or did he have a piece of the larger pie too? We have allegations of Joe Biden and Biden Crime Family offshore accounts with substantial amounts of laundered money, but the FBI and the DOJ for over four years left the potential witnesses abandoned. As far as I know, they have never even been interviewed. We just don't know.

What we do know is that there is a pattern. The complexity of the enterprises, the overlapping LLC names, getting a foot in the door through one individual and then cutting that person out of the golden oil well when it finally gushes, moving money through different bank accounts—all that suspicious activity, to use a banking world term, raises questions about something called "pattern and practice"— another RICO component.

And finally, the activities described in this chapter and this book are not the only ones that took place, either during Joe's government tenure or in his brief few years as a private citizen. There are many more ways the Biden Crime Family made money. Let's look at the role loans played in their enrichment.

CHAPTER 7

WHAT ABOUT THOSE LOANS? AND THOSE TAXES?

To say that millions of dollars have passed through James Biden's hands in his seventy-five years would be an understatement. We've already seen some of his paydays—$610,000 from Americore, and nearly $1.5 million from the China deals, for example. At one point, James was worth an estimated $7 million.[472] And from that first $5000 check he accepted for Joe Biden's campaign back in 1972, his brother, either by name or in person, has been a big part of James's financial success.

Contributing largely to that success have been donors willing— some would say, waiting—to give money to the Biden Crime Family. Remember what James boasted to the Paradigm group the day the Bidens took over? "We've got people all around the world who want to invest in Joe Biden. . . . We've got investors lined up in a line of 747s filled with cash ready to invest in this company." He wasn't kidding.

In James's case, much of that investment has taken the form of loans. Why loans? Well, as a former IRS official turned accountant to the stars once instructed a colleague of mine, anybody can get—or give—a personal loan to anybody for any reason. *Investopedia* reveals another huge advantage. "Personal loans can be made by a bank, an employer, or through peer-to-peer lending networks, and *because they must be repaid, they are not taxable income.*"[473] There aren't any requirements for paperwork if your brother lends you, say $200,000. Or collateral if a friend helps you out to the tune of maybe $800,000.

Over his lifespan, James Biden had a lot of wealthy friends willing to help him out. In 2020, *ProPublica* put together a table of "Key Loans to Jim Biden."[474] Take a look:

Lender	Loan Amount	Loan Made	Loan Repaid
Joel Boyarsky Donor and fundraiser Businessman and former Jim Biden employer	Up to $200,000	1997	2000
Leonard Barrack Donor Attorney and former Sara Biden employer	$353,000	2000	2004
Thomas Knox Donor and fundraiser Businessman	$400,000	2004	2013
WashingtonFirst Bank William Oldaker, co-founder Campaign lawyer and lobbyist	$1,000,000	2006	2014
John Hynansky Donor Businessman	$500,000[475]	2015	2019

(continued next page)

Trustar Bank William Oldaker, co-founder Former Biden campaign lawyer Lobbyist	$250,000	2019	Still Open

Now, that chart is over four years old and there very well could be a few more names and numbers added to it. But it does document $2,703,000 that James Biden received from donors, fundraisers and lobbyists over the course of twenty-seven years. It also says that many of the loans were paid off. Let's drill down on a couple of these transactions and add a little more to the story.

We'll start with John Hynansky.

Born in Germany to Ukrainian parents, he grew up in Delaware after moving there in the late 1940s. He started out as a car salesman,[476] like Joe Biden Sr., but established his own dealership, now the Winner Auto Group, in 1973.[477] The firm expanded into John's parents' homeland of Ukraine in 1992, going from selling just Fords, to hawking luxury brands like Porsche, Bentley, Land Rover, and Jaguar.[478] The dealerships made Hynansky a wealthy man—so wealthy that he bought one of the DuPont mansions in Greenville, the tony part of Wilmington where Joe Biden still has his main residence.[479]

In fact, "The Hynanskys and the Bidens also overlapped in the small world of Delaware's upper crust, where Hynansky's daughter, Alexandra, grew up as a close friend of the senator's sons, according to a person who knows both families. Joe Biden was prominently seated at Alexandra Hynansky's wedding, according to the person, who also attended. 'John made a point of noting that Biden was present, and thanked him,' the person said."[480]

Joe was equally complimentary, calling Hynansky "[m]y very good friend" in a speech in Kiev in 2009.[481] Hynansky had been a very good friend indeed, contributing over $100,000[482] to various Biden campaigns as far back as 1987. John's son, Michael Hynansky, even loaned his Lear jet to Joe back when he was still a senator.[483]

The money stream didn't just flow one way though. A few months after that speech in Kiev, "Hynansky scored his first international development loan from the U.S. Overseas Private Investment Corporation, or OPIC, a federal body whose board was appointed by President Obama. Hynansky used the $2.5 million to break ground on a new headquarters and massive distribution center outside Kiev that prepares eight thousand cars for sale every year. In 2012, Hynansky landed another $20 million in OPIC funding to expand his dealership facilities, federal records show, helping him corner roughly 25 percent of the luxury car market in Ukraine. . . . The terms of the OPIC loans state that all cars sold at his dealerships would be imported from Europe, not the United States, which meant that American-based automakers would not benefit from the taxpayer-backed venture."[484]

This all took place while VP Joe was "point man" in Ukraine. And once he became president, Joe didn't forget his "good friend." In 2022, as the current Ukraine-Russia war was about to break out, "The Biden administration helped Hynansky's team in Ukraine prepare for the invasion, including placing calls to his top executive in Kiev 13 days in advance of Russian tanks crossing the border."[485]

So when James and Sara Biden found themselves in a financial bind after purchasing a six bedroom, seven bath vacation home for $2.5 on remote Keewaydin Island near Naples, FL—an island with no cars, no roads and no bridges, that you need a boat to reach[486]—Hynansky was only too happy to help. "Over the next few years . . . Hynansky . . . floated Sara and Jim Biden 'loans' totaling $900,000."[487]

The funds went towards paying their back taxes (they "missed federal tax payments of $589,000 in 2013 and $30,000 in 2014, according to IRS liens filed against the house"[488]) and costly repairs that were discovered when Joe came to visit the "Biden Bungalow," including "a leaky cistern that left the house without running water."[489] That was just to start. In the end, after 2017's Hurricane Irma wreaked more damage, the Bidens took a loss on the place, finally unloading it in 2018 for a mere $1.35 million.[490] Their mortgage holder, 1018 PL LLC, issued a "release of mortgage" on February 21, 2018. The document is signed by "John Hynansky, managing member." What's interesting is that "Hynansky did not acknowledge full payment and satisfaction of the loans."[491]

Back in 2019, when asked about this, a Biden spokesperson claimed "they had settled the debt with Hynansky in full."[492] James told a different story to the House Oversight Committee looking into impeaching Joe Biden in February 2024. At that time, he said, "I think I have an outstanding balance with John, who is not pressing. He's a very wealthy guy."[493] James was a little fuzzy on just how much he owed the eighty-one-year-old auto magnate, who he described as a "character" who "walks in and has a cigarette holder and has the coat draped over his back,"[494] estimating that it was somewhere in the neighborhood of $97,000. How much really remains unpaid is unknown.

The Keewaydin Island house wasn't the only real estate purchase that sent James to Joe's circle of backers for funds.[495] The 1997 loan from Joel Boyarsky went to help pay for a $650,000 home near Philadelphia. Besides being James's boss, Boyarsky was also the national finance chair for Joe when he ran for president the first time in 1987 but had to drop out.[496]

A second look at that *ProPublica* chart shows just how closely several of the loans overlapped. Boyarsky's $200,000 was paid off in 2000, the same year Leonard Barrack—also a Joe Biden donor and Sara Biden's law firm boss—ponied up $350,000. Of that, $145,000 went to the IRS for James' back taxes. While Boyarsky remained upbeat about his former employee, when interviewed by *ProPublica*, Barrack was not so positive. He sued the couple, claiming that he "had hired Sara at Jim Biden's request to court local government and pension fund clients" but that the couple had "used law firm resources to fuel their consulting company, the Lion Hall Group." At issue was also $250,000 that went to pay for several of the couple's vacations.[497]

Barrack did get paid off in 2004, the same year another Joe Biden donor, Thomas Knox, gave James $400,000. And then there was William Oldaker. Through two of his banks, James obtained $1.25 million. Oldaker was not only a Biden campaign lawyer, he was also Hunter Biden's partner in the lobbying firm of Oldaker, Biden and

Belair. I've already mentioned a bit of the story behind that $1 million loan in 2006. That went to pay off Simmons-Cooper, the firm that pulled out of the Paradigm fiasco that James, Hunter and Beau got themselves into. What should have been a straightforward bank loan, with proper collateral, undoubtedly would not have gone through had the borrowers' last names been different. The $1 million was secured by James and Sara's Pennsylvania home . . . which was valued at $1.1 million and already had three mortgages on it totaling $1.5 million. Hunter pledged his house too. Since it was fairly new, the mortgage on it was nearly as much as the purchase price, leaving very little equity to guarantee the loan.[498]

"These transactions illuminate the well-synchronized tango that the Biden brothers [Joe and James] have danced for half a century. They have pursued overlapping careers—one a presidential aspirant with an expansive network of well-heeled Democratic donors; the other an entrepreneur who helped his brother raise political money and cultivated the same network to help finance his own business deals,"[499] concluded *ProPublica*.

I want to touch on two other "loans" that James Biden was questioned about during his February 2024 appearance in front of the House committee, both involving characters from the Americore disaster. First, the committee members wanted to know about several deposits in April 2019 into the Lion Hall bank account. The money, totaling $225,000, came from Third Friday,[500] the hedge fund run by Michael Lewitt, who was sued in 2022 for embezzling $20 million from his investors. The vehicle he used to siphon off the money "involved the use of 'sham' loans to third parties," according to the lawsuit.[501] Lion Hall was not named in the proceedings. However, in front of his congressional questioners, Biden was adamant that the $225,000 was an actual loan—not a payout for a hidden percentage of another LLC connected to the Americore affair. He wasn't sure if there were loan documents to back up that claim; his lawyer insisted there were, although none were produced. Asked when the loan was to be repaid, he said the entire amount was "forgiven by Michael Lewitt."[502]

That's not what Lewitt says. He told *Politico* in March 2024 that "Jim Biden's debts were assumed by a third-party benefactor whom he declined to name, and remain unpaid."[503]

There's also the "loan" from Joey Langston, who helped out his old buddy James during a rough patch in 2016 and 2017. As James tells it, "I was in financial distress. And Langston I know to be a very wealthy man." The "financial distress" was caused by a "very expensive health issue" concerning one of his three children. James explained, "I said, Joey, I am anticipating getting a substantial amount of money in the immediate short term . . . I was supposed to be paid from a deal . . . that didn't materialize. . . . A deal ain't done until it's done, okay? And so I said, I feel that I'll be able to pay you back this within the next, you know, three to six months, something like that. And he said, well, how much? And I said, you know, $400,000. And then he said, no problem. . . . I subsequently paid him back his $400,000. And it wasn't a document, a written document, but he loaned me, personally, as a friend."[504] When questioned further, it turned out that the amount was $800,000, of which James has only remunerated $400,000. And at the time Langston fronted the money, he was trying to get his conviction for bribery overturned.[505]

It's been mentioned, but I want to emphasize the fact that with many of these "loans," there's no documentation and no payment schedule. Which means that James Biden may never pay back the large sums that these affluent financiers have advanced him over the years. Why is that pertinent?

Here's another very important point about personal loans. If you don't pay back the money in full, it *is* considered taxable income and you need to pay taxes to the IRS. The rule is, a "debt is canceled when a lender allows a borrower to not pay back part or all of the loan. . . . Once a debt is forgiven, it is considered income. Borrowers should receive a 1099-C tax form."[506] So should James Biden need to worry that the IRS will come knocking on his door again with a bill? Well, there are some exceptions to the rule. For example, in general, "if a loan is forgiven as a gift by a private lender, the borrower has no income to report."[507] There are other stipulations as well, having to do with lifetime gift tax exemptions, mortgage debt, and student loan relief. But, as anyone who's gotten a chunk of money knocked off their debts knows, you should look for an IRS form in the mail—and you'll need to pay Uncle Sam.

Maybe not if your last name is Biden. Joe's repeated demand of the wealthy is that they "pay their fair share." Except when it's coming out of his pocket. "Biden avoided paying Medicare taxes on speech and book-sale income in 2017 and 2018 by using a dubious accounting tactic employed by wealthy people to avoid paying for federal health programs. Biden and first lady Jill Biden routed more than $13 million through 'S corporations' and counted less than $800,000 of it as salary eligible for the Medicare tax—exempting the rest from what would have been a 3.8 percent rate. He should have paid the tax on the share of this income that was earned as a result of his own labor, experts say."[508]

We've already seen some of James Biden's tangles with the IRS over the years and the amounts that he's ended up paying.

And then there's Hunter, who went to court in September 2024 over his tax problems. He was "charged with failing to pay $1.4 million in taxes between 2016 and 2019, while also filing false tax reports. He allegedly used the funds to live lavishly, including spending millions of dollars on drugs, escorts, luxury cars, and other high-priced items. He is charged with three felonies and six misdemeanors."[509]

Perhaps not as well publicized as the indictment and trial is the fact that Hunter's back tax bill had already been paid by Hollywood donor/entertainment lawyer Kevin Morris, who made millions by making deals for the creators of *South Park*.[510] In addition to the outstanding IRS fees, Morris covered Hunter's "rent on a house, legal fees for other attorneys, payments to Hunter Biden's ex-wife, child support and outstanding payments for a Porsche."[511] Morris, who's one of Hunter's lawyers as well as his benefactor, also bought thirteen of his client's paintings from the Georges Bergès Gallery in New York for about $1 million.[512] That brings the total that Morris fronted Hunter to "more than $6.5 million."[513]

And—shades of Uncle Jim and his financiers—at first there was no paperwork for the loans, only a retainer agreement for Morris's legal representation. Morris testified to the House Oversight Committee in January 2024 that "the loans would often occur before a written agreement was in place, but that lawyers later drafted promissory notes for the money that included interest, terms and default provisions. The money is due back to Morris in 2025."[514] Stay tuned on that front.

Meanwhile, at the September tax trial, Hunter "shocked a Los Angeles courtroom,"[515] as well as prosecutors, including special counsel David Weiss, "when he unexpectedly copped to an entire tax evasion case, which could land him behind bars for up to 17 years."[516] The reason Hunter pled guilty to all nine charges, he said, was that "I will not subject my family to more pain, more invasions of privacy and needless embarrassment. . . . For all I have put them through over the years, I can spare them this, and so I have decided to plead guilty."[517]

A cynic might wonder if there were other motivating factors, like the possibility that the defendant's "sugar brother" Morris may be running out of cash,[518] or that Hunter may gamble on being let off the hook by either the judge when he is sentenced in December, or by his dad, who could commute his sentence or pardon him entirely before leaving office in January 2025—despite current vows not to do so.[519] Only time will tell which wins out—Joe's concern for his legacy, his love for his son, or possibly his ability, as the Biden Crime Family Godfather, to mastermind one last behind-the-scenes deal.

PART 2

THE PROSECUTION

Now that you've seen the evidence—what the Biden Crime Family actually did, how they operated—let's talk about how to prosecute them. While recent events—like Joe Biden declining to run for a second term as President of the United States, and the Supreme Court ruling that presidents cannot be prosecuted for official acts committed while in office—may have a bearing on what could be included in our indictment, there are still cases to be made and Biden Crime Family principals that, in my view, should be held accountable.

CHAPTER 8

THE CASES

The RICO Case

Our primary goal here is to show that the Biden Crime Family is, indeed, a crime syndicate that operates no differently than, say, the Bonannos or the Colombos did back when the Cosa Nostra ran New York.

First, let's review the definition of the Racketeer Influenced and Corruptions Organizations Act (RICO):

The "RICO statute expressly states that it is unlawful for any person to conspire to violate any of the subsections of 18 U.S.C.A. § 1962."[520] (That's the statute on Prohibited Activities.[521]) "The government need not prove that the defendant agreed with every other conspirator, knew all of the other conspirators, or had full knowledge of all the details of the conspiracy. . . . All that must be shown is: (1) that the defendant agreed to commit the substantive racketeering offense through agreeing to participate in two racketeering acts; (2) that he knew the general status of the conspiracy; and (3) that he knew the conspiracy extended beyond his individual role."[522]

Next, let's re-introduce our defendants:

1. Joe Biden, 46th president of the United States, former vice president of the United States (2009–2017), senator from Delaware (1973–2009).
2. Hunter Biden, son of Defendant 1.
3. James Biden, younger brother of Defendant 1.
4. Francis "Frank" Biden, youngest brother of Defendant 1.

Potential co-conspirator:

1. Sara Biden, wife of Defendant 2.

Now, let's outline our case.

Point 1: Was There a conspiracy?

As noted earlier in this narrative, the biggest question has always been, what was the Biden business? The answer, according to the *Wall Street Journal*[523], and testified to by Hunter's business partners Tony Bobulinski and Devon Archer,[524] is the Biden "brand." Perhaps, more accurately, the "brand" was selling the influence that emerges from access to Joe Biden's public office.[525] Here's how MarcoPolo put it: "The business model for Hunter and Joe's siblings was simple but required walking a high and delicate tightrope: sell Joe's influence over the American government as its (sic) pResident (and previously as its vice president and the senior Senator from Delaware) and execute the 'Delaware Way' while attracting as little law enforcement attention as possible."[526]

I'm going to digress for just a minute to define "the Delaware Way." *Mother Jones* explained it like this: "Elected officials from both parties prided themselves on what they called 'the Delaware Way'—a willingness to put aside partisanship for the good of the state, which invariably meant aiding its business climate. Revenue from corporate taxes and LLCs kept government coffers full, and the state's low income tax rates kept voters happy. . . . [Joe] Biden did not create this system, but he used his influence to strengthen and protect it."[527] *Politico* added, "Biden has held up 'the Delaware Way,' the nickname for the state's cozy political culture, as a model for bipartisan cooperation."[528]

But there's another side to "the Delaware Way." "[M]ention the second smallest US state to corruption fighters, and they'll tell you of . . . a place where extreme corporate secrecy enables corrupt people, shady companies, drug traffickers, embezzlers and fraudsters to cover their tracks when shifting dirty money from one place to another. It's a haven for transnational crime.

"Low taxes, the state's business-friendly laws and a sophisticated court system for hearing business disputes draw thousands of brand-name corporations to Delaware. . . . In many cases, firms flock there for legitimate business reasons—but not everyone is squeaky clean. Delaware is also home to thousands of anonymous shell companies thanks to its strict corporate secrecy rules. . . . No data is collected on beneficial owners, and company formation agents based in the state can act as nominee directors. It's a cinch for a criminal to set up a shell corporation to launder illicit money, and gain access to the US banking system."[529]

With that in mind, let's return to the question of conspiracy. Who knew about the Biden family business model? Certainly Hunter and James Biden did. They were in several businesses together, from Paradigm Global Partners to the CEFC. Frank used the MO in his Mavericks scheme.

What about Joe? The House Oversight Committee compiled a list of Joe's changing stories about his knowledge of the family business. Here are a few excerpts:

August 28, 2019: First of all, I have never discussed with my son, or my brother, or anyone else, anything having to do with their businesses, period.

August 9, 2023: Reporter: There's this testimony now where one of your son's former business associates is claiming that you were on speakerphone a lot with them talking business. . . . President Biden: I never talked business with anybody and I knew you'd have a lousy question.[530]

And this wasn't on the House list, but here's the updated iteration from White House press secretary Karine Jean-Pierre:

> July 24, 2023: The president was never in business with his son.[531]

Putting the lie to these claims is a mountain of photos, emails, books, contemporaneous news stories, depositions, and other evidence that says otherwise. In this narrative we've recounted just a few of the innumerable meetings, conversations, phone calls, and meals that Joe had with Hunter and James's business associates. As Tony Bobulinski said about his late night meeting with Joe in the Beverly Hilton Hotel bar, "The only reason why I was there was because . . . I was a partner of the Biden family's in this operating business."[532]

None of this is new, though. As far back as the 1970s, when James couldn't make the payments on the loans he obtained to keep his Seasons Change disco afloat, his brother—a one-time member of the Senate banking committee—called the bank to find out "how the guy in charge of loans let it get this far."[533] Joe stayed at James and Sara's Keewaydin Island home, the one he was able to buy with the loan from Biden donor/friend John Hynansky. Sara Biden told an investigator looking into her husband's Iraq dealings that he and Joe "told each other everything."[534] Certainly Joe knew enough about Frank's business affairs to pull him aside during his 2020 presidential campaign and give him this big brotherly advice, "For Christ's sake, watch yourself."[535]

What stands out, though, as the most convincing evidence of conspiracy is Hunter's email to his daughter, found on the "Laptop from Hell." That's the one where Hunter texts his oldest daughter Naomi, "I Hope you all can do what I did and pay for everything for this entire family Fro 30 years. It's really hard. But don't worry unlike Pop I won't make you give me half your salary."[536]

Conclusion: On the question of conspiracy, "the government need not prove that the defendant agreed with every other conspirator, knew all of the other conspirators, or had full knowledge of all the details of the conspiracy."[537] Given the evidence above, it must be concluded that Joe, James, Hunter, and Frank were part of a conspiracy. In fact, the House Impeachment Inquiry report issued in August 2024 agreed with this conclusion, stating that "[O]verwhelming evidence demonstrates that President Biden participated in a conspiracy to monetize his office of public trust to enrich his family."[538]

Point 2: Were there racketeering activities?

Now we need to look into the second part of the RICO statute to see if "the defendant[s] agreed to commit the substantive racketeering offense through agreeing to participate in two racketeering acts." What racketeering acts might relate to the Biden Crime Family?

First let's look at bribery, as defined by 18 US Code § 201.

Whoever –

(1) directly or indirectly, corruptly gives, offers or promises anything of value to any public official or person who has been selected to be a public official, or offers or promises any public official, or any person who has been selected to be a public official to give anything of value to any other person or entity, with intent—

(A) to influence any official act; or

(B) to influence such public official or person who has been selected to be a public official to commit or aid in committing, or collude in, or allow, any fraud, or make opportunity for the commission of any fraud, on the United States; or

(C) to induce such public official or such person who has been selected to be a public official to do or omit to do any act in violation of the lawful duty of such official or person.[539]

As I said in the Introduction, what started me on this journey was seeing a video clip of what struck me as Joe Biden confessing to committing a classic case of bribery. In light of what we know now about Joe's role in Ukraine and Hunter's position with Burisma, let's see if the statement fits the definition of bribery—offering something of value in exchange for official action, or "quid pro quo."

"I went over for the 12th, 13th time [and] I was supposed to announce that there is another billion dollar loan guarantee . . . " There's the "thing of value," a billion dollar loan guarantee.

" . . . And I had gotten a commitment from [Ukraine's president Petro] Poroshenko and from [prime minister Arseniy] Yatsenyuk . . . " They would be the public officials.

" . . . that they would take action against the state prosecutor . . . " There's the official action he wants influenced, or the "quo."

" . . . and they didn't. So they're walking out to the press conference and I said we're not going to give you the billion dollars. . . . I said I'm leaving in six hours. If the prosecutor is not fired you're not getting the money. Well son of a bitch. He got fired!"[540] That makes it clear that, in return for a billion dollars, the Ukrainian president reluctantly capitulated to Joe Biden's demand. He bribed them to fire the prosecutor and they did. There's a case for extortion[541] here too, but in my opinion, bribery is a better fit. So check bribery for one act of racketeering.

Next, let's consider fraud, which also qualifies as a racketeering activity. Both the Merriam-Webster dictionary[542] and the law have many ways of defining fraud[543]. There's bank fraud, wire fraud, mail fraud, scheme or artifice to defraud—the list goes on. Many of the businesses the Bidens were involved in ended in litigation for fraud. Here's a brief recap:

- Mavericks Education—Frank Biden was the president of this company.
- Americore—James Biden was a "consultant" here.
- Paradigm Global Advisors—James, Hunter, and Beau Biden took over this hedge fund.

Paradigm was the first company where the Bidens employed their "bait and switch" strategy. What I mean by that is, they set up a partnership with one person or entity—in this case it was Anthony Lotito.

Once their foot was in the door, they would go around the back of their initial partner, make a new deal with the main entity (James Park and Paradigm here), and cut out the initial partner when the money came in. James did it when he negotiated with Saudi Arabia for Hill International. Hunter and James did it when they excised Tony Bobulinski from the CEFC partnership. And Bobulinski is not shy about declaring that the Bidens "knowingly and aggressively defrauded me."[544]

So we have two provable racketeering acts: bribery and fraud. A little more murky would be allegations of money laundering. The final report by the House Oversight Committee looking into the impeachment of Joe Biden stops short of declaring outright that the Biden Crime Family committed money laundering. But it did find "a web of over 20 companies—most were limited liability companies formed during Joe Biden's vice-presidency."[545] In this narrative, we've shown how the Bidens use variations on the same name with their LLCs: BG Equity (Paradigm), Rosemont Capital/Seneca (Burisma) and Hudson West (CEFC).

The House also traced some of the payments from foreign sources as proof of money laundering. Among their findings[546]:

- Bank records show the Biden family, their business associates, and their companies received over $10 million from foreign nationals' companies.
- Despite creating many companies after Vice President Biden took office, the Biden family used business associates' companies to receive millions of dollars from foreign companies.
- After foreign companies sent money to business associates' companies, the Biden family received incremental payments over time to different bank accounts. These complicated financial transactions appear to conceal the source of the funds and reduce the conspicuousness of the total amounts made into the Biden bank accounts.

- As the Committee traces additional financial transactions, the Committee continues to identify new Biden family members who may have benefited financially from the foreign companies.

So while that may not be 100 percent proof of money laundering (the *Washington Post*, for one, insists that most of the "shell" companies named were legitimate[547]) it certainly raises enough questions to put money laundering on the list of possible racketeering activities. A grand jury investigation would likely supply a number of additional witnesses and documentary corroboration for this.

Tax evasion is also considered a racketeering activity.[548] Hunter's least serious tax crimes (including a few that did not involve Joe Biden) are already established, and now that he's pled guilty on nine felony and misdemeanor counts, he faces jail time. Whether he ever serves it remains to be seen, as we said earlier. But what about James's loans? Those large sums that remain unpaid may actually be taxable income. There's also the question of Joe and that $240,000 he received as a "loan repayment" from his brother. Eric Schwerin, who was Joe's bookkeeper and tax preparer for seven years, says he doesn't recall any such "loans." He said there may have been one in 2017, after he left that post.[549] *Politico* said it's seen bank records showing wire transfers to James "made from an account that appeared to belong to Joe Biden"[550] months before the repayment checks, and after Schwerin left. But there is no written documentation of a loan, not even a hand scribbled note to say that Joe Biden lends this sum to his brother James Biden. And if it ends up being proven that this was not a loan repayment, then Joe would be subject to taxation. According to Rep. Ralph Meuser (R-PA-9), "they broke the law because they did not document the loan properly. That's fraud. That's tax evasion. . . . And by the way, that's five years of jail in the state of Delaware."[551]

Conclusion: Were there racketeering activities? I think we can say a definite "yes" to bribery and fraud. Money laundering and tax evasion would need further investigation, but there are so many possibilities and surely a number would be provable. But you only need two predicates (crimes) to convict.

Before we leave our outline of the RICO case, I want to mention a legal concept that may have bearing on this called "pattern and practice." Mostly this is used in discrimination cases, i.e. does the defendant have a "pattern and practice" of systematically discriminating against a particular group of people in, say, housing, employment or school segregation.[552] It's also used in civil rights litigation looking into the question of, for example, does a police department have a "pattern and practice" of using excessive force or unlawfully stopping a particular group.[553] Why I bring it up here is to point out patterns in the Biden Crime Family business dealings. They target an opportunity (Paradigm, Hillstone International, Americore, CEFC), engage with partners (Anthony Lotito, Hill International, several people in the Americore case, Bobulinski, Gilliar et al in CEFC), make promises that never materialize (and these partners believe the declarations because, after all, they come from a Biden), then collect the money and exit, leaving the companies and the partners in litigation or bankruptcy. This has been the pattern and the practice of the Biden Crime Family since way back in the 1970s—over fifty years—which is why we've dredged up all these old stories. It may not be strictly illegal but all of this would be admissible in proving the existence of a RICO enterprise.

Influence Peddling, Corruption and the Biden Crime Family

Another point I want to make, even if it may fall slightly outside our RICO case outline, is that, strictly speaking, possibly the correct term for what the Biden Crime Family has been engaged in over the five decades that Joe has been in office is influence peddling.[554] And in the United States, that's not, in and of itself, illegal.[555]

To state the obvious, it's also not illegal to be related to a person in power. It's not even illegal to create the illusion that, *because* you're related to a person in power, that you can have that person do "favors" for friends or business associates. The entire Biden clan has always proudly pointed to the closeness of their family connection. "There's an axiom often repeated in his Senate years by Joe Biden's staff: 'Joe says that when someone helps his family, it's just like helping Joe,' recited Sam Waltz, a Wilmington business consultant who covered Biden's first Senate reelection campaign as a young reporter."[556]

When does "helping out" Joe's family cross the line from legal to illegal? There have been many instances where that line has been very, very fuzzy. The question here is, are the activities described below illegal?

- Was it illegal, for example, for Hunter to be earning money for years as the manager of an investment firm set up by a friend of his brother, Beau, when that associate owned an asbestos firm and Joe sat on the Senate judiciary committee that was blocking asbestos litigation reform?[557]
- What about the $100,000 that James received in 1998 for "advice" on how to get the landmark, multi-billion dollar Tobacco Master Settlement Agreement through the Senate? Did the payment to James convince Joe to change his mind and vote for the bill? As tobacco attorney, Richard "Dickie" Scruggs, said years later, "[H]e did not know whether James Biden had talked to his brother about his vote, 'but I hope he did.'"[558]
- Way back in the 1980s, there was an accusation that Joe was "the Senator from MBNA," due to his "pretty cozy relationship [with the credit card giant.] John Cochran, the company's vice-chairman and chief marketing officer, did pay top dollar for Biden's house, and MBNA gave Cochran a lot of money—$330,000—to help with expenses related to the move. A few months after the sale, as Biden's re-election effort got under way, MBNA's top executives contributed generously to his campaign in a series of coordinated donations that sidestepped the limits on contributions by the company's political action committee."[559] And all that was before Hunter got his cushy MBNA job right out of college.

- Finally, what, if anything, did Joe have to do with James, Frank, and Ashley getting lucrative government grants? Ditto firms owned by Biden doners like John Hynansky's Winner Group and Scott Green's the Lafayette Group?

The underlying question here—was Joe Biden's vote and/or influence for sale, even he didn't benefit directly? Are there any similarities to the 2024 case of New Jersey Senator Robert Menendez? He was accused—and convicted on sixteen felony counts—of "selling out his office for lucrative bribes, including cash and gold bars."[560] Menendez tried to make the distinction that it was his wife, not him, who received the money. Prosecutors didn't buy the difference. "In its indictment, the government claimed Menendez and his wife, Nadine Menendez, accepted hundreds of thousands of dollars of bribes in exchange for using his power and influence as a U.S. senator to enrich and protect three New Jersey businessmen and benefit Egypt's government from roughly 2018 to 2022."[561] Note that the government is also prosecuting Nadine Menendez. Her trial is postponed, pending her recovery from surgery for breast cancer.

Georgetown University Law professor Jonathan Turley, who has often testified before Congress, described where the line between legal and illegal can be drawn. In his September 28, 2023 statement before the House Oversight Committee looking into impeaching Joe Biden, he called Hunter and James's paydays from Ukraine, Romania, Kazakhstan and China a violation of 18 US Code § 201—or bribery.

> Many have insisted that the House has not shown that the President personally accepted money from these sources to be considered a benefit for the purposes of bribery or other impeachable offenses. . . . [T]here is a suggestion that, absent a direct payment or gift, the benefits accrued by Hunter Biden and his associates would not implicate Joe Biden. If President Biden was aware of money going to his family in exchange for influence or access, it would constitute an impeachable offense. Putting aside references in e-mails to Hunter paying bills for his

father, transfers to his close family members are also a benefit
. . . To say that millions of dollars going to his family would
not be considered a benefit to Joe Biden is legally and logically
absurd.[562]

Citing cases, including one in which he had personally participated,
the law professor further explained, "It is widely accepted that benefits
given to family members can constitute bribes.[563] Even clothing for a
spouse[564] or a rigged victory for a son in a golfing contest[565] have been
treated as sufficient for bribery charges. The direct benefit claim also
contradicts the past position of the House on impeachable offenses.
I served as lead counsel in the last judicial impeachment tried before
the Senate. My client, Judge G. Thomas Porteous, was impeached by
the House for, among other things, benefits received by his children,
including gifts related to a wedding."[566,567]

Turley later wrote: "After years of denying influence peddling
with the help of an obligating media, even some Democrats are now
admitting that Hunter and his uncles have been selling influence . . . .
After Hunter Biden's former business associate Devon Archer admitted that they were selling the 'Biden brand,' the Bidens' defenders
immediately insisted that it was merely 'illusory.' In other words,
these corrupt figures wanted to buy influence and access, but they
were just chumps fleeced by the Bidens. . . . It is a curious defense that
we are not corrupt because we just ripped off dupes who were corrupt
people . . . . The problem, of course, is that influence peddling is a
form of corruption. Indeed, it is a form of corruption that is so damaging to good government that the United States has pushed global
agreements to ban influence peddling in other countries. . . . Under
federal case law, money and gifts going to one's family is often treated
as a benefit for the purposes of corruption or bribery."[568]

Outside the United States, gifts to the family of a prominent leader
don't always have the same meaning as they do here. Because so much
of the Biden Crime Family's income came from foreign sources while
Joe Biden was vice president, it's important to understand how influence peddling is seen in different parts of the world. We've already

talked about the role of *guanxi* in China, the system of rewarding those with the right relationships and contacts. (See Chapter 3.) Other countries—like those in the EU—include "trading in influence" as one of the more "classic bribery offenses."[569]

When writing about Devon Archer's House Oversight Committee testimony in conjunction with Hunter and Burisma, a reporter from the *Atlantic* explained where the line between familial relationships and corruption is crossed.

> Asked whether Hunter might have been explicitly "using his dad [to] add value in the eyes of Burisma officials," Archer explained the impact of nonverbal signaling. "He would not be so overt," he said. "It's pretty obvious if you're, you know . . . the son of a vice president."
>
> I spent a decade in a country where this sort of signaling was the primary mode of communication among members of a corrupt ruling elite. I watched Afghanistan's President Hamid Karzai send opposing messages to separate audiences during a single speech in 2010. To his international backers, he spelled out his willingness to tackle corruption by calling for new legislation (calculated to appeal to wordy Westerners who love drafting laws). To members of his network, Karzai indicated his intent to keep providing protection by sharing the platform with two notorious warlords, members of his cabinet who were involved in drug trafficking and spiriting away millions of dollars in national revenue.
>
> That Afghanistan experience makes plain to me what was wrong about the Bidens' behavior, even if it wasn't illegal. There is absolutely no evidence that Joe Biden, as vice president, changed any aspect of U.S. foreign policy to benefit Burisma or any of its principals. But Hunter Biden's position on that board of directors served to undermine the very U.S. anti-corruption policy his father was promoting. As George Kent, who then headed the U.S. embassy's anti-corruption effort in Kyiv, put it in a classified cable: Hunter's presence on the Burisma board

undercut the anti-corruption message the VP and we were advancing in Ukraine, b/c Ukrainians heard one message from us then saw another set of behavior, with the family association with a known corrupt figure.[570]

And that's from the *Atlantic*.

FARA Violations

While we're still discussing the Biden' foreign interactions, I want to touch on their FARA violations. That's the Foreign Agents Registration Act, which "requires the registration of, and disclosures by, an 'agent of a foreign principal' who, either directly or through another person, within the United States (1) engages in 'political activities' on behalf of a foreign principal; (2) acts as a foreign principal's public relations counsel, publicity agent, information-service employee, or political consultant; (3) solicits, collects, disburses, or dispenses contributions, loans, money, or other things of value for or in the interest of a foreign principal; or (4) represents the interests of the foreign principal before any agency or official of the U.S. government."[571]

It's a simple enough thing to do, but Hunter never did complete the registration. In fact, he was adamant that he and Uncle James not do so. On May 1, 2017, when discussing setting up the deal with CEFC, he texted Tony Bobulinski, "'No matter what it will need to be a U.S. company at some level in order for us to make bids on federal and state-funded projects. Also we don't want to have to register as foreign agents under the FCPA [Foreign Corrupt Practices Act] which is much more expansive than people who should know choose not to know. James has very particular opinions about this so I would ask him about the foreign entity.'"[572]

But Hunter did violate FARA in many instances, some of which were noted by the *New York Post*. "Those include convening DC dinners in 2014 and 2015 attended by his father and his associates from Kazakhstan, Russia and Ukraine, and bringing Mexican associates to the vice president's residence, and setting up meetings for them with Obama-Biden administration officials."[573] Besides those, as Rep. Lisa

McClain (R-MI) pointed out in Chapter 4, "In March 2016, Biden, who is not registered as a foreign agent under FARA meets with the US Ambassador to Romania—red flag—then, coincidentally, over $1 million flows to the Bidens."[574]

In spite of these well documented examples, to date, neither Hunter nor James have been charged with FARA violations, and it's not looking like that will change.[575] The *Post* speculated that may be because the offenses were too old. It wasn't too late, though, for the white shoe law firm of Cravath, Swaine and Moore to belatedly register as foreign agents in January 2024, in conjunction with their work on behalf of Burisma eight years before.[576] Maybe they were trying to avoid the penalties that, as the *Post* points out, "can result in significant prison terms."[577] Just ask Paul Manafort. He spent nearly two years in jail after his FARA convictions.[578]

Joe Biden's Classified Documents Case

Finally, let's consider a criminal act committed by Joe Biden that was discovered, investigated, and will not be prosecuted. I'm talking about Biden's classified documents case. Briefly, the "incident,"[579] as Wikipedia is now calling it, started in November 2022 when Joe's personal attorneys were cleaning out a closet at the Penn Biden Center for Diplomacy and Global Engagement in Washington, DC., where Biden sometimes kept an office, and found a trove of classified documents. (To digress for just a second, this think tank with Biden's name on it, founded in 2018, saw donations from Chinese entities and individuals triple from mid-2022 to mid-2023, when it took in $25 million in contributions. The previous reporting period (mid-2021 to mid-2022) saw just $8.6 million in contributions.[580] Further, when the *Washington Examiner* was able to uncover the identities of the donors, they found that some of those donors "have ties to Hunter Biden's past deals and the Chinese government."[581] Given the identity of these "donors," to think the CCP had no access to this building where classified US secrets were kept would be naïve.)

More classified documents were found during subsequent searches of Biden's Wilmington and Rehoboth Beach houses, some stuffed into "mangled" boxes in the garage next to his beloved green 1967 Corvette Stingray.[582]

The discovery posed two major problems for Biden—one legal, the other political. The legal problem was that the documents dated from his days as a senator and vice president. Neither position authorized him to take and store those documents on his personal property. Taking them home was in and of itself a federal crime. That's a violation of 18 U.S.C. § 793(e), a section of the Espionage Act that "that proscribes unauthorized retention and disclosure of national defense information."[583] Possible penalties for those violations include both fines and imprisonment.[584]

The political problem was that, just three months before Biden's top secret documents came to light, the FBI had raided Donald Trump's home at Mar-a-Lago and seized some classified material there. Interviewed by *60 Minutes* on September 8, 2022, Biden said he thought to himself, "How could anyone be that irresponsible."[585] And yet here he was, much more irresponsible and without any legal justification.

In January 2023, Attorney General Merrick Garland appointed a special prosecutor to look into the case.[586] His name was Robert Hur, a former US Attorney and chief federal prosecutor in Maryland. A little over a year later, Hur issued his findings.

Trump was assigned a special prosecutor too—Jack Smith— in November 2022. The following June, he was hit with a thirty-seven-count indictment, charging him with "willfully" retaining "the nation's most sensitive documents" and showing "some of them on at least two occasions."[587] (That case was dismissed in July 2024,[588] but Smith and the Justice Department have since appealed the ruling.[589])

Biden's outcome was much different. Hur's 388-page report, delivered on February 5, 2024, declared that "Our investigation uncovered evidence that President Biden willfully retained and disclosed classified materials after his vice presidency when he was a private citizen."[590] So Biden "willfully" kept classified materials and "disclosed" them to someone, in this case, Mark Zwonitzer, his ghostwriter on the 2017 memoir *Promise Me, Dad*. But—and this is a big BUT—"We have also considered that, at trial, Mr. Biden would likely present himself to a jury, as he did during our interview of him, as a sympathetic, well-meaning, elderly man with a poor memory. Based on our direct interactions with and observations of him, he is someone for whom many jurors will want to identify reasonable doubt. It would be difficult to convince a jury that they should convict him—by then a former president well into his eighties—of a serious felony that requires a mental state of willfulness. . . . We conclude the evidence is not sufficient to convict, and we decline to recommend prosecution of Mr. Biden."[591]

There's a concept in criminal law called *mens rea*, Latin for "guilty mind." Hur even refers to it in his report. "*Mens rea* is the state of mind statutorily required in order to convict a particular defendant of a particular crime. . . . The mens rea requirement is premised upon the idea that one must possess a guilty state of mind and be aware of his or her misconduct; however, a defendant need not know that their conduct is illegal to be guilty of a crime."[592]

So did Joe have a "guilty mind" when he took home classified information? Reading through the Hur report, it seems Biden was absolutely aware that he wasn't entitled to have the material stashed, for example, in a junked-up corner of his garage next to his sports car, or a think tank funded by donors with ties to our enemies, the CCP, among other places. He also admitted that, while checking around a house he rented in Virginia for material for *Promise Me, Dad*, he "just found all the classified stuff downstairs."[593] Whether he believed it was illegal or not is debatable. The important conclusion is that this Justice Department didn't exonerate[594] him of the crime. It just declined to prosecute, without ever considering that much of this material was available to Red China who had paid the Biden Crime Family millions of dollars.

In addition, Hunter's laptop email adds the highly persuasive evidence that half of his income, including the millions from China, went to Joe Biden. This all makes these crimes actions that imperiled our national security and that were committed before there was evidence of Joe Biden's dementia. It doesn't seem justified to let Biden get away with imperiling the security of the United States simply because he's become an old man. The report does not conclude that Joe was incapable of participating in his own defense, which is the legal standard for determining whether or not a defendant can stand trial. It just says Biden is having lapses of memory and that's not enough to prevent a trial of such historic importance.

Conclusion

So where are we left in our prosecution of the Biden Crime Family? At its core, this is a case against a group of people who, over 50 years, has taken multiple millions from corrupt foreign oligarchs and even from our nation's worst enemies to help them further their schemes, defrauded and left bankrupt an unknown number of businesses and business partners, accepted "loans" with no terms or payback date from political donors, benefitted from big government contracts at taxpayer expense, all just so they can enjoy a privileged life.

These quotes sum it up well: "Over his decades in office, 'Middle-Class Joe's' family fortunes have closely tracked his political career," stated *Politico* in 2019.[595] Agreed *Real Clear Politics* two years later, what "should be obvious by now, is that the Biden family has gotten rich from plying all these political connections. Actually, they have only one connection: Joe Biden."[596]

You've been presented with a lot of evidence. I've outlined a straightforward RICO case, and then added some other information, much of which, if this were a courtroom, would be considered relevant and admissible. But it also speaks to the character—or lack thereof—of the people we want to hold accountable.

There's one last legal concept I want to mention, and that's "pattern of racketeering activity" or PORA. One law firm summarized the Supreme Court definition of PORA in the 1985 case of Sedima, S.P.R.L. v. Imrex Co, 473 U.S. 479. "The Court looked at the legislative history . . . indicating that RICO pattern was not designed to cover merely sporadic or isolated unlawful activity, but rather activity which demonstrated 'relationship' and the 'threat of continuing activity.'"[597] The Bidens have surely demonstrated that their activities are continuous; as noted, those activities span more than five decades.

As for "racketeering"? Here's the Merriam-Webster definition: "a pattern of illegal activity . . . that is carried out in furtherance of an enterprise . . . which is owned or controlled by those engaged in such activity."[598] We posit that the evidence you've seen adds up to a pattern of racketeering.

Is there conspiracy? As we said earlier, there's no doubt that Hunter, James, and Frank have cooperated—another name for conspired—on various ventures. At the center of all of it is Joe. So check the box for conspiracy. And that's what you need for a RICO indictment.

PART 3

DOES PROSECUTING THE BIDEN CRIME FAMILY STILL MATTER?

On July 21, 2024, when Joe Biden did something no presidential candidate had done since Lyndon Baines Johnson in 1968 and declared that he was withdrawing from the race, I seriously thought, why bother continuing with this book? The goal originally was to show the public what this corrupt family has done over fifty years, and to provide a blueprint for holding them accountable, to use a favorite phrase of the Left. After all, was it worth pursuing James and Frank Biden, who are both elderly and have squirreled away enough money to comfortably live out the rest of their years? Hunter, once his current legal woes are behind him—possibly with a pardon from his dad before he leaves office—is young enough to find a job in an honest profession. With their power base removed, how much more havoc could the Biden Crime Family wreak?

And then I thought about all those Mafia capos that went to jail, and how their syndicates just carried on. In some cases, they flourished. Even with Joe out of office, there's still a wide network of people with money that he's taken care of over the decades. Only the rest of the Biden Crime Family knows how vast that network is, what favors are owed. So there could be a lot more havoc still to come, especially if Kamala Harris ascends to the presidency and continues the policies of the Biden-Harris regime.

CHAPTER 9

YES, IT STILL MATTERS

I also thought about everything that Biden (with the aid of his VP Harris) have done in a short three and a half years to destroy the American way of life. Despite the recent Supreme Court ruling that he cannot be legally prosecuted for his official acts while he's president, Biden should still have to answer for what he's done. Any Republican (probably any Independent and even a few Democrats now) knows the litany.

There's inflation, like we haven't seen in forty years.[599] After spending most of his term denying there was a crisis at the US/Mexico border, Biden and his do-nothing "border-czar" Harris were finally forced to pay attention to the invasion they caused when the illegal aliens they welcomed began to overwhelm sanctuary cities, and even Democrat mayors like New York's Eric Adams started publicly denouncing[600] the administration's policies. No one knows for sure just how many have invaded our country, but the estimate as of February 2024 is over 10 million.[601] More frightening is the fact that we have no idea what their agendas might be. While many claim they're here for a better life (not, by the way, a valid reason for requesting asylum), we do know that over seven hundred on the known or suspected terror watch list were caught in fiscal 2023[602] alone. The Department of Homeland Security even admits that a human smuggling network affiliated with ISIS brought in four hundred immigrants; 150 of them were arrested but fifty have disappeared[603] without a trace into the 3,119,885 square miles of the United States. And then there's the issue of migrant crime. These days, every town is a border town, from El Paso, TX to Aurora, CO, to Athens, GA, to New York, NY. Stories of murders, gang takeovers of apartment buildings, rapes, robberies, and worse, committed by those who crossed the border illegally, is all over the media. Despite the Democrats' insistence that "the immigrant crime narrative is racist,"[604] well, as they say, who are you gonna believe, them or your lyin' eyes.

Scarier is the heavy hand of the US government on American lives under Biden and Harris. We all remember the pandemic-era mask mandates, workers compelled to choose between taking experimental COVID "vaccine" shots and keeping their jobs, businesses forced to shutter permanently because they were not deemed "essential" during the pandemic. There are the EV mandates,[605] the thousands of new agents the IRS is hiring,[606] intimidating social media platforms into censoring content the administration didn't like,[607] the imposition of regulations on everything from minimum staffing regulations on nursing homes to banning noncompete agreements to a demand for federal agencies to purchase sustainable products.[608]

The Helpful Hand of the DOJ

But perhaps the most frightening aspect of the Biden-Harris administration is how they and the Justice Department under Attorney General Merrick Garland have weaponized the legal system to pursue, imprison, bankrupt, and attempt to silence anybody who dares to speak up against these draconian policies.

There are the more than 1,200 charged and over 460 jailed for offenses including "assaults on federal officers, obstructing law enforcement and seditious conspiracy"[609] in conjunction with the January 6, 2021, riot at the US Capitol. Over three years on, officials say they're still pursuing eighty more people. Thankfully, the Supreme Court decision in June that the Justice Department overcharged these people[610] may curb this pursuit.

It can't be stated strongly enough that Biden's lawfare and the two-tiered justice system under Garland is an assault on American democracy. In fact, Robert F. Kennedy Jr. stated just that when he appeared on Erin Burnett's *Outfront* on CNN. "I make the argument that President Biden is a much worse threat to democracy [than President Trump]," he said. "And the reason for that is President Biden is the first candidate and the first president in history has used the federal agencies to censor political speech or censor his opponent."[611]

Obviously, I have a personal stake in this argument, having fought the Bidens for many years through my attempts to bring to light their corruption in everything from the Ukraine, to Hunter's laptop, to their theft of the 2020 presidential election. They, in turn, have sued me, sent me to bankruptcy court, and tried to force me to sell my homes. The Biden-Harris administration used the Deep State and corrupt bar associations to take away my law license, which I've had since 1969, denying my ability to make a living as a lawyer.

I have never been disciplined by the bar association and my record is unblemished. As a matter of fact, I have prosecuted some of the most significant cases of the 20th century, including but not limited to, handling John Hinckley, Jr. after the attempted assassination of President Ronald Reagan, prosecution of two Nazi war criminals, dismantling the five families of the Mafia, corruption in Mayor Ed Koch's administration and Wall Street crime.

Of course, I'm but one of their political opponents. They've indicted and attempted to disbar legal friends and colleagues like John Eastman and Jeffrey Clark for their work on trying to correct the stolen election results. Others, like Peter Navarro and Steve Bannon, actually had to serve four months in federal prisons for misdemeanor of contempt of Congress—*while their cases were on appeal!* Were charges brought against Merrick Garland, who Congress also voted to hold in contempt? Not on your life.[612]

And it's not only public figures they've gone after. Just six days into the Biden-Harris administration in 2021, a Florida social media influencer was arrested by eight FBI and other law enforcement agents for the "crime" of posting memes mocking Hillary Clinton supporters on Twitter (now X).[613] They said he conspired to "spread disinformation" on the presidential election. The 2016 election. The felony charges could have sent him to jail ten years. He got seven months but his case is pending appeal.[614] Then there's the seventy-five-year-old grandmother with a medical condition sentenced to jail for two years for protesting outside an abortion center.[615] These are the actions of a fascist regime.

So is the lawfare leveled against President Donald J. Trump. Altogether he's faced eighty-eight criminal charges[616] (and he became a convicted felon when a Manhattan jury proclaimed him guilty on thirty-four of those spurious charges).[617] There are also the civil suits in New York that may cost him over $440 million.[618] The cases already adjudicated are all on appeal, others are dismissed or delayed until after the November election.

None of this corrupt use of the federal government really comes as a surprise to those who dare to stand in Joe Biden's way. Remember Bill Stevenson, Jill Biden's first husband? In Chapter 1, he told the story of how, when he refused to give her the house after she left him for Joe Biden, he and his brother were indicted for a tax charge.[619] On the other hand, there's David Weiss, the special counsel who originally signed off on Hunter Biden's "sweetheart" plea deal[620] which would have allowed the first son to escape punishment for gun charges and not paying his taxes. Weiss has been familiar with the Bidens since his earliest days as a US Attorney in Delaware in the 1980s. He even worked with Beau Biden at one point.[621] Thanks to Judge Maryellen Noreika, who refused to be a "rubber stamp,"[622] Hunter was not the beneficiary of the Delaware Way, and did not receive immunity—or even a slap on the wrist—for his gun and tax crimes.

Media Complicity

Why aren't these stories about Joe Biden as well-known as some others? Well, the mainstream media would prefer to repeat the myth of "Joe from Scranton," the tragedy of his first wife and daughter perishing in a car crash at Christmas time, his brain aneurisms, his son Beau's passing from brain cancer, rather than tell the whole story about the Biden Crime Family. To be fair, Joe wasn't always as protected by the press as he has been since he assumed the presidency. Over the years, there were journalists and media outlets that did write about the Bidens' grift; for some it was almost a regular beat and we've quoted them in this book. For the most part, though, it was ignored or excused.

One cannot underestimate the media's role in allowing the Biden Crime Family to get away with their five-decade crime spree. A *New York Post* headline says it all: "The media mob's free pass for the Bidens at any sign of scrutiny is no accident—they're all in on it."[623] Author Michael Goodwin wrote:

> From the get-go, they made certain the public would never know the full story of Biden's involvement in his family's influence-peddling schemes. By ignoring or discrediting enormous amounts of evidence showing the president played a direct role and shared in the booty, they withheld key facts and deprived the probe of the oxygen needed to sustain broad public support. . . . The media ignores all this and more for the most disgraceful reason: they don't want to do anything that would help Donald Trump. That's how much they hate him. They would rather protect a failing, corrupt president, one compromised by the millions of dollars his family received from China alone, than do anything that might lead to a second Trump presidency. . . . Their protection racket is a break with history and journalism itself. Not long ago, when prominent media organizations had even a fraction of the documentation amassed against Biden, there was fierce competition to get the big story first. . . . Instead of throwing their best reporters into the fray, the big outlets circle the wagons around the president and echo White House talking points. They aren't practicing journalism. They are doing public relations . . . They aren't even curious about how the Bidens got so rich and what exactly they were selling to foreign powers. In any other era, if you described this fact pattern to even a rookie journalist, the race to get the whole

story would begin immediately. Yet America's best and brightest media know those facts and more, yet still look the other way. That's the real scandal.[624]

Goodwin points out our other obstacle to exposing the Biden Crime Family. The Department of Justice and Attorney General Merrick Garland "did everything he could to keep from prosecuting Hunter Biden and prevented investigators from following the money, lest it incriminate the father."[625] And it wasn't just Merrick Garland's DOJ.

When I presented my evidence on Joe and Hunter Biden's Ukraine misdeeds to those Assistant US Attorneys in Pittsburgh in January 2020, Trump's DOJ under AG Bill Barr stalled the investigation. Barr, along with FBI Director Christopher Wray, also covered up the existence of Hunter's laptop for eight critical months in a consequential election year.[626] I'm still wondering why that happened, and hope to find out.

But that was the presidential election of 2020. This is 2024, when we find ourselves living in perhaps one of the most head-spinning moments in American history. What's the quote? "There are decades when nothing happens and weeks where decades happen."[627] The summer of 2024 has been one of those "weeks where decades happen."

It started with that staple of presidential campaigns, the candidate debate—although, in hindsight, there had been warning signs for weeks before the scheduled faceoff between Donald Trump and Joe Biden on June 27 in Atlanta. June had already been an awkward month for Biden, sparking rumblings that he was too old for a second term in the White House. International news organizations caught him on tape fumbling for a chair at D-Day commemorations in Normandy,[628] appearing to wander in the wrong direction in Italy with G7 leaders after watching a skydiving demonstration,[629] looking like a zombie at a White House Juneteenth celebration,[630] and being guided off stage by Barack Obama at an LA fundraiser.[631] Press secretary Karine Jean-Pierre tried to downplay actual news footage, calling those video news clips "cheap fakes."[632] But it was impossible to deny what the 51.27

million viewers[633] who tuned in to the CNN debate saw—an old man who shuffled onto the stage, looking feeble and confused.

From the moment he rasped out his first comments (his handlers said he had a cold), it was clear that this was not the strong and vibrant image that the leader of the free world should project. It was closer to—but much worse than—the Joe Biden described by Robert Hur in his classified documents report as an "elderly man with a poor memory."[634]

The rest of Biden's debate performance did nothing to dispel the picture. In fact, it made it worse. He struggled to make a coherent sentence. When asked a question on abortion that should have been a layup Democrat talking point, his word salad answer wandered onto the third-rail topic of immigration.[635] When listening to a Trump reply, Biden's slack jaw, open mouth, half-closed eyes, and blank stare were frightening to watch. CNN moderators Jake Tapper and Dana Bash did their best to help stop the trainwreck, cutting short his rambling answers with a "Thank you, President Biden."[636]

Pro Biden TV pundits watching Trump annihilate this feeble man for ninety minutes were in shock. Van Jones on CNN looked like he had lost his best friend. NBC's Chuck Todd said, "There's a full-on panic about this performance."[637] On MSNBC, former Missouri senator Claire McCaskill said, "Joe Biden had one thing he had to do tonight. And he didn't do it. He had one thing he had to accomplish. And that was reassure America, that he was up to the job at his age. And he failed at that tonight."[638] Her co-anchor, Nicole Wallace, added, "I think conversations range from whether he should be in this race tomorrow morning to what was wrong with him."[639]

It seemed like the only person who thought Joe hadn't blown his chances of a second presidential term was First Lady Jill Biden. At a Waffle House watch party with supporters afterwards, she buoyed his spirits, in a tone that she may have used as a teacher reassuring a confused child, "Joe you did such a great job. You answered every question. You knew all the facts."[640]

The next morning, even the left-leaning mainstream media began calling for Biden to give up the nomination. No fewer than four *New York Times* columns—some, penned by his staunchest advocates—said he had to go.[641] There was speculation as to which political leaders would need to convince him to bow out. Would he listen to the Clintons? The Obamas? Chuck Schumer? Nancy Pelosi?

Then the tide began to change. Biden had a midday campaign rally in North Carolina. The Biden that showed up on that stage was 180° from the one viewers saw the night before. He was angry Joe Biden. He was forceful Joe Biden. He addressed his devastating performance of the previous night by saying "I don't debate as well as I used to." Then he echoed an old theme from his childhood. "When you get knocked down, you get back up."[642]

Within hours, the narrative shifted to, "oh he had a bad night" and "nobody should be judged on one bad night." The *New York Times* went from calling his debate performance "heartbreaking"[643] to "disjointed."[644] Even Obama offered support on X, writing, "Bad debate nights happen. Trust me, I know."[645] Other Dems, even one rumored to be Biden's replacement, chimed in. "This president has delivered. We need to deliver for him at this moment."[646] By the end of the day, the media pundits and the Democrat politicians decided they were sticking with Joe. Joe said he wasn't quitting either, declaring that he would even show up for the second debate slated in September.[647] Democrat presidential candidate crisis, averted . . . temporarily.

The drumbeat for Joe to go wasn't completely muffled though. The White House spin machine went into warp speed to shut that down before it could get any louder. He did OK at a couple rallies, then rolled the dice on a much hyped post-Independence Day interview with ABC TV's *Good Morning America* co-host, George Stephanopoulos. But even Bill Clinton's former communications director couldn't stop the train wreck. When George asked if he realized how badly the debate was going, Biden offered this explanation:

"I realized—'bout partway through that, you know, all—I get quoted the *New York Times* had me down, at ten points before the debate, nine now, or whatever the hell it is. The fact of the matter is, what I looked at is that he also lied 28 times. I couldn't—I mean, the way the debate ran, not—my fault, no one else's fault, no one else's fault."[648]

A few minutes after that word salad, he was asked if he'd take a cognitive test. "Look," the man with the nuclear codes answered. "I have a cognitive test every single day. Every day I have that test. Everything I do. You know, not only am I campaigning, but I'm running the world." He went on to say that he "put NATO together" and that the November election is "about the character of the President. The character of the President's gonna determine whether or not this Constitution is employed the right way." And when Stephanopoulos pressed him on bowing out of the race if he could be convinced he couldn't defeat Trump, Biden answered, "if the Lord Almighty came down and said, 'Joe, get outta the race,' I'd get outta the race. The Lord Almighty's not comin' down."[649]

The campaign gamble on Biden acing his media performances was about as successful as Charles Barkley in Vegas.[650] It got worse when he told a Black radio station host that "I'm proud to be as I said the first vice president first black woman . . . serve with a black president proud to . . . the first black woman the Supreme Court . . . there's just so much that we can do because together we . . . there's nothing . . . look this is the United States of America." That fourteen-minute interview cost host Andrea Lawful-Sanders of WURD in Philadelphia her job when it came out that the Biden campaign had given her the four questions to ask.[651] Midwest Black radio host Earl Ingram confirmed that he had the same experience. "They gave me the exact questions to ask," Ingram, whose *The Earl Ingram Show* is broadcast statewide across twenty Wisconsin outlets, told the Associated Press. "There was no back and forth."[652]

Biden had another chance to redeem himself at the NATO summit in Washington DC. The hole just got deeper. When introducing Ukrainian president Volodymyr Zelenskyy at a speech, he called him "President Putin."[653] Later, in another appearance, he declared that he "wouldn't have picked Vice President Trump to be vice president,"[654] when he clearly meant to say Kamala Harris. "Joe must go" was increasingly being spoken aloud by members of the Democrat political class.

More serious was the financial impact. "Wealthy donors to President Joe Biden are withholding $90 million in pledged contributions to the main super PAC supporting his candidacy in protest of his decision to stay in the race."[655]

And then Donald Trump survived an assassination attempt. The 45th president was at a campaign rally in western Pennsylvania's Butler Farm Show Grounds on July 13 when, at 6:11pm, twenty-year-old would-be-assassin Thomas Matthew Crooks aimed an AR-15-style rifle at him from a rooftop about 130 yards away[656] and fired off eight shots.[657] One bullet hit Trump's ear.[658] He grabbed at the side of his head with his hand, then immediately dropped behind the protective barrier on the stage, Secret Service agents rushing to cover him. Seconds later, Secret Service snipers on another rooftop "neutralized" Crooks with one round.[659]

About forty-two seconds after "taking a bullet for democracy," as Trump would later put it, he scrambled to his feet, the Secret Service detail trying to hurry him offstage to a waiting car. But before he went, blood streaking his face, Trump stopped, pumped his fist in the air, and urged the stunned and frightened crowd to "Fight! Fight! Fight!"[660] That image, of a wounded Trump looking every bit the strong and vibrant leader his political opponent was not, immediately reverberated around the world.[661] Barely forty-eight hours later, with a bandage over his wounded ear, Trump strode into the Republican National Convention hall in Milwaukee to thunderous applause.[662] Three days later he left, the official 2024 Republican nominee for President of the United States, very much looking poised to reassume that office in November.

The attention swiveled back to Biden, who stubbornly refused to quit. His July 15 interview with Lester Holt on NBC did him no favors. He headed to Las Vegas for a series of campaign events. And then, moments before appearing at a scheduled speech on July 17 before a Latino conference, it was announced that he tested positive for COVID and was going back to Delaware to isolate.[663] He still defiantly declared that he would be back on the campaign trail soon.

Recuperating at his Rehoboth Beach house, on July 20 he met with aides who brought him very bad news. Not only were thirty-one Democrats calling for him to step aside, funding had "slowed considerably" and the campaign's polls "showed his victory in November was gone."[664] The next day, in a tweet on X, he announced it was over, saying "while it has been my intention to seek reelection, I believe it is in the best interest of my party and the country for me to stand down."[665] And just like that, Joe's fifty years in politics was done.

In the post-mortem over these moments in history, one glaring point emerges. Despite the fact that his deteriorating health was now exposed to the entire world, the Biden Crime Family wanted him to continue his quest for a second term. "The president's family . . . had been dead set against him dropping out, recalling crisis after crisis over the course of Biden's political career in which they had banded together and bounced back. Jill Biden and son Hunter Biden in particular seethed against the top Democrats—including some longtime friends—who they felt were betraying a loyal party leader and public servant."[666]

These events occurred in July 2024. I'm going to take you back to January 2019—not quite five and a half years earlier. This was months before Joe announced his candidacy on April 25. On his much maligned laptop, Hunter Biden has the following text exchanges with Dr. Keith Ablow,[667] a controversial psychiatrist who was his doctor at the time. They're talking about a podcast and Hunter offered his father as the first guest:

Ablow: Does he recall details tho, with the dementia and all?
Hunter: Not much these days, but since it's all fake news anyway I don't see the problem.
Ablow: Is he a go for sure—running?
Hunter: According to inside sources which I can neither confirm nor deny/he is in it to win it.[668]

In another exchange they return to the topic of Joe's candidacy, with the psychiatrist offering a quotable quote:

Ablow: "Any man who can triumph over dementia is a giant. Think what he could do for our nation's needed recovery." Dr. Keith Ablow.

Hunter: You're such an asshole but that made me laugh out loud.

Ablow: "Perhaps he can help us remember all we intended to be as a people, since he can now remember his address." I wanna be Surgeon General. . . .

Hunter: He doesn't need to know where he lives Keith that's the only thing the secret service get right at least 75 percent of the tine. (sic)[669]

There you have it. The Biden Crime Family knew *months before he ran for office in 2019*, that Joe Biden had dementia.

Now, in this book we've meticulously detailed the shady grifts, the decades of fraudulent schemes, and the undeniably illegal activities of the Biden Crime Family. But this is probably the most egregious crime of all that they committed—allowing, aiding, and abetting an impaired man that they knew was in cognitive decline to run for and become the President of the United States. This may be the biggest cover-up and worst crime of all. Think of all the needless death— Afghanistan, now over a million in the Ukraine war[670], Gaza, the fentanyl, migrant march deaths. And it could have been avoided.

The full extent of what Jill and Hunter Biden knew and how they orchestrated the cover-up[671] must eventually come to light. I could go on to make a case about this being elder abuse, and asking how could they do this to someone they profess to love. But in the words of Stephen K. Bannon, this family is "a pack of feral dogs." Nothing should surprise me or anyone else.

But the Biden Crime Family did not do this alone. People who encountered Joe Biden on a daily basis—everybody from the White House West Wing staff, to spokespersons like Karine Jean-Pierre and John Kirby, cabinet officials and more[672]—insisted he was "sharp," "on his game" and "robust." And what about Kamala Harris, the woman who said she was always the "last person in the room."[673] What did she know?

As late as August 29, in her much-hyped first post-nomination TV inter-view, here's what she had to say. "I have spent hours upon hours with him, be it in the Oval Office or the Situation Room. He has the intel-ligence, the commitment and the judgment and disposition that I think the American people rightly deserve in their president."[674] And then she pivoted into trashing Trump. No full throated defense, no words to assure Americans that her boss—who still holds the number one position for several more months—is up to the job. And no truth either. Only verbal air.

But Jill, Hunter, Val, James, and Frank Biden, aides, government leaders, Kamala Harris, and whoever else propped him up and hid the truth of his condition[675] for four—perhaps five or more[676]—years *must* answer for this. We've somehow lived through the nightmare of Joe Biden's America. The politicians and the media who forced him out are now calling him a statesman and a hero, saying that is his legacy. It is not. The emperor's lack of new clothes has been exposed, as we've shown in this book.

And the Biden Crime Family also needs to answer for the fifty years they sold out America for money. Most especially for the last four years. I've given you the evidence. I've given you the law. I've given you the arguments. Now you must render your verdict.

ENDNOTES

1   Scott Wong and Ali Vitali, "As Biden dug in on continuing his campaign, Nancy Pelosi kept the pressure on," NBC News, July 22, 2024. https://www.nbcnews.com/politics/2024-election/nancy-pelosi -helped-pressure-joe-biden-end-2024-campaign-rcna162943

2   "Pelosi Statement on President Joe Biden," Congresswoman Nancy Pelosi, July 21, 2024 https://pelosi.house.gov/news/press-releases/pelosi -statement-president-joe-biden

3   Tamar Lapin, "VP Harris says she was last person in the room before Biden's withdrawal decision," *New York Post*, April 25, 2021. https:// nypost.com/2021/04/25/harris-was-last-voice-in-the-room-for -afghanistan-withdrawal/

4   Katherine Donlevy, "Nearly 17K first responders are suffering cancers, diseases linked to 9/11 over two decades later," *New York Post,* September 10, 2024. https://nypost.com/2024/09/10/us-news /nearly-17k-first-responders-are-suffering-cancers-diseases-linked -to-9-11-over-two-decades-later/. See also: Jennifer Bisram, "22 years later, the fight continues for those battling 9/11-related illnesses," CBS News, September 9, 2023. https://www.cbsnews.com/newyork/news /september-11th-related-illnesses-advocates/

5   Selwyn Raab, *Five Families: The Rise, Decline, and Resurgence of America's Most Powerful Mafia Empires* (St. Martin's Press, New York, 2005), Page xi.

6   Jon Levine et al, "Notorious Gambino mob 'Gemini Twins' hitman linked to 11 murders, dismemberments paroled after getting life sentence," *New York Post,* December 9, 2023. https://nypost.com /2023/12/09/news/gambino-mob-hitman-anthony-senter-paroled-set -for-2024-release/

7   Al Guart, "Crazy Joe Gallo Eats His Last Clam," *New York Post,* November 16, 2001. https://nypost.com/2001/11/16/crazy-joe-gallo-eats-his-last -clam/

8   Joseph Bonanno, *A Man of Honor* (Simon and Schuster, New York, 1983), Page 147.

9   Ibid. Page 11.

10   Ibid. Page 39.

11   "Mafia Commission Trial," Wikipedia. https://en.wikipedia.org/wiki/Mafia_Commission_Trial

12   James Barron, "Tangled Strands: Anatomy Of The New York City Scandal," *New York Times*, March 23, 1987. https://www.nytimes.com/1987/03/23/nyregion/tangled-strands-anatomy-of-the-new-york-city-scandal.html

13   "109. RICO Charges," U.S. Department of Justice. https://www.justice.gov/archives/jm/criminal-resource-manual-109-rico-charges#:~:text=All%20that%20must%20be%20shown,United%20States%20v.

14   "It shall be unlawful for any person who has received any income derived, directly or indirectly, from a pattern of racketeering activity or through collection of an unlawful debt in which such person has participated as a principal within the meaning of section 2, title 18, United States Code, to use or invest, directly or indirectly, any part of such income, or the proceeds of such income, in acquisition of any interest in, or the establishment or operation of, any enterprise which is engaged in, or the activities of which affect, interstate or foreign commerce." "18 U.S. Code § 1962 - Prohibited activities," Legal Information Institute, Cornell Law School. https://www.law.cornell.edu/uscode/text/18/1962

15   "109. RICO Charges," U.S. Department of Justice. https://www.justice.gov/archives/jm/criminal-resource-manual-109-rico-charges#:~:text=All%20that%20must%20be%20shown,United%20States%20v.

16   The text was one of thousands on Hunter Biden's laptop, the so-called "Laptop from Hell," that he left to be repaired at a computer shop in Delaware and never retrieved. A screen shot of the text appears on the "Report on the Biden Laptop," MarcoPolo501c3.org, page 205. https://bidenreport.com/#p=209 Typos and misspellings are all Hunter's. Plus, that wasn't the only communication on the laptop where Hunter claimed to be the family support. In an inebriated text to his uncle James Biden in 2017, Hunter – on an anti-Jill Biden rant – wrote, "I suooorted [supported] my GM family including some of the costs you [Jill] should have used your salary to lay [pay] for - for the last 24 years." See: Alex Diaz, "'GO F**K YOURSELF' Hunter Biden called Jill Biden a 'vindictive moron' and blasted her teaching skills in foul-mouthed argument over rehab," *The*

Sun, July 8, 2022. https://www.the-sun.com/news/5733242/hunter -biden-jill-biden-vindictive-moron-argument-rehab/

17   Stephanie Saul, "Politics, Money, Siblings: The Ties Between Joe Biden and Valerie Biden Owens," *New York Times*, February 25, 2020. https://www.nytimes.com/2020/02/25/us/politics/valerie-joe-biden -sister.html

18   "Recorded interview between Special Counsel Robert Hur…and President Joseph R. Biden, Jr.," *Washington Post* October 8, 2023. https:// www.washingtonpost.com/documents/bc7aadda-757b-4b92-b17a -77a77a907674.pdf?itid=lk_inline_manual_3

19   Andrew E. Kramer et al, "Secret Ledger in Ukraine Lists Cash for Donald Trump's Campaign Chief," *New York Times*, August 14, 2016. https://www.nytimes.com/2016/08/15/us/politics/what-is-the-black -ledger.html

20   Marshall Cohen, "The Steele dossier: A reckoning," CNN, November 18, 2021. https://www.cnn.com/2021/11/18/politics/steele-dossier-reckoning /index.html

21   "Joe Biden on Defending Democracy," Council on Foreign Relations, January 23, 2018. https://www.youtube.com/watch?v=Q0_AqpdwqK 4&t=3108s. Ironically, the discussion took place at the Penn Biden Center for Diplomacy and Global Engagement at the University of Pennsylvania in Washington, DC. That's the same place where top secret, classified documents from Biden's Senate days and his vice-presidency were found in a locked closet in 2022. Add in the fact that the University has recently seen a major increase in donations from China, including some by people and institutions associated with the Chinese Communist Party. See: Joe Schoffstall, Cameron Cawthorne, "UPenn, which hosts Biden's think tank, sees Chinese donations soar, including from CCP-linked sources," Fox News, January 18, 2024. https://www.foxnews.com/politics/university-housing-bidens-think-tank-recently-experienced-a-surge-of-chinese-donations-records-show

22   Jonathan Turley, "The grifter defense: The Bidens move to embrace influence peddling with a twist," *The Hill*, December 21, 2023. https:// thehill.com/opinion/white-house/4369903-the-grifter-defense-the -bidens-move-to-embrace-influence-peddling-with-a-twist/

23   Bonanno, *A Man of Honor*, Page 147.

24   Joe Biden, *Promises to Keep* (Random House, New York, 2008), Page 13.

25   Ibid., Page 13.

26   Raab, *Five Families*, Page 5.

27   Bonanno, *A Man of Honor*, Page 123.

28   There's a discrepancy in the spelling of the Sheene surname. The Bidens, in their various memoirs, spell it Sheen. But Adam Entous, in his insightful profile of the Biden clan, explains the Sheenes feel the misspelling is "intentional." The article delves into the Biden family's financial boom and bust, and their difficult relationship with alcohol. It also unearths the tale of the time that bootlegger/Sheene business partner Arthur Briscoe, following the suggestion of his mob-connected girlfriend/wife Marie Gaffney, engaged Luciano family crime boss Frank Costello to help "keep the unions in line" at their Maritime Welding & Repair Company. Adam Entous, "The Untold History of the Biden Family," *New Yorker,* August 15, 2022. https://www.newyorker.com /magazine/2022/08/22/the-untold-history-of-the-biden-family

29   Ben Schreckinger, *The Bidens* (Hachette Book Group, New York, 2021), Page 15.

30   Biden, *Promises to Keep*, page 36.

31   Jack Dutton, "Did Joe Biden Cheat in Law School? What He Has Said About 'Stupid' Mistake'," *Newsweek*, May 20, 2022. https://www .newsweek.com/did-joe-biden-cheat-law-school-what-he-has-said -about-stupid-mistake-1708548

32   Ibid.

33   "Biden's Law School Ranking Not as He Said," *Los Angeles Times*, September 21, 1987. https://www.latimes.com/archives/la-xpm-1987 -09-21-mn-6104-story.html

34   Richard Ben Cramer, *What It Takes: The Way to the White House*, (Random House, New York, 1992), Page 784 (Kindle version.)

35   Schreckinger, *The Bidens*, Page 26.

36   Elisabeth Egan, "Hunter Biden's Memoir: 7 Takeaways From 'Beautiful Things'," *New York Times*, March 30, 2021. https://www.nytimes .com/2021/03/30/books/hunter-biden-beautiful-things-memoir.html

37   *American Spectator* has the details. "A few weeks after Biden was re-elected in November 1996, there came yet another tie between the senator and MBNA when the company hired Biden's son Hunter (the younger Biden is a Yale Law School graduate who was admitted to the bar this year). MBNA officials seem delighted with their new executive. 'Hunter Biden is an outstanding young man,' a bank spokesman says. 'We're very fortunate to have him here at MBNA.' Beyond that, the company is not eager to talk. First, a spokesman declined to discuss Biden's salary. Then, when asked what young Biden is doing for the bank, the spokesman paused and said, 'That's not something we get into details on.' When pressed, the spokesman said, 'He's a talented young guy that we are grooming for a management position.' The spokesman said Hunter Biden has been 'moving around the bank' as part of his

introduction into the business. Hunter Biden himself declined to discuss his salary or his job." Byron York, "The Senator From MBNA (From Our January, 1998 Issue)," *American Spectator*, September 5, 2015. https://spectator.org/63981_senator-mbna-our-january-1998-issue/; A later story has Hunter entering MBNA's "management training program in late 1996 and exiting as a senior vice president in 1998 for a job in Washington at the Commerce Department." See: Jasper Craven, "Hunter Biden Snagged a Cushy Bank Job After Law School. He's Been Trading on His Name Ever Since," *Politico*, January 24, 2024. https://www.politico.com/news/magazine/2024/01/26/hunter-biden-first-nepotism-job-00137308

38 Luke Darby, "How Biden Helped Strip Bankruptcy Protection From Millions Just Before a Recession," *GQ*, October 23, 2019. https://www.gq.com/story/joe-biden-bankruptcy-bill

39 Joseph N. Distefano, "Joe Biden's Friends and Backers Come Out on Top—at the Expense of the Middle Class," *The Nation*, November 7, 2019. https://www.thenation.com/article/archive/biden-delaware-way-graft/

40 According to his 2021 memoir, *Beautiful Things*, Hunter was forced to abandon his lobbyist career by the Obama administration so there was no appearance of conflict of interest. That did not go over well with the Second Son, who wrote that quitting felt like "riding the escalator without an exit. I once again had huge expenses and no savings, and now I had to bust my ass to build another career from scratch." See: Alex Thompson, "Exclusive: Michelle Obama's private frustration with the Bidens," *Axios*, June 27, 2024. https://www.axios.com/2024/06/27/michelle-obama-private-frustration-bidens-2024-election

41 Roberts also reportedly "mentored" Barack and Michelle Obama's daughter, Sasha. See: C. Douglas Golden, "Hunter Biden Claimed Lunden Roberts Was a Basketball 'Mentor' to His Daughter and Sasha Obama," *Western Journal*, June 15, 2021. https://www.westernjournal.com/hunter-biden-claimed-lunden-roberts-basketball-mentor-daughter-sasha-obama/

42 Kayla Tausche et al, "Why it took four years for the Bidens to acknowledge their seventh grandchild," CNN, August 2, 2023. https://www.cnn.com/2023/08/02/politics/joe-biden-seventh-grandchild-hunter-biden/index.html

43 "A 'miracle': Hunter Biden says a blind date with his future wife rescued him from crack addiction," CBS News, April 5, 2021. https://www.cbsnews.com/news/hunter-biden-crack-addition-future-wife-blind-date/

44 Biden, *Promises to Keep*, Pages 59, 70–71.

45   Ibid. Page 70.

46   Ralph Moyed, "James Biden surrenders nightclub because of debts," *The Morning News*, June 15, 1977. https://www.newspapers.com/article/the-morning-news-james-biden-seasons-ch/46795020/

47   "Jill Biden Denies Ex-Husband's Claim She Had Affair With Joe Biden Before They Split," *Inside Edition*, September 22, 2020. https://www.insideedition.com/jill-biden-denies-ex-husbands-claim-she-had-affair-with-joe-biden-before-they-split-61971

48   Martin Gould, "EXCLUSIVE: 'Joe Biden stole Jill from me': Her first husband tells how she CHEATED with Democrat candidate he once considered a friend and that they have LIED about how they started dating for years," *Daily Mail*, August 17, 2020. https://www.dailymail.co.uk/news/article-8635281/Jill-Biden-cheated-husband-Joe-ex-claims.html

49   Ibid.

50   Germania Rodriguez Poleo, "Jill Biden's ex-husband - who claims she cheated on him with Joe - slams 'Biden crime family' for targeting Trump despite Hunter's 'tax crimes' and brands President 'dangerous'," *Daily Mail*, July 27, 2023. https://www.dailymail.co.uk/news/article-12344539/Jill-biden-ex-husband-Bill-Stevenson-Trump.html

51   According to the "Report on the Biden Laptop" on MarcoPolo501c3.org, Frank has a second – unacknowledged – daughter named Megan Elizabeth Jester Walker (b. 1977). See: "Report on the Biden Laptop," MarcoPolo501c3.org, page 595. https://bidenreport.com/#p=599 Her mother was Judith Lynn Rodgers (1945-2022). Frank is nowhere mentioned in her obituary. See: "Judith Lynn Rodgers, enjoyed helping others," *Cape Gazette*, September 8, 2022. https://www.capegazette.com/article/judith-lynn-rodgers-enjoyed-helping-others/245722

52   Ryan Parry, "Meet Frank Biden, Joe's 'penniless' brother who has snubbed mourning family he owes $1m - but who dined at the White House, boasts of his links to the former VP and vacations at $1,000-a-night ranch," *Daily Mail*, February 6, 2020. https://www.dailymail.co.uk/news/article-7961825/Meet-Frank-Biden-Joes-brother-place-inner-circle-resume-raises-questions.html

53   A scan of traffic collision report is included in the *Daily Mail* story. See: Ryan Parry et al, "EXCLUSIVE: Joe Biden's brother Frank owes dead man's family $1 MILLION for 80mph car crash - but has never paid a cent in 20 years and the Democratic candidate did NOTHING to help," *Daily Mail*, February 6, 2020. https://www.dailymail.co.uk/news/article-7908559/Joe-Bidens-brother-Frank-owes-1-million-dead-mans-family-2020-Democrat-did-help.html

54 Ibid.

55 Ibid.

56 Ibid.

57 Ibid. All the details mentioned in this paragraph are in this story.

58 Adam Entous, "The Untold History of the Biden Family," *New Yorker*, August 15, 2022. https://www.newyorker.com/magazine/2022/08/22 /the-untold-history-of-the-biden-family

59 Photo of letter from Joe Biden's Chief of Staff, Luis Navarro on September 24, 2008. See: Ryan Parry, "EXCLUSIVE: Joe Biden's brother Frank owes dead man's family $1 MILLION for 80mph car crash - but has never paid a cent in 20 years and the Democratic candidate did NOTHING to help," *Daily Mail*, February 6, 2020. https:// www.dailymail.co.uk/news/article-7908559/Joe-Bidens-brother -Frank-owes-1-million-dead-mans-family-2020-Democrat-did-help.html

60 Ibid.

61 "Remarks by the President and the Vice President in Presentation of the Medal of Freedom to Vice President Joe Biden," White House Archives, January 12, 2017. https://obamawhitehouse.archives.gov/the-press -office/2017/01/12/remarks-president-and-vice-president -presentation-medal-freedom-vice

62 Biden, *Promises to Keep*, Page 115.

63 "Report on the Biden Laptop," MarcoPolo501c3.org, page 50. https:// bidenreport.com/#p=55 See also: In that misspelled, expletive-laden text to his uncle James we mentioned in the last chapter, Hunter went a little further in expressing his feelings about Jill, claiming he told her, "'Yang ow [you know] what mom you're a f**king moron. A vindictive moron.... And you do know the drunkest I've ever been is still smarter than you could ever even comprehend and you're a shut (sic) grammar teacher that wouldn't survive one class in a ivy graduate program. So go f**k yourself Jill let's all agree I don't like you anymore than you like me.'" Alex Diaz, "'GO F**K YOURSELF' Hunter Biden called Jill Biden a 'vindictive moron' and blasted her teaching skills in foul-mouthed argument over rehab," *The Sun*, July 8. 2022. https://www.the-sun.com/news/5733242/hunter -biden-jill-biden-vindictive-moron-argument-rehab/

64 Associated Press, "Biden shushes wife after secretary of state slip," *The Guardian*, January 19, 2009. https://www.theguardian.com/world/2009 /jan/19/joe-jill-biden-vp-secretary-of-state

65 David Kamp, "Why Joe Biden Didn't Run...And Why He's Not Ruling Out 2020," *Vanity Fair*, October 25, 2017. https://www.vanityfair.com /news/2017/10/why-joe-biden-didnt-run-for-president-and-why-hes -not-ruling-out-2020

66   Leena Kim, "Beau Biden, the Late Son of Joe Biden, Is Still a Strong Presence in His Father's Life," *Town & Country*, January 5, 2021. https://www.townandcountrymag.com/society/politics/a33638261 /who-was-beau-biden-joe-biden-son/

67   Schreckinger, *The Bidens*, Page 114.

68   Cris Barrish, "Beau Biden defends handling of duPont heir sex case," *The News Journal*, April 3, 2014. https://www.delawareonline .com/story/news/crime/2014/04/03/beau-biden-defends-handling -du-pont-heir-sex-case/7255629/

69   Tigani was a wealthy Delaware beer distributor who amassed contributions for first, Beau Biden's 2006 attorney general campaign, then Joe's 2008 presidential campaign, by bundling checks from his employees and their families, then reimbursing those contributors using company money. That was a flagrant – criminal – violation of campaign finance law. See: Ben Schreckinger, "Delaware Beer Distributor: I Wore a Wire to Probe Biden's Fundraising," *Politico*, July 21, 2020. https://www.politico.com/news/magazine/2020/07/21 /christopher-tigani-joe-biden-fundraising-373724

70   Dan Dagalyn, "Biden addresses possible link between son's fatal brain cancer and toxic military burn pits." PBS, January 10, 2018. https://www.pbs.org/newshour/health/biden-addresses-possible-link -between-sons-fatal-brain-cancer-and-toxic-military-burn-pits

71   Josh Boswell, "EXCLUSIVE: Inside Hallie Biden's toxic relationship with President's family - from twisted affair with Hunter who lavished her with expensive gifts and put her on his payroll to her crack cocaine addiction and rehab stints paid for by JOE," *Daily Mail*, March 20, 2023. https://www.dailymail.co.uk/news/article-11869515/Hallie-Bidens -toxic-relationship-Hunter-father-law-Joe.html

72   "Mandatory Reports Related to Child Abuse and Neglect," Division of Professional Regulation, Delaware.gov. https://dpr.delaware.gov/ boards/investigativeunit/mandatorychild/ See also: "Title 16, Health and Safety, Regulatory Provisions Concerning Public Health, Chapter 9. Abuse of Children." The Delaware Code Online. https://delcode .delaware.gov/title16/c009/sc01/index.html

73   Frances Dean and KF, "The Real Reason Ashley Biden Was Arrested Twice," Nicki Swift, October 15, 2023. https://www.nickiswift.com /237844/the-real-reason-ashley-biden-was-arrested-twice/

74   "Sen. Biden's Daughter Arrested in Altercation," *LA Times*, August 4, 2002. https://www.latimes.com/archives/la-xpm-2002-aug-04-na -briefs4.1-story.html

75   Brianna Morris-Grant, "In the last days of the 2020 US election, a plot unfolded to expose a diary by Joe Biden's daughter," ABC News Australia,

April 10, 2024. https://www.abc.net.au/news/2024-04-10/biden
-daughter-diary-sentencing/103689610

76   Patrick Howley, "FULL RELEASE: Ashley Biden Diary Reveals Child
      Sex Trauma, Drug Abuse, Resentment For Joe–Whistleblower," *National
      File*, October 26, 2020. https://nationalfile.com/full-release-ashley
      -biden-diary-reveals-child-sex-trauma-drug-abuse-resentment-for-joe
      -whistleblower/ Page 25.

77   Victor Nava, "DOJ demands prison time for Ashley Biden diary
      thief," *New York Post*, April 4, 2024. https://nypost.com/2024/04/03
      /us-news/doj-demands-prison-time-for-ashley-biden-diary-thief/

78   Larry Neumeister, "Florida woman is sentenced to a month in jail
      for selling Biden's daughter's diary," Associated Press, April 9, 2024.
      https://apnews.com/article/biden-diary-aimee-harris-fa1081c11
      b34a18f7d216f9cac8bf4e6

79   Kayla Webley Adler, "Ashley Biden Knows Who She Is," *Elle*, March 28,
      2023. https://www.elle.com/culture/a43251490/ashley-biden-interview
      -2023/

80   Krein and two of his siblings, Steven and Bari, founded StartUp Health
      in 2011 with a friend, Unity Stokes. When it "barely had a website,"
      two of the founders met in the Oval Office with Biden and Barack
      Obama and to announce the launch. See: Peter Schweizer, "How five
      members of Joe Biden's family got rich through his connections," *New
      York Post*, January 20, 2020. https://nypost.com/2020/01/18/how-five
      -members-of-joe-bidens-family-got-rich-through-his-connections/

81   Maegan Vazquez, "Biden son-in-law faces conflict of interest concerns
      following coronavirus response investments," CNN, February 10, 2021.
      https://www.cnn.com/2021/02/10/politics/joe-biden-howard-krein
      -startup-health/index.html

82   Matt Viser, "In politics and life, Biden's sister has been at his side,"
      Washington Post, January 11, 2021. https://www.washingtonpost.com
      /politics/valerie-joe-biden-sister/2021/01/09/49cefb24-4171-11eb
      -9453-fc36ba051781_story.html

83   "Family Affair – Senate," Citizens For Responsibility and Ethics in
      Washington, 2008. https://www.scribd.com/document/48891779
      /Family-Affair-Senate-2008

84   Ibid.

85   Meredith Newman, "Joe Biden's family tree: An introduction to
      Delaware's most famous family," *Delaware News Journal*, April 25, 2019.
      https://www.delawareonline.com/story/news/politics/joe-biden
      /2019/04/25/joe-biden-running-2020-a-look-at-biden-family/3013958002/

86   Hillel Italie, "Valerie Biden Owens, the president's sister, has a book
      deal," Associated Press, June 24, 2021. https://apnews.com/article/joe

-biden-valerie-biden-owens-entertainment-government-and-politics
-arts-and-entertainment-46752afe6875e0cd0285d16676238c16

87   "President Obama Announces More Key Administration Posts,"
     White House Archives, September 13, 2016. https://obamawhitehouse
     .archives.gov/the-press-office/2016/09/13/president-obama-announces
     -more-key-administration-posts

88   "Valerie Biden Owens, Chair of the Biden Institute at the University
     of Delaware," LinkedIn. https://www.linkedin.com/in/valerie-biden
     -owens/

89   Schreckinger, "Biden Inc.," *Politico*, August 2, 2019. https://www
     .politico.com/magazine/story/2019/08/02/joe-biden-investigation
     -hunter-brother-hedge-fund-money-2020-campaign-227407/

90   "Missy Owens, Strategic Leader | Environmental and Sustainability
     Policy | Social Impact | Communications | Federal & Diplomatic
     Relations," LinkedIn. https://www.linkedin.com/in/missyowens/

91   "Casey (Owens) Castello, Experience Innovation, Operations, and
     General Management at Starbucks," LinkedIn. https://www.linkedin
     .com/in/casey-owens-castello/ Casey was also quite helpful to her
     cousin Hunter in his China dealings. More on that in Chapter 3.

92   Paul Sperry, "Who Is Sara Biden" Joe's In-Law Emerges as Central
     Figure in Foreign Cash Deals," *RealClearInvestigations*, December 11,
     2023.   https://www.realclearinvestigations.com/articles/2023/12/11
     /who_is_sara_biden_joes_in-law_emerges_as_central_figure_in
     _foreign_cash_deals_996942.html

93   Jon Levine, "Joe Biden's family racks up arrests for drugs, drunk
     driving — but no jail time," *New York Post*, July 11, 2020. https://
     nypost.com/2020/07/11/joe-bidens-family-has-a-long-rap-sheet/

94   "Report on the Biden Laptop," MarcoPolo501c3.org, page 623.
     https://bidenreport.com/#p=627

95   Morgan Phillips, "Biden tapped big donor friend to get his niece Caroline
     an $85,000-a-year job while she was on probation for shoplifting -
     and she slammed it as minimum wage because she wouldn't accept
     anything below $180,000," *Daily Mail*, January 26, 2023. https://
     www.dailymail.co.uk/news/article-11680881/Biden-tapped-big-donor
     -friend-niece-Caroline-85-000-year-job.html

96   Victor Nava, "Biden donor offered prez's convict niece Caroline $85K
     job she called 'below minimum wage'," *New York Post*, January 26, 2023.
     https://nypost.com/2023/01/26/bidens-niece-caroline-blasted-85k
     -a-year-job-at-a-donors-company-as-below-minimum-wage/

97   "Report on the Biden Laptop," MarcoPolo501c3.org, page 359.
     https://bidenreport.com/#p=363

98 "Biden Delivers Remarks at Heroes Ball," ABC News, January 21, 2013. https://abcnews.go.com/Politics/video/inauguration-2013-vice-president-biden-delivers-remarks-heroes-18280411

99 Bonanno, *A Man of Honor,* Page 149.

100 Ibid., Page 152.

101 Raab, *Five Families,* Page 93.

102 "Raskin & Comer Shouting Match Sends House Hearing Off the Rails," CNN-News 18, April 18, 2024. https://www.youtube.com/watch?v=TbRH8btiQv8

103 "Interview of: Anthony Bobulinski," Committee On Oversight And Accountability Joint With The Committee On The Judiciary, U.S. House Of Representatives, February 13, 2024. https://oversight.house.gov/wp-content/uploads/2024/02/Bobulinski-Transcript.pdf

104 Ukraine's ranking on the Corruption Perception Index in 2022. "Corruption Perceptions Index," Transparency International, 2022. https://www.transparency.org/en/cpi/2022/index/ukr

105 Isha Mehrota, "Ukraine is one of the most corrupt countries in Europe. The war with Russia hasn't changed that," *Firstpost,* February 2, 2023. https://www.firstpost.com/explainers/ukraine-one-of-the-most-corrupt-countries-in-europe-russia-war-volodymyr-zelenskyy-12091652.html See also: Farah Stockman, "Corruption Is an Existential Threat to Ukraine, and Ukrainians Know It," *New York Times,* September 10, 2023. https://www.nytimes.com/2023/09/10/opinion/ukraine-war-corruption.html#:~:text=Ukrainians%20consider%20corruption%20the%20country%27s,Institute%20of%20Sociology%20this%20year.

106 "Nukes & Crooks," *Eastern Europe,* (Lonely Planet Global Limited, January, 2022), Page 451.

107 Tanya Kozyreva and Jason Leopold, "Here's How Ukraine's Ousted Government Got Away With $40 Billion," *BuzzFeed News,* July 12, 2018. https://www.buzzfeednews.com/article/tanyakozyreva/ukraines-ousted-regime-made-40-billion-disappear-and-no

108 Serhii Plokhy, *The Gates of Europe: A History of Ukraine* (Hachette Book Group, New York, 2021), Page 328

109 Plokhy, *Gates of Europe,* Pages 329, 330.

110 Plokhy, *Gates of Europe,* Page 331.

111 Plokhy, *Gates of Europe,* Page 326.

112 Pekka Sutela, "The Underachiever: Ukraine's Economy Since 1991," Carnegie Endowment, March 9, 2012. https://carnegieendowment.org/research/2012/03/the-underachiever-ukraines-economy-since-1991?lang=en

113 Oliver Bullough, "Welcome to Ukraine, the most corrupt nation in Europe," *The Guardian*, February 6, 2015. https://www.theguardian.com/news/2015/feb/04/welcome-to-the-most-corrupt-nation-in-europe-ukraine

114 Allegedly. Figures put Yanukovych's stolen loot at somewhere between $40 and $70 billion. But who's counting?

115 Plokhy, *Gates of Europe*, Page 338.

116 As we all know, war broke out again in 2022 when Russia invaded the same area of Ukraine.

117 "Petro Poroshenko," Wikipedia. https://en.wikipedia.org/wiki/Petro_Poroshenko.

118 Plokhy, *Gates of Europe*, Page 351.

119 "Burisma," Wikipedia. https://en.wikipedia.org/wiki/Burisma

120 Peter Baffoe, "The Trump Impeachment Inquiry And The Infamous Company Nobody's Ever Heard Of," *The Acronym*, October 16, 2019. https://sites.imsa.edu/acronym/2019/10/16/the-Burisma-story/

121 Polina Ivanova and Pavel Polityuk, "Ukraine agency says allegations against Burisma cover period before Biden joined," Reuters, September 27, 2019. https://www.reuters.com/article/world/ukraine-agency-says-allegations-against-Burisma-cover-period-before-biden-joined-idUSKBN1WC1LV/

122 Paul Sonne and Laura Mills, "Ukrainians See Conflict in Biden's Anticorruption Message," *Wall Street Journal*, December 7, 2015. https://www.wsj.com/articles/ukrainians-see-conflict-in-bidens-anticorruption-message-1449523458

123 "Mykola Zlochevsky," Wikipedia. https://en.wikipedia.org/wiki/Mykola_Zlochevsky

124 I have my own thoughts about that. One of the reasons Poroshenko was so hot to get to Zlochevsky was not because he was hell bent on eliminating corruption but because he was a bigger crook than all the other oligarchs – the Godfather, to go back to our Mafia analogy. There's a $5 million bribe that Zlochevsky paid to get the NABU gang off his back. See: Ilya Zhegulev, "Ukraine alleges $5 million bribe over Burisma, no Biden link," Reuters, June 13, 2020. But, given that Burisma's revenue in 2018 alone was estimated to be $400 million, according to Wikipedia, I think Poroshenko figured he was owed more than a paltry $5 million. See: "Burisma," Wikipedia. https://en.wikipedia.org/wiki/Burisma

125 "Ep. 3 The Trial: Witness One. EXCLUSIVE interview with Viktor Shokin," *Rudy Giuliani's Common Sense*, January 31, 2020. https://www.youtube.com/watch?v=eKDYhb3kaMk

126 Rosemont Seneca Partners was just one of many LLCs with the name Rosemont, created by Hunter and his business partners. In fact, a search on the State of Delaware's Division of Corporations website turns up over 50 companies with the name Rosemont in it. See: https://icis.corp.delaware.gov/Ecorp/EntitySearch/NameSearch.aspx. The MarcoPolo website lists at least 7 Rosemonts in which Hunter was involved, all established between 2009 and 2014. See: "Report on the Biden Laptop," MarcoPolo501c3.org, page 54. https://bidenreport. com/#p=59 Also note that when the money from Burisma started coming in, it was paid to Rosemont Seneca Bohai's bank account. See: "Report Of The Impeachment Inquiry Of Joseph R. Biden Jr., President Of The United States Of America," Committee on Oversight and Accountability Committee on the Judiciary Committee on Ways and Means, August 19, 2024. https://oversight.house.gov/wp-content /uploads/2024/08/2024.08.19-Report-of-the-Impeachment-Inquiry -of-Joseph-R.-Biden-Jr.-President-of-the-United-States.pdf. This was not the first time Hunter and his various partners created a web of overlapping LLCs with similar names. He and James did that when they took over Paradigm Global Advisors in 2006, setting up corporations with variations on the name BG Equity.

127 Devon Archer was Hunter Biden's partner in many of the latter's schemes. Before they met, Archer's roommate at Yale was Christopher Heinz, son of the deceased Senator Henry J. Heinz and Teresa Heinz Kerry; an heir to the Heinz ketchup empire billions; and – in this context and during this time period – most notably, the stepson of Obama's Secretary of State John Kerry. Heinz and Archer (who was a senior advisor in Kerry's 2004 presidential campaign) formed their own private equity company, Rosemont Capital, in 2009. Rosemont Capital was a 50% partner in Archer and Hunter's Rosemont Seneca Partners. Reportedly concerned about corruption in Ukraine and the propriety of Hunter being on the Burisma board, Heinz resigned from Rosemont. See: Steven Richards and John Solomon, "Road to Hunter Biden's Burisma riches was paved in Moscow with effort to court Russian oligarchs," *Just The News*, February 29, 2024. https:// justthenews.com/accountability/political-ethics/hdall-roads-lead- moscow-hunters-Burisma-gig-was-born-failed-venture; and Paul Sonne et al, "The gas tycoon and the vice president's son: The story of Hunter Biden's foray into Ukraine," *Washington Post*, September 28, 2019. https://www.washingtonpost.com/world/national-security/the-gas -tycoon-and-the-vice-presidents-son-the-story-of-hunter-bidens-foray -in-ukraine/2019/09/28/1aadff70-dfd9-11e9-8fd3-d943b4ed57e0 _story.html

128 "Interview of Devon Archer," Committee On Oversight And Accountability, U.S. House Of Representatives, July 31, 2023. https://oversight.house.gov/wp-content/uploads/2023/08/Devon-Archer -Transcript.pdf

129 Tim Hains, "Schweizer: Biden's Son Cashed In On VP Being Point Man For Obama In Ukraine And China," *RealClearPolitics*, October 4, 2019. https://www.realclearpolitics.com/video/2019/10/04/schweizer _bidens_son_cashed_in_on_vp_being_point_man_for_obama_in _ukraine_and_china.html

130 Paul Sonne and Laura Mills, "Ukrainians See Conflict in Biden's Anticorruption Message," *Wall Street Journal*, December 7, 2015. https://www.wsj.com/articles/ukrainians-see-conflict-in-bidens -anticorruption-message-1449523458

131 Ibid.

132 "Read Trump's phone conversation with Volodymyr Zelensky," CNN, September 26, 2019. https://www.cnn.com/2019/09/25/politics/ donald-trump-ukraine-transcript-call/index.html

133 John Solomon, "Timeline of key events in Ukraine scandal that led to Trump impeachment," *Just The News*, February 23, 2020. https://justthenews.com/accountability/political-ethics/timeline-key-events -ukraine-scandal-led-trump-impeachment

134 Ilya Timtchenko, "Prosecutors put Zlochevsky, multimillionaire ex-ecology minister, on wanted list," *Kyiv Post*, January 18, 2015. https:// www.kyivpost.com/article/content/reform-watch/prosecutors-put -zlochevsky-multimillionaire-ex-ecology-minister-on-wanted-list-3777 19.html

135 "Remarks by Vice President Joe Biden and Ukrainian President Petro Poroshenko at a Bilateral Meeting," U.S. Embassy in Ukraine, December 7, 2015. https://ua.usembassy.gov/remarks-vice-president -joe-biden-ukrainian-president-petro-poroshenko-bilateral-meeting/

136 James Risen, "Joe Biden, His Son and the Case Against a Ukrainian Oligarch," *New York Times*, December 8, 2015. https://www.nytimes .com/2015/12/09/world/europe/corruption-ukraine-joe-biden-son -hunter-biden-ties.html

137 "Court seizes property of ex-minister Zlochevsky in Ukraine," *InterFax-Ukraine*, February 4, 2016. https://en.interfax.com.ua/news /general/322395.html

138 As part of the investigation into Burisma, the Ukrainian Prosecutor General planned to interrogate members of the executive board, specifically including Hunter Biden. See: John Solomon, "Joe Biden's 2020 Ukrainian nightmare: A closed probe is revived," *The Hill*, April 1, 2019. https://thehill.com/opinion/white-house

/436816-joe-bidens-2020-ukrainian-nightmare-a-closed-probe-is
-revived

139 "Poroshenko asks Shokin to resign as prosecutor general," *InterFax-
Ukraine*. February 16, 2016 https://en.interfax.com.ua/news/general
/325051.html

140 John Solomon, "Latvian government says it flagged 'suspicious' Hunter
Biden payments in 2016," *John Solomon Reports*, December 17, 2019.
https://johnsolomonreports.com/latvian-government-says-it-flagged
-suspicious-hunter-biden-payments-in-2016/ See also: "Ep. 2 The
Trial: Opening Statement," *Rudy Giuliani's Common Sense*, January 29,
2020. https://www.youtube.com/watch?v=tCO3nW3cnHM

141 "Readout of Vice President Biden's Calls with Prime Minister Arseniy
Yatsenyuk and President Petro Poroshenko of Ukraine," U.S. Embassy
in Ukraine, February 19, 2016. https://ua.usembassy.gov/readout-vice
-president-bidens-calls-prime-minister-arseniy-yatsenyuk-president
-petro-poroshenko-ukraine-021916/ Prior to this period of time, Biden
had only talked to the Ukrainian president once, maybe twice every few
months.

142 "Ukrainian President's Ally Approved For Top Prosecutor's Post," Radio
Free Europe/Radio Liberty. May 12, 2016. https://www.rferl.org/a/
ukraine-prosecutor-general-lutsenko-no-legal-background/27731069
.html

143 "Foreign Affairs Issue Launch with Former Vice President Joe Biden,"
Council on Foreign Relations, January 23, 2018. https://www.cfr.org/
event/foreign-affairs-issue-launch-former-vice-president-joe-biden

144 "Burisma," Wikipedia. https://en.wikipedia.org/wiki/Burisma. See also:
"Repeated failures by Ukraine General Prosecutor's Office show politics at
work, serious reform needed," Anti-Corruption Action Centre, January
18, 2017. https://antac.org.ua/en/news/Burisma-group-of-companies
-are-still-under-criminal-investigation-in-ukraine-despite-case-against
-mykola-zlochevskyi-was-dumped-by-the-general-prosecutor-s-office/

145 Polina Ivanova et al, "What Hunter Biden did on the board of Ukrainian
energy company Burisma," Reuters, October 18, 2019. https://www
.reuters.com/article/world/us-politics/what-hunter-biden-did-on-the
-board-of-ukrainian-energy-company-Burisma-idUSKBN1WX1P6/

146 "Remarks by Vice President Joe Biden at a Joint Press Availability
with Ukrainian President Petro Poroshenko," U.S. Embassy in
Ukraine, January 17, 2017. https://ua.usembassy.gov/remarks-vice
-president-joe-biden-joint-press-availability-ukrainian-president
-petro-poroshenko/

147 Investigative journalist John Solomon put together a very detailed
timeline of the events leading up to Trump's first impeachment

trial. Follow it to see the individuals and organizations in Ukraine that conspired to keep Donald Trump from being elected in 2016, who prevented the US electorate in 2020 from discovering the extent of Hunter and Joe Biden's multi-million dollar involvement with at least one corrupt Ukrainian oligarch. See: John Solomon, "Timeline of key events in Ukraine scandal that led to Trump impeachment," *Just The News*, February 23, 2020. https://justthenews.com/accountability/political-ethics/timeline-key-events-ukraine-scandal-led-trump-impeachment

148 "Ep. 3 The Trial: Witness One. EXCLUSIVE interview with Viktor Shokin," *Rudy Giuliani's Common Sense*, January 31, 2020. https://www.youtube.com/watch?v=eKDYhb3kaMk

149 Ibid

150 "Interview of Devon Archer," Committee On Oversight And Accountability, U.S. House Of Representatives, July 31, 2023. https://oversight.house.gov/wp-content/uploads/2023/08/Devon-Archer-Transcript.pdf

151 Alan Apter is an investment banker who became Burisma's board chairman. Paul Sonne et al, "The gas tycoon and the vice president's son: The story of Hunter Biden's foray into Ukraine," *Washington Post*, September 28, 2019. https://www.washingtonpost.com/world/national-security/the-gas-tycoon-and-the-vice-presidents-son-the-story-of-hunter-bidens-foray-in-ukraine/2019/09/28/1aadff70-dfd9-11e9-8fd3-d943b4ed57e0_story.html

152 "Ep. 2 The Trial: Opening Statement," *Rudy Giuliani's Common Sense*, January 29, 2020. https://www.youtube.com/watch?v=tCO3nW3cnHM

153 "Ep. 3 The Trial: Witness One. EXCLUSIVE interview with Viktor Shokin," *Rudy Giuliani's Common Sense*, January 31, 2020. https://www.youtube.com/watch?v=eKDYhb3kaMk

154 Ibid.

155 David L. Stern and Robyn Dixon, "Ukraine court forces probe into Biden role in firing of prosecutor Viktor Shokin," *Washington Post*, February 27, 2020. https://www.washingtonpost.com/world/europe/ukraine-court-forces-probe-into-biden-role-in-firing-of-prosecutor-viktor-shokin/2020/02/27/92710222-5983-11ea-8efd-0f904bdd8057_story.html

156 Veronika Melkozerova, "Ukraine police close Biden probe initiated by ousted prosecutor," NBC News, November 10, 2020. https://www.nbcnews.com/politics/politics-news/ukraine-police-closes-biden-probe-initiated-ousted-prosecutor-n1247320

157 Thomas Catenacci, "Former Ukraine prosecutor makes explosive claims against Joe and Hunter Biden in new interview," Fox News,

August 25, 2023. https://www.foxnews.com/politics/former-ukraine
-prosecutor-makes-explosive-claims-joe-hunter-biden-new-interview

158 Our source for those bank records was willing to turn them over but
quite understandably feared for her life and would only cooperate on
the condition that she be admitted into the US witness protection
program. Bob and I tried to get the Pittsburgh authorities to contact
her, but they ultimately did not follow up.

159 Scott Neuman, "Biden Visits Ukraine In Show Of U.S. Support," NPR,
April 21, 2014. https://www.npr.org/sections/thetwo-way/2014/04
/21/305634031/biden-visits-ukraine-to-offer-energy-economic-aid

160 "Report on the Biden Laptop," MarcoPolo501c3.org, page 143.
https://bidenreport.com/#p=147. Note that Hunter is looking to
figure out ways to further line his pockets by adding legal fees on top of
his $83k/month as a board member. At the time he's still employed as
a lawyer for Boise Shiller (BSF).

161 "Report on the Biden Laptop," MarcoPolo501c3.org, page 147.
https://bidenreport.com/#p=151

162 "Report on the Biden Laptop," MarcoPolo501c3.org, page 150.
https://bidenreport.com/#p=155

163 "Report on the Biden Laptop," MarcoPolo501c3.org, page 163.
https://bidenreport.com/#p=167

164 John Solomon and Steven Richards, "FBI knew since 2016 Hunter
Biden's team nearly scored $120 million Ukrainian deal while Joe
was VP," *Just The News*, June 17, 2024. https://justthenews.com
/accountability/political-ethics/hld-hunter-biden-was-proposed
-board-member-120-million-Burisma

165 "Interview of Jason Galanis," Committee On Oversight And
Accountability Joint With The Committee On The Judiciary, U.S.
House Of Representatives, February 23, 2024. https://oversight.house
.gov/wp-content/uploads/2024/03/Jason-Galanis-Transcript.pdf

166 Email from Devon Archer to Jesica Lindgren at public affairs
consultancy firm Blue Star Strategies laying out Zlochevsky's aims.
https://justthenews.com/sites/default/files/2024-06/2015.10.20%20
-%20Re-Burisma%20Proposal.pdf

167 The email from Pozharskyi to Archer. https://justthenews.com/sites/
default/files/2024-06/HunterBidenLichstensteinUkrainewantsHB-1.pdf

168 Richard Morgan, "'Porn's New King' busted for ripping off Indians,"
New York Post, May 12, 2016. https://nypost.com/2016/05/12/porns
-new-king-busted-for-ripping-off-tribe-in-60m-scam/ Note that it was
the third time in 9 years that Jason Galanis was accused of financial
fraud.

169 Kaja Whitehouse and Samantha Tomaszewski, "'Porn's New King' pleads guilty to manipulating company shares," *New York Post*, July 21, 2016. https://nypost.com/2016/07/21/porns-new-king-pleads-guilty -to-manipulating-company-shares/. John went to jail for his tax shelter scheme in 1988 and got out in 2001. At the time I called him a "career white-collar criminal." Besides Jason, his sons Jared and Derek appear to have followed in his criminal footsteps.

170 "Hunter Biden's name used to legitimize sale of fraudulent tribal bonds," *Native Sun News Today*, January 27, 2020. https://www .nativesunnews.today/articles/hunter-bidens-name-used-to-legitimize -sale-of-fraudulent-tribal-bonds/. Archer was convicted and unsuccessfully appealed his case all the way to the Supreme Court. As of this writing, he has yet to see jail time. See: "Supreme Court Rejects an Appeal From a Former Business Partner of Hunter Biden," *US News and World Report*, January 22, 2024. https://www.usnews.com/news /politics/articles/2024-01-22/supreme-court-rejects-an-appeal-from -a-former-business-partner-of-hunter-biden; Steve Korris, "Devon Archer to get new hearing on prison sentence for fraud, conspiracy," *Madison-St. Clair Record*, May 24, 2024. https://madisonrecord. com/stories/659305295-devon-archer-to-get-new-hearing-on-prison -sentence-for-fraud-conspiracy

171 Peter Schweizer, "How five members of Joe Biden's family got rich through his connections," *New York Post*, January 20, 2020. https:// nypost.com/2020/01/18/how-five-members-of-joe-bidens-family-got -rich-through-his-connections/

172 Letter from Chairmen James Comer and Jim Jordan to SEC Chairman Gary Gensler. https://oversight.house.gov/wp-content/ uploads/2024/06/6.18.2024-Letter-to-the-SEC-re-Hunter-Biden.pdf

173 John Solomon and Steven Richards, "FBI knew since 2016 Hunter Biden's team nearly scored $120 million Ukrainian deal while Joe was VP," *Just The News*, June 17, 2024. https:// justthenews.com/accountability/political-ethics/hld-hunter-biden -was-proposed-board-member-120-million-Burisma

174 Marc Caputo, "Poll: Majority says Biden son's Ukraine job was inappropriate," *Politico*, February 13, 2020. https://www.politico.com/ news/2020/02/13/biden-Burisma-poll-ukraine-115096

175 Josh Lederman, "Biden's trip to China with son Hunter in 2013 comes under new scrutiny," NBC News, October 2, 2019. https:// www.nbcnews.com/politics/2020-election/biden-s-trip-china-son -hunter-2013-comes-under-new-n1061051

176 Peter Schweizer, *Red-Handed*, (Harper, 2022.) Kindle version - page 10.

177 "'It has nothing to do with me,' [Hunter] wrote in 2011 about some of his developing connections with Chinese investors, "and everything to do with my last name." Matt Viser, "Hunter Biden's career of benefiting from his father's name," *Washington Post*, November 18, 2023. https://www.washingtonpost.com/politics/2023/11/18/hunter-biden-family-name/. See also: John Solomon, "Hunter Biden friend tells Congress how first family's name scored Chinese deal worth millions," KTBS, February 13, 2024. https://www.ktbs.com/news/national_politics/hunter-biden-friend-tells-congress-how-first-family-s-name-scored-chinese-deal-worth-millions/article_5163b3b0-777b-5324-a490-d2d729c89629.html

178 Peter Schweizer, *Secret Empires* (Harper Collins, New York, 2018), Pages 27, 28.

179 Stephanie Saul, "Politics, Money, Siblings: The Ties Between Joe Biden and Valerie Biden Owens," *New York Times*, February 28, 2020. https://www.nytimes.com/2020/02/25/us/politics/valerie-joe-biden-sister.html

180 Jessica Chasmar, Cameron Cawthorne, "Biden's niece updated Hunter's company on Chinese sovereign wealth fund during stint at Treasury: emails," Fox News, September 11, 2023. https://www.foxnews.com/politics/vp-bidens-niece-updated-hunters-company-chinese-sovereign-wealth-fund-treasury-emails

181 Steven Nelson, "Joe Biden wrote letter to Hunter biz partner Devon Archer after 2011 China lunch — despite claims of never discussing son's business," *New York Post*, August 2, 2023. https://nypost.com/2023/08/02/joe-biden-told-hunter-biz-partner-devon-archer-happy-you-guys-are-together-after-2011-china-lunch/

182 There are too many articles to cite about this, but here's one: Steven Nelson, "Biden insists he told truth about not talking foreign biz with Hunter — despite mounting evidence," *New York Post*, June 26, 2023. https://nypost.com/2023/06/26/biden-insists-he-and-hunter-never-talked-foreign-biz-despite-mounting-evidence/

183 "Remarks by Vice President Joe Biden to the Opening Session of the U.S.-China Strategic & Economic Dialogue," White House Archives, May 9, 2011. https://obamawhitehouse.archives.gov/the-press-office/2011/05/09/remarks-vice-president-joe-biden-opening-session-us-china-strategic-econ

184 Ibid.

185 Peter Schweizer, "Inside the shady private equity firm run by Kerry and Biden's kids," *New York Post*, March 15, 2018. https://nypost.com/2018/03/15/inside-the-shady-private-equity-firm-run

-by-kerry-and-bidens-kids/. Remember that when all this was going down, Chris Heinz' stepdad, John Kerry, was Secretary of State.

186   Eliana Dockterman, "The True Story Behind *Black Mass*," *Time*, September 21, 2015. https://time.com/4043186/black-mass-true-story/

187   "Thornton Group and Rosemont Seneca senior executives visited the senior executives of China's financial/fund industry," Thornton Group LLC, April 12, 2010. https://archive.ph/www.thorntonai.com

188   Ibid. In the photo caption, Michael Lin, the Thornton CEO, is identified as Lin Junliang. See also: "Thornton Group LLC, Financial Services, Boston, MA," LinkedIn. https://www.linkedin.com/company/thornton-group-llc/; "Michael Lin, Co-Founder and Chief Executive officer," Management Team, Thornton Group, https://web.archive.org/web/20131202060735/http://www.thorntonai.com/english/team-a-2.html; and Jennifer Van Laar, "Are Hunter Biden's China Travels With Michael Lin Related to the Loss of 30 CIA Assets?" *RedState*. October 20, 2020. https://redstate.com/jenvanlaar/2020/10/29/are-hunter-bidens-china-travels-with-michael-lin-related-to-the-loss-of-30-cia-assets-n271683

189   "Michael Lin Connected Biden with Beijing," *Chinascope*, October 17, 2020. http://chinascope.org/archives/24965

190   The Wikipedia entry for BHR lists only Hunter, Devon and Jonathan Li as its founders. Chris Heinz's name is notably absent. See: "BHR Partners," Wikipedia. https://en.wikipedia.org/wiki/BHR_Partners

191   Josh Lederman, "Biden's trip to China with son Hunter in 2013 comes under new scrutiny," NBC News, October 2, 2019. https://www.nbcnews.com/politics/2020-election/biden-s-trip-china-son-hunter-2013-comes-under-new-n1061051

192   Michael Forsythe et al, "How Hunter Biden's Firm Helped Secure Cobalt for the Chinese," *New York Times*, December 7, 2021. https://www.nytimes.com/2021/11/20/world/hunter-biden-china-cobalt.html. See also: "'Sugar Brother' Admits He Still Owns 10% Stake in Hunter's Chinese Equity Firm," *Headline USA*, January 24, 2024. https://headlineusa.com/hunter-sugar-brother-own-stake-bhr/ and "Report Of The Impeachment Inquiry Of Joseph R. Biden Jr., President Of The United States Of America," Committee on Oversight and Accountability Committee on the Judiciary Committee on Ways and Means, August 19, 2024. https://oversight.house.gov/wp-content/uploads/2024/08/2024.08.19-Report-of-the-Impeachment-Inquiry-of-Joseph-R.-Biden-Jr.-President-of-the-United-States.pdf

193   Adam Entous, "Will Hunter Biden Jeopardize His Father's Campaign?" *New Yorker*, July 1, 2019. https://www.newyorker.com/magazine/2019/07/08/will-hunter-biden-jeopardize-his-fathers

-campaign Later, Joe also wrote college recommendation letters for Li's daughter and son when they applied to some of the top universities in the US. See: Emily Crane and Miranda Devine, "Biden wrote college recommendation letters for kids of Chinese exec tied to Hunter," *New York Post*, April 6, 2022. https://nypost.com/2022/04/06/biden-wrote -college-rec-for-son-of-chinese-exec-tied-to-hunter/

194 "Q&A : BHR Partners' Jonathan Li & Xin Wang," BHR Partners, March 4, 2016. http://www.bhrpe.com/show.php?catid=42&id=112

195 Peter Schweizer, "Inside the shady private equity firm run by Kerry and Biden's kids," *New York Post*, March 15, 2018. https:// nypost.com/2018/03/15/inside-the-shady-private-equity-firm -run-by-kerry-and-bidens-kids/

196 David Barboza, "Family of Chinese Regulator Profits in Insurance Firm's Rise," *New York Times*, December 30, 2012. https://www.nytimes .com/2012/12/31/business/global/chinese-regulators-family-profited -from-stake-in-insurer.html

197 "Anti-corruption campaign under Xi Jinping," Wikipedia. https:// en.wikipedia.org/wiki/Anti-corruption_campaign_under_Xi_Jinping

198 Frank Fang, "How Xi Jinping's Anti-Corruption Campaign Has Put China's Financial Institutions on Notice," *Epoch Times*, November 2, 2017. https://www.theepochtimes.com/how-xi-jinpings-anti -corruption-campaign-has-put-chinas-financial-institutions-on-notice _2346850.html

199 "Report on the Biden Laptop," MarcoPolo501c3.org, page 93. https:// bidenreport.com/#p=97

200 Hillary Clinton, "America's Pacific Century," *Foreign Policy*, October 11, 2011. https://foreignpolicy.com/2011/10/11/americas-pacific-century/

201 Steve Clemons, "Biden Gets China," *The Atlantic*, January 2, 2012. https:// www.theatlantic.com/politics/archive/2012/01/biden-gets-china /250747/

202 "China's Island Building in the South China Sea: Damage to the Marine Environment, Implications, and International Law," U.S.- China Economic and Security Review Commission, April 12, 2016. https://www.uscc.gov/research/chinas-island-building-south-china -sea-damage-marine-environment-implications-and

203 RFA Staff, "New photos show China's artificial islands are highly developed military bases," Radio Free Asia, October 31, 2022. https://www.rfa.org/english/news/southchinasea/china-artificial -islands-10312022043801.html

204 John W. Rollins, "U.S.–China Cyber Agreement," CRS Insight, October 16, 2015. https://sgp.fas.org/crs/row/IN10376.pdf

205 Derek M. Scissors, "Can Biden Stop China's Intellectual Property Theft?," *The National Interest*, October 14, 2021. https://nationalinterest.org/blog/reboot/can-biden-stop-chinas-intellectual-property-theft-194751

206 "Strike Hard Campaign against Violent Terrorism," Wikipedia. https://en.wikipedia.org/wiki/Strike_Hard_Campaign_Against_Violent_Terrorism

207 Ramtin Arablouei and Rund Abdelfatah, "Who The Uyghurs Are And Why China Is Targeting Them," NPR, May 31, 2021. https://www.npr.org/2021/05/31/1001936433/who-the-uyghurs-are-and-why-china-is-targeting-them

208 Katie Rogers and Edward Wong, "For Biden and Xi, a Long Relationship With Rising Mutual Suspicion," *New York Times*, November 11, 2022. https://www.nytimes.com/2022/11/11/us/politics/biden-china-g20-bali.html

209 Time Staff, "Read the Full Transcript of President Joe Biden's Interview With TIME," *Time*, June 5, 2024. https://time.com/6984968/joe-biden-transcript-2024-interview/

210 For example, it took a week for Biden to order a Chinese spy balloon to be shot down – after it had traversed nearly all of the US. See: Helene Cooper et al, "U.S. Shoots Down Surveillance Balloon," *New York Times*, February 5, 2023. https://www.nytimes.com/live/2023/02/04/us/china-spy-balloon. He's allowed Xi to bully Taiwan. See: Brendan Cole, "Is Biden 'Too Soft' on China?," *Newsweek*, October 6, 2023. https://www.newsweek.com/biden-jinping-xi-china-trump-1831731. During the 2023 San Francisco summit between the two leaders, Biden did not offer any push back when Xi claimed he was going to retake Taiwan. See: Kristen Welker et al, "Xi warned Biden during summit that Beijing will reunify Taiwan with China," NBC News, December 20, 2023. https://www.nbcnews.com/news/china/xi-warned-biden-summit-beijing-will-reunify-taiwan-china-rcna130087. And he's doing very little to counter China's escalating aggression towards the Philippines in the South China Sea. See: Tim Rogan, "US must resist China's aggression toward the Philippines," *Washington Examiner*, August 29, 2024. https://www.washingtonexaminer.com/opinion/beltway-confidential/3135767/us-must-resist-china-aggression-toward-philippines/

211 "Elite Capture, Why America Is Losing in the Political Warfare Arena, and What Can Be Done," The Heritage Project, April 5, 2023. https://www.heritage.org/the-oversight-project/countering-ccp-influence/elite-capture-why-america-losing-the-political

212 "Chinese Money Keeps Coal Mines Humming - Heard on the Street," BHR Partners, February 18, 2016. http://www.bhrpe.com/show.php?catid=42&id=114

213 Michael Forsythe et al, "How Hunter Biden's Firm Helped Secure Cobalt for the Chinese," *New York Times*, December 7, 2021. https://www.nytimes.com/2021/11/20/world/hunter-biden-china-cobalt.html

214 Kevin Clemens, "Understanding the Role of Cobalt in Batteries," *Design News*, February 16, 2023. https://www.designnews.com/electronics/understanding-the-role-of-cobalt-in-batteries

215 Peter Schweizer, "6 facts about Hunter Biden's business dealings in China," *New York Post*, October 10, 2019. https://nypost.com/2019/10/10/6-facts-about-hunter-bidens-business-dealings-in-china/

216 "US engineer gets two years in jail for leaking nuclear secrets to China," Sky News, September 1, 2017. https://news.sky.com/story/us-engineer-gets-two-years-in-jail-for-leaking-nuclear-secrets-to-china-11016090. See also: Jamie Satterfield, "Secrecy surrounds sentencing of Chinese government operative in nuclear tech spy case," *Knox News*, August 29, 2017. https://www.knoxnews.com/story/news/crime/2017/08/29/secrecy-surrounds-sentencing-chinese-government-operative-nuclear-tech-spy-case/611490001/; and "U.S. Nuclear Engineer Sentenced to 24 Months in Prison for Violating the Atomic Energy Act," U.S. Department of Justice, August 31, 2017. https://www.justice.gov/opa/pr/us-nuclear-engineer-sentenced-24-months-prison-violating-atomic-energy-act

217 Letter from Senator Chuck Grassley (R-IA), Chairman of the Senate Committee on Finance, to Secretary of the Treasury Steven Mnuchin, August 14, 2019. https://justthenews.com/sites/default/files/2020-09/2019-08-14%20CEG%20to%20Treasury%20%28AVIC%20CFIUS%29.pdf. Grassley quotes several sources in his letter to back up his facts and figures. See also: Chris Sweeney, "Equity Firm Sells Henniges," *Rubber & Plastics News*, September 17, 2015. https://www.rubbernews.com/article/20150917/NEWS/150919961/equity-firm-sells-henniges.; "Chinese FDI in the United States: 3Q 2015 Update," Rhodium Group, November 12, 2015. https://rhg.com/research/chinese-fdi-in-the-united-states-3q-2015-update/; Bill Gertz, "Stolen F-35 Secrets Now Showing Up in China's Stealth Fighter," *The Washington Free Beacon*, March 13, 2014. https://freebeacon.com/national-security/stolen-f-35-secrets-now-showing-up-in-chinas-stealth-fighter; and David Z. Morris, "Hackers Stole Restricted F-35 Data from an Australian Contractor," *Fortune*, October 14, 2017. https://fortune.com/2017/10/14/hacked-f-35-data/.

218 "China – CEFC," House Committee on Oversight and Accountability, July 10, 2023. https://oversight.house.gov/timeline/china-cefc/

219 "The Secretive China Energy Giant That Faces Scrutiny: QuickTake," NDTV, April 3, 2018. https://www.ndtvprofit.com/quicktakes/the -secretive-china-energy-giant-that-faces-scrutiny-quicktake

220 Alexander Bowe, "China's Overseas United Front Work," U.S.- China Economic and Security Review Commission, August 24, 2018. https://www.uscc.gov/sites/default/files/Research/China%27s%20 Overseas%20United%20Front%20Work%20-%20Background%20 and%20Implications%20for%20US_final_0.pdf

221 Peter Schweizer, *Blood Money* (Harper Collins, New York, 2024), Page 43.

222 For example, the August 19, 2024 "Report Of The Impeachment Inquiry Of Joseph R. Biden Jr., President Of The United States Of America," stated that "Hunter Biden described Chairman Ye to James Biden as a 'protégé' of President Xi Jinping," and that Joe Biden "was aware that his family had been in business with certain Chinese entities since 2014 and in fact made millions of dollars from China." See: "Report Of The Impeachment Inquiry Of Joseph R. Biden Jr., President Of The United States Of America," Committee on Oversight and Accountability Committee on the Judiciary Committee on Ways and Means, August 19, 2024. https://oversight.house.gov/wp-content /uploads/2024/08/2024.08.19-Report-of-the-Impeachment-Inquiry -of-Joseph-R.-Biden-Jr.-President-of-the-United-States.pdf

223 Brooke Singman, "Joe Biden allegedly considered joining board of CCP-linked company, witness testifies from prison," Fox News, February 23, 2024. After scouring Hunter's "Laptop from Hell," the *New York Post*'s Miranda Devine reported that Hunter's associate James Gilliar suggested Joe would join the board of a second Chinese company as well. See: Miranda Devine, "'More money than God': Chinese titan lavished Hunter Biden with 3-carat gem, offer of $30 million," *New York Post*, November 30, 2021. https://nypost.com/2021/11/28 /chinese-titan-lavished-hunter-biden-with-3-carat-gem-offer-of-30 -million/

224 Schweizer, *Red-Handed*, Page 32.

225 "Report on the Biden Laptop," MarcoPolo501c3.org, page 110. https://bidenreport.com/#p=115

226 The accounts of this are too numerous to detail. See, for starters, "Report on the Biden Laptop," MarcoPolo501c3.org, https://bidenreport .com/#p=1; Miranda Devine, *Laptop From Hell*, Liberatio Protocol, New York/Nashville, 2021; and Hunter Biden, *Beautiful Things: A Memoir*, Gallery Books, April 6, 2021.

227 Daniel Bates, "Revealed: Hunter Biden raked in $6M in just nine months from Chinese business dealings - and that doesn't include the

2.8 carat-diamond he got as a gift," *Daily Mail*, December 10, 2020. https://www.dailymail.co.uk/news/article-9040381/Hunter-Biden -raked-6m-nine-months-Chinese-business-dealings.html

228 "Interview of John Robinson Walker," Committee On Oversight And Accountability Joint With The Committee On The Judiciary, U.S. House Of Representatives, January 26, 2024. https://oversight.house .gov/wp-content/uploads/2024/02/Walker-Transcript.pdf

229 "James Gilliar, Joe Biden's handler of dirty cash," *Blitz*, July 28, 2022. https://weeklyblitz.net/2022/07/28/james-gilliar-joe-bidens-handler -of-dirty-cash/

230 Sophie Beach, "Beijing, CEFC, And The Czech Republic," *China Digital Times*, August 15, 2018. https://chinadigitaltimes.net/2018/08 /chinese-influence-in-europe-cefc-and-the-czech-republic/

231 "James Biden, Memorandum of Interview," Department of Treasury, September 29, 2022. https://justthenews.com/sites/default/files/2023 -09/T19%20Exhibit%20401-Memo-FINAL%20Memo%20of%20 Interview%20w%20James%20B%20SPORTSMAN-09.29.2022 _KPM%20Unredacted_Redacted.pdf

232 "Report on the Biden Laptop," MarcoPolo501c3.org, page 108. https:// bidenreport.com/#p=113

233 Miranda Devine, "'More money than God': Chinese titan lavished Hunter Biden with 3-carat gem, offer of $30 million," *New York Post*, November 30, 2021. https://nypost.com/2021/11/28/chinese-titan-lavished-hunter -biden-with-3-carat-gem-offer-of-30-million/

234 Ibid.

235 "Joe Biden's Son Hunter Kicked Out of Navy for Cocaine," NBC News, October 16, 2014. https://www.nbcnews.com/news/us-news /joe-bidens-son-hunter-kicked-out-navy-cocaine-n227811

236 Miranda Devine, "'More money than God': Chinese titan lavished Hunter Biden with 3-carat gem, offer of $30 million," *New York Post*, November 30, 2021. https://nypost.com/2021/11/28/chinese-titan -lavished-hunter-biden-with-3-carat-gem-offer-of-30-million/

237 "Patrick Ho," Wikipedia. https://en.wikipedia.org/wiki/Patrick_Ho

238 "Influential Chinese businessman helps strengthen Georgia-China friendship," *Agenda.GE*, October 18, 2016. https://agenda.ge/en/news /2016/2559#gsc.tab=0

239 "Interview of Anthony Bobulinski," Committee On Oversight And Accountability Joint With The Committee On The Judiciary, U.S. House Of Representatives, February 13, 2024. https://oversight.house .gov/wp-content/uploads/2024/02/Bobulinski-Transcript.pdf

240 Ibid.

241 "Interview of Mervyn Yan," Committee On Oversight And Accountability Joint With The Committee On The Judiciary, U.S. House Of Representatives, January 25, 2024. https://oversight.house .gov/wp-content/uploads/2024/02/Mervyn-Yan-Transcript.pdf

242 Ibid

243 See, for starters, Peter Schweizer, *Red-Handed: How American Elites Get Rich Helping China Win* (Harper, New York, January 25, 2022); Ben Schreckinger, *The Bidens: Inside the First Family's Fifty-Year Rise to Power* (Hachette Book Group, New York, 2021); any number of stories in the *Daily Mail*, https://www.dailymail.co.uk/ushome/index.html; "Report on the Biden Laptop," MarcoPolo501c3.org. https://bidenreport. com/#p=1; and "Report Of The Impeachment Inquiry Of Joseph R. Biden Jr., President Of The United States Of America," Committee on Oversight and Accountability Committee on the Judiciary Committee on Ways and Means, August 19, 2024. https://oversight .house.gov/wp-content/uploads/2024/08/2024.08.19-Report-of-the -Impeachment-Inquiry-of-Joseph-R.-Biden-Jr.-President-of-the -United-States.pdf

244 "Interview of John Robinson Walker," Committee On Oversight And Accountability Joint With The Committee On The Judiciary, U.S. House Of Representatives, January 26, 2024. https://oversight.house .gov/wp-content/uploads/2024/02/Walker-Transcript.pdf.   Walker also talks about additional work for the CEFC that Hunter and co. did while Joe Biden was still vice president.

245 See: Miranda Devine, "'More money than God': Chinese titan lavished Hunter Biden with 3-carat gem, offer of $30 million," *New York Post*, November 30, 2021. https://nypost.com/2021/11/28/chinese-titan -lavished-hunter-biden-with-3-carat-gem-offer-of-30-million/ and Adam Entous, "Will Hunter Biden Jeopardize His Father's Campaign?" *New Yorker*, July 1, 2019. https://www.newyorker. com/magazine/2019/07/08/will-hunter-biden-jeopardize-his-fathers -campaign. Hunter also told the *New Yorker* that "I knew it wasn't a good idea to take it. I just felt like it was weird." Still, Hunter had also gone to the dinner with a gift. In his testimony before the House Oversight Committee on February 28, 2024, Hunter claimed that the bottle of 1967 Macallan scotch he gave to Ye was "worth far more than the diamond he gave to us." Hunter was so dismissive of the gem that he gave it to his uncle, James Biden. See: "Interview of Robert Hunter Biden," Committee On Oversight And Accountability Joint With The Committee On The Judiciary, U.S. House Of Representatives, February 28, 2024. https://oversight.house.gov/wp-content/uploads/2024/02 /Hunter-Biden-Transcript_Redacted.pdf

246 "Interview of John Robinson Walker," Committee On Oversight And Accountability Joint With The Committee On The Judiciary, U.S. House Of Representatives, January 26, 2024. https://oversight.house .gov/wp-content/uploads/2024/02/Walker-Transcript.pdf

247 See: "Report Of The Impeachment Inquiry Of Joseph R. Biden Jr., President Of The United States Of America," Committee on Oversight and Accountability Committee on the Judiciary Committee on Ways and Means, August 19, 2024. https://oversight.house.gov/wp-content /uploads/2024/08/2024.08.19-Report-of-the-Impeachment-Inquiry -of-Joseph-R.-Biden-Jr.-President-of-the-United-States.pdf

248 "Majority Staff Report Supplemental," Committee on Finance, Committee on Homeland Security and Governmental Affairs, November 18, 2020. https://www.finance.senate.gov/imo/media/doc/2020-11-18 %20HSGAC%20-%20Finance%20Joint%20Report%20 Supplemental.pdf. The 2020 report notes two wire transfers, each for $3 million, for a total of $6 million, between HK Limited and Robinson Walker LLC. However, the Biden recipients aren't named in this 2020 review.

249 Committee on Oversight and Accountability Majority Staff, "New Evidence Resulting from the Oversight Committee's Investigation into the Biden Family's Influence Peddling and Business Schemes," Committee on Oversight and Accountability, March 16, 2023. https://oversight.house.gov/wp-content/uploads/2023/03/Bank -Records-Memo-3.16.23.pdf. The Committee was unclear about that First Clearing LLC wire transfer. A Google search turned up the Firstclearing.com website, which states that "First Clearing is a trade name used by Wells Fargo Clearing Services," for "broker-dealers and registered investment advisors." See: First Clearing.com. https://www .firstclearing.com. And Hunter Biden has a long association with Wells Fargo, as evidenced by transactions on his infamous laptop.

250 "Interview of Anthony Bobulinski," Committee On Oversight And Accountability Joint With The Committee On The Judiciary, U.S. House Of Representatives, February 13, 2024. https://oversight.house .gov/wp-content/uploads/2024/02/Bobulinski-Transcript.pdf The next set of Bobulinski quotes are also taken from this transcript.

251 Miranda Devine, "Hunter Biden and CEFC China firm's million-dollar deals revealed on laptop," *Daily Telegraph*, November 29, 2021. https://www.dailytelegraph.com.au/news/hunter-biden-and-cefc -china-firms-milliondollar-deals-revealed-on-laptop/news-story/c7217 31db79a46b3ce24c9432b34b67e?amp&nk=aea36d08dcec64a6c246f f85191ddaf0-1720142233

252 "Report on the Biden Laptop," MarcoPolo501c3.org, page 579. https://bidenreport.com/#p=583

253 "Interview of Anthony Bobulinski," Committee On Oversight And Accountability Joint With The Committee On The Judiciary, U.S. House Of Representatives, February 13, 2024. https://oversight.house. gov/wp-content/uploads/2024/02/Bobulinski-Transcript.pdf

254 See: "Interview of Robert Hunter Biden," Committee On Oversight And Accountability Joint With The Committee On The Judiciary, U.S. House Of Representatives, February 28, 2024. https://oversight. house.gov/wp-content/uploads/2024/02/Hunter-Biden-Transcript _Redacted.pdf and "Interview of James Brian Biden," Committee On Oversight And Accountability Joint With The Committee On The Judiciary, U.S. House Of Representatives, February 21, 2024. https:// oversight.house.gov/wp-content/uploads/2024/06/James-Biden -Transcript-1.pdf

255 "Interview of John Robinson Walker," Committee On Oversight And Accountability Joint With The Committee On The Judiciary, U.S. House Of Representatives, January 26, 2024. https://oversight.house .gov/wp-content/uploads/2024/02/Walker-Transcript.pdf

256 The most concise chronology of the next series of texts was compiled by a semi-retired mining consultant with degrees from the University of Toronto and Oxford named Stephen McIntyre who blogs about climate. His compilation is housed here: https://www.scribd.com/ document/482411681/Hunter-Biden-CEFC-Chronology. Unless otherwise noted, I'm citing this as my main source for these written exchanges simply because it IS the most concise. The same material is available via a host of other outlets, including but not limited to "Report on the Biden Laptop," MarcoPolo501c3.org. https://bidenreport.com /#p=1

257 Brooke Singman, "Hunter Biden associate texts hint at push to 'get Joe involved,' make it look like 'truly family business'," Fox News, December 17, 2020. https://www.foxnews.com/politics/hunter-biden -ex-associate-get-joe-involved-family-business

258 Arlette Saenz, "Joe Biden announces he is running for president in 2020," CNN, April 25, 2019. https://www.cnn.com/2019/04/25/politics /joe-biden-2020-president/index.html

259 "Report on the Biden Laptop," MarcoPolo501c3.org, page 108. https://bidenreport.com/#p=113

260 "Interview of Anthony Bobulinski," Committee On Oversight And Accountability Joint With The Committee On The Judiciary, U.S. House Of Representatives, February 13, 2024. https://oversight.house .gov/wp-content/uploads/2024/02/Bobulinski-Transcript.pdf

261 On June 6, Hunter texted Gilliar, "Explain to me one thing Tony brings to MY table that I so desperately need that I'm willing to sign over my family's brand and pretty much the rest of my business lift?...Why in gods name would I give this marginal bully the keys to my family's only asset? Why?" Rowan Scarborough, "Newly released text messages show Joe Biden had involvement in son Hunter's business dealings," *Washington Times*, October 24, 2020. https://www.washingtontimes.com/news /2020/oct/24/bobulinski-texts-joe-biden-involved-son-business-/

262 "Report on the Biden Laptop," MarcoPolo501c3.org, page 119. https://bidenreport.com/#p=123

263 See: Alexandra Stevenson et al, "A Chinese Tycoon Sought Power and Influence. Washington Responded," *New York Times*, December 12, 2018. https://www.nytimes.com/2018/12/12/business/cefc-biden-china -washington-ye-jianming.html and Clifford Krauss, "Russia Uses Its Oil Giant, Rosneft, as a Foreign Policy Tool," *New York Times*, October 29, 2017. https://www.nytimes.com/2017/10/29/business /energy-environment/russia-venezula-oil-rosneft.html. The deal eventually fell through, requiring the CEFC to cough up €225 million in compensation. See: "China's CEFC paid out compensation after Rosneft stake deal fell through," Reuters, November 19, 2018. https://www.reuters.com/article/idUSKCN1NO1RV/. That's about $257,760,000 in November, 2018 dollars. See: "Euro (EUR) To US Dollar (USD) Exchange Rate History for 2018," Exchange-Rates.org. https://www.exchange-rates.org/exchange-rate-history/eur-usd-2018

264 Katherine Clarke, "A Top Chinese Oilman Vanishes, and a Manhattan Buying Binge Ends," *Wall Street Journal*, October 25, 2018. https://www .wsj.com/articles/a-top-chinese-oilman-vanishes-and-a-manhattan -buying-binge-ends-1540478781

265 "Report on the Biden Laptop," MarcoPolo501c3.org, page 119. https://bidenreport.com/#p=123

266 "Report on the Biden Laptop," MarcoPolo501c3.org, page 120. https://bidenreport.com/#p=125

267 Geoff Earle et al, "Joe was 'sitting next to Hunter when he demanded payment from Chinese businessman': IRS whistleblower claims president's son used his father's name to threaten associate in damning WhatsApp message," *Daily Mail*, June 22, 2023. https:// www.dailymail.co.uk/news/article-12224355/I-sitting-father-Hunter -Bidens-WhatsApp-Chinese-associate.html

268 These WhatsApp messages are part of a trove of documents released by the House Ways and Means Committee in conjunction with evidence provided by IRS whistleblowers Gary Shapley and Joseph Ziegler in May, 2024. They gave the Committee nearly 100 pages

of new documentation to show that Hunter Biden did not tell the truth when he testified before Congress in February, 2024. https://gop -waysandmeans.house.gov/wp-content/uploads/2024/05/6-Exhibit -801-Chat-62-with-attachments_WMRedacted.pdf

269 Why Hunter would claim this message went to Henry Zhao is a mystery. Henry, who served as Group Chairman of the Harvest Fund Management Company in Singapore, had nothing at all to do with CEFC or this deal. See: "Dr. Henry Zhao, Group Chairman, Harvest Fund Management Co., Ltd," Harvest Advisors Group. https://harvestadvisors .sg/leadership/?lang=zh-hans

270 "Interview of Robert Hunter Biden," Committee On Oversight And Accountability Joint With The Committee On The Judiciary, U.S. House Of Representatives, February 28, 2024. https://oversight.house .gov/wp-content/uploads/2024/02/Hunter-Biden-Transcript _Redacted.pdf

271 Josh Boswell, "Hunter Biden is seen smirking in a photo taken at Joe's Delaware home the SAME day he sent Chinese business partner damning text saying, 'I am sitting here waiting for the call with my father'," *Daily Mail*, June 23, 2023. https://www.dailymail.co.uk/news /article-12227585/Hunter-Biden-seen-photo-taken-outside-Joes -Delaware-home-day-sent-damning-text.html. See also: Talia Lakritz, "The Bidens own a vacation home in Rehoboth Beach, Delaware. Take a look inside the 1,108-person town," *Business Insider*, July 31, 2023. https://www.businessinsider.com/biden-vacation-home-rehoboth -beach-delaware-2023-7?op=1#president-joe-biden-and-first-lady-jill -biden-purchased-a-vacation-home-in-rehoboth-beach-delaware -in-2017-1

272 James Lynch, "Biden Business Associate Admits He Wasn't Really Sure What Hunter Actually Brought To The Table, Comer Says," *Daily Caller*, January 25, 2024. https://gop-waysandmeans.house.gov /wp-content/uploads/2023/09/T9-Exhibit-1i-HWM-Apple-iCloud -Email-regarding-HW3-Income-08.02.2017_Redacted.pdf Note that the typos and any missing words are all Hunter's.

273 "Hunter Biden, Burisma, and Corruption: The Impact on U.S. Government Policy and Related Concerns," U.S. Senate Committee on Homeland Security and Governmental Affairs and U.S. Senate Committee on Finance Majority Staff Report, September 18, 2020. https://www.hsgac.senate.gov/wp-content/uploads/imo/media/doc /HSGAC_Finance_Report_FINAL.pdf. Just like the Rosemont Seneca LLCs in Ukraine, there were several variations on the Hudson West corporate name. In fact, there are no fewer than 11 Hudson West entities that were registered with the state of Delaware's Division of

Corporations between February, 2015 and January, 2018. See: State of Delaware, Department of State, Division of Corporations. https://icis .corp.delaware.gov/eCorp/EntitySearch/NameSearch.aspx. All have the same registered agent and address with a one exception. That is Hudson West LLC, registered to a Jai Qi Bao on April 9, 2018. See: State of Delaware, Department of State, Division of Corporations. https://icis.corp.delaware.gov/eCorp/EntitySearch/NameSearch.aspx. Bao was a "flirty" assistant to Hunter Biden who told him, as the CEFC deal was winding down, to "Keep as much money as you can." See: Josh Boswell, "EXCLUSIVE: 'Your doggy chain necklace is waiting for you.' Flirty messages from Hunter Biden's Chinese-American secretary, 29, who worked for him when he partnered with the 'spy chief of China' are revealed," *Daily Mail,* May 10, 2021, https://www.dailymail .co.uk/news/article-9522591/Hunter-Bidens-close-relationship -Chinese-American-secretary-revealed.html. She was also alleged to have been previously employed by a CCP-affiliated company prior to her job with Hunter. See: Steven Nelson, "Hunter Biden's 'flirty' Chinese secretary who urged 'Uncle Joe' to run is new GOP focus," *New York Post,* October 26, 2022. https://nypost.com/2022/10/26 /hunter-bidens-chinese-secretary-who-urged-joe-to-run-is-new-gop -focus/. As for all those Hudson West LLCs, the reason for the many overlapping corporate names is unclear, but one has to wonder if the actual purpose was money laundering, as these government reports did. See: Committee on Oversight and Accountability Majority Staff, "Second Bank Records Memorandum from the Oversight Committee's Investigation into the Biden Family's Influence Peddling and Business Schemes," Committee on Oversight and Accountability, May 10, 2023. https://oversight.house.gov/wp-content/uploads/2023/07/Bank -Memorandum-5.10.23.pdf.-SECOND.pdf and "Report Of The Impeachment Inquiry Of Joseph R. Biden Jr., President Of The United States Of America," Committee on Oversight and Accountability Committee on the Judiciary Committee on Ways and Means, August 19, 2024. https://oversight.house.gov/wp-content/uploads /2024/08/2024.08.19-Report-of-the-Impeachment-Inquiry-of-Joseph -R.-Biden-Jr.-President-of-the-United-States.pdf.

274 James Lynch, "Biden Business Associate Admits He Wasn't Really Sure What Hunter Actually Brought To The Table, Comer Says," *Daily Caller,* January 25, 2024. https://dailycaller.com/2024/01/25/biden -business-associate-admit-hunter-brought-table-comer/

275 "Hunter Biden, Burisma, and Corruption: The Impact on U.S. Government Policy and Related Concerns," U.S. Senate Committee on Homeland Security and Governmental Affairs and U.S. Senate

Committee on Finance Majority Staff Report, September 18, 2020. https://www.hsgac.senate.gov/wp-content/uploads/imo/media/doc /HSGAC_Finance_Report_FINAL.pdf

276 "Interview of Anthony Bobulinski," Committee On Oversight And Accountability Joint With The Committee On The Judiciary, U.S. House Of Representatives, February 13, 2024. https://oversight.house .gov/wp-content/uploads/2024/02/Bobulinski-Transcript.pdf

277 Ibid.

278 See: Sinohawk: "Limited Liability Company Agreement Of Sinohawk Holdings LLC." https://www.yaacovapelbaum.com/wp-content/uploads /2020/12/sinohawk-jv-operating-agreement-2.pdf and Hudson West III: Exhibit 2-A: Amended And Restated Limited Liability Company Agreement Of Hudson West III LLC. https://gop-waysandmeans.house .gov/wp-content/uploads/2023/09/T12-Exhibit-2A-First-HW3 -Agreement-Executed-Provided-by-Cathay-Bank.pdf

279 This was Bobulinski's interpretation. Legally, whether or not it was actually fraud depends on the corporation formulator's intent. "Interview of Anthony Bobulinski," Committee On Oversight And Accountability Joint With The Committee On The Judiciary, U.S. House Of Representatives, February 13, 2024. https://oversight.house .gov/wp-content/uploads/2024/02/Bobulinski-Transcript.pdf

280 "Influence Peddling: Examining Joe Biden's Abuse of Public Office," GOP Oversight Committee, YouTube, March 20, 2024. https://www .youtube.com/watch?v=lMUe53nbk6w&t=9s

281 Donalds meant to say September 3, 2017, as the video clearly shows.

282 "Hunter Biden, Burisma, and Corruption: The Impact on U.S. Government Policy and Related Concerns," U.S. Senate Committee on Homeland Security and Governmental Affairs and U.S. Senate Committee on Finance Majority Staff Report, September 18, 2020. https://www.hsgac.senate.gov/wp-content/uploads/imo/media/doc /HSGAC_Finance_Report_FINAL.pdf

283 Daniel Bates, "Revealed: Hunter Biden raked in $6M in just nine months from Chinese business dealings—and that doesn't include the 2.8 carat-diamond he got as a gift," *Daily Mail,* December 10, 2020. https://www.dailymail.co.uk/news/article-9040381/Hunter-Biden -raked-6m-nine-months-Chinese-business-dealings.html. By the way, Hunter's laptop shows that he lied under penalty of perjury on his application for that line of credit. He says that the company was not subject to backup withholding. "In fact, Owasco P.C. owed thousands of dollars due to undeclared income from Burisma." "Report on the Biden Laptop," MarcoPolo501c3.org, page 123. https://bidenreport.com /#p=127

284 "Hunter Biden, Burisma, and Corruption: The Impact on U.S. Government Policy and Related Concerns," U.S. Senate Committee on Homeland Security and Governmental Affairs and U.S. Senate Committee on Finance Majority Staff Report, September 18, 2020. https://www.hsgac.senate.gov/wp-content/uploads/imo/media/doc/HSGAC_Finance_Report_FINAL.pdf

285 "Report on the Biden Laptop," MarcoPolo501c3.org, page 124. https://bidenreport.com/#p=129. See also: "Swedish emails reveal new facts on Joe Biden's keys to Hunter's office," *Dagens Nyheter*, February 24, 2021. https://www.dn.se/sverige/swedish-emails-reveal-new-facts-on-joe-biden-s-keys-to-hunter-s-office/. The short-lived Biden Foundation closed in April, 2019 when Joe announced his presidential run. "Biden Foundation," Wikipedia. https://en.wikipedia.org/wiki/Biden_Foundation

286 "Patrick Ho," Wikipedia. https://en.wikipedia.org/wiki/Patrick_Ho

287 Jack Davis, "Hunter Biden Talks About Working Closely with the 'Spy Chief of China' in Newly Unearthed Recording: Report," *The Western Journal*, May 27, 2022. https://www.westernjournal.com/hunter-biden-talks-working-closely-spy-chief-china-newly-unearthed-recording-report/ In 2002, Ho was appointed Secretary for Home Affairs, a senior post in the Preparatory Committee for the Hong Kong Special Administrative Region (SAR.) An SAR is what the People's Republic of China calls certain regions that maintain separate legal, administrative and judicial systems from the rest of the country. Hong Kong is an SAR. So is Macau, for example.

288 Jenni Marsh, "Disgraced former Hong Kong politician jailed for 3 years for bribing African leaders at the UN," CNN, March 25, 2019. https://www.cnn.com/2019/03/25/asia/patrick-ho-sentencing-intl/index.html

289 Alexandra Stevenson et al, "A Chinese Tycoon Sought Power and Influence. Washington Responded," *New York Times*, December 12, 2018. https://www.nytimes.com/2018/12/12/business/cefc-biden-china-washington-ye-jianming.html

290 Erica Davies, "SPY GAMES: Hunter Biden associate Patrick Ho was SPY suspect as clip 'shows Hunter discuss 'f***ing spy chief of China'," *The Sun*, October 28, 2020. https://www.the-sun.com/news/1699111/hunter-biden-associate-patrick-ho-spy-china/

291 Matthew Goldstein, "Ex-Hong Kong Official Convicted in Bribe Case Involving Chinese Oil Company," *New York Times*, December 5, 2018. https://www.nytimes.com/2018/12/05/business/cefc-china-patrick-ho.html

292 Xie Yu, "Exclusive | Guosheng puts CEFC under state ward as crackdown intensifies on freewheeling private businesses," *South China Morning Post,* March 2, 2018. https://www.scmp.com/business /companies/article/2135420/guosheng-puts-cefc-under-state-ward -crackdown-intensifies

293 Eric Ng and Xie Yu, "Update | China detains CEFC's founder Ye Jianming, wiping out US$153 million in value off stocks," *South China Morning Post*, March 1, 2018. https://www.scmp.com/business /companies/article/2135238/china-detain-cefc-founder-ye-jianming -stocks. Rather than corruption, it's possible that the CCP was not happy with the $4.9 billion Ye and the CEFC spent in 3 years, most of which was financed by the state-owned China Development Bank, according to the *South China Morning Post*. See: Xie Yu, "Exclusive | Guosheng puts CEFC under state ward as crackdown intensifies on freewheeling private businesses," *South China Morning Post,* March 2, 2018. https:// www.scmp.com/business/companies/article/2135420/guosheng-puts-cefc-under-state-ward-crackdown-intensifies. It's also possible that Xi Jinping himself was not thrilled with Ye's international profile, which included being named "an economic policy advisor for Czech President Milos Zeman and 'special honorary advisor' to the U.N. General Assembly." See: Ji Tainqin and Han Wei, "In Depth: Investigation Casts Shadow on Rosneft's China Investor CEFC," *Caixin Global,* March 1, 2018. https://www.caixinglobal.com/2018-03-01/investigation-casts -shadow-on-rising-oil-star-101215272.html

294 "Chinese business tycoons, executives who disappeared from public view," Reuters, February 21, 2023. https://www.reuters.com/world/china/chinese -business-tycoons-executives-who-disappeared-public-view-2023-02-21/

295 "Interview of Mervyn Yan," Committee On Oversight And Accountability Joint With The Committee On The Judiciary, U.S. House Of Representatives, January 25, 2024. https://oversight.house .gov/wp-content/uploads/2024/02/Mervyn-Yan-Transcript.pdf

296 Alexandra Stevenson et al, "A Chinese Tycoon Sought Power and Influence. Washington Responded," *New York Times*, December 12, 2018. https://www.nytimes.com/2018/12/12/business/cefc-biden-china -washington-ye-jianming.html

297 Josh Boswell, "EXCLUSIVE: 'I think you're clear': VOICEMAIL from Joe Biden to Hunter about *NY Times* report on his Chinese business dealings proves he DID speak to his son about his relationship with criminal dubbed the 'spy chief of China'," *Daily Mail*, June 27, 2022. https://www.dailymail.co.uk/news/article-10938637/Voicemail -Joe-Biden-Hunter-proves-president-DID-speak-Chinese-business -dealings.html

298 "Interview of Anthony Bobulinski," Committee On Oversight And Accountability Joint With The Committee On The Judiciary, U.S. House Of Representatives, February 13, 2024. https://oversight.house .gov/wp-content/uploads/2024/02/Bobulinski-Transcript.pdf

299 Nectar Gan and James Griffiths, "The great power race between the US and China is on. And Beijing is confident of winning," CNN, April 30, 2021. https://www.cnn.com/2021/04/30/china/biden-xi-china -us-mic-intl-hnk/index.html

300 Nadège Rolland, "China's Vision For A New World Order," National Bureau of Asian Research, January, 2020. https://www.nbr.org/wp -content/uploads/pdfs/publications/sr83_chinasvision_jan2020.pdf

301 "Hunter Biden, Burisma, and Corruption: The Impact on U.S. Government Policy and Related Concerns," U.S. Senate Committee on Homeland Security and Governmental Affairs and U.S. Senate Committee on Finance Majority Staff Report, September 18, 2020. https://www.hsgac.senate.gov/wp-content/uploads/imo/media/doc /HSGAC_Finance_Report_FINAL.pdf

302 CNOOC was later blacklisted by the Trump administration for drilling in disputed areas of the South China Sea where the CCP had created islands upon which it built military bases. Just about the time Hunter and Archer were working on their deal, CNOOC also touched off an international incident when they moved one of their oil rigs into waters claimed by South Vietnam. See: Matthew Pennington, "US Slaps Sanctions on China Oil Giant Over South China Sea Activity," Radio Free Asia, January 14, 2021. https://www.rfa.org/english/news/china/ usa-southchinasea-01142021173722.html and "Hai Yang Shi You 981 standoff," Wikipedia. https://en.wikipedia.org/wiki/Hai_Yang _Shi_You_981_standoff

303 "Energy in Kazakhstan," Wikipedia. https://en.wikipedia.org/wiki /Energy_in_Kazakhstan

304 "Kazakhstan energy profile," IEA 50, April, 2020. https://www.iea.org /reports/kazakhstan-energy-profile

305 "Government of Kazakhstan", Wikipedia. https://en.wikipedia.org /wiki/Government_of_Kazakhstan Described as a "dictator," the Communist Party member Nazarbayev started his rule while Kazakhstan was still part of the Soviet Union, becoming the country's first president after it achieved independence in 1991. He was dubbed "Elbasy" or "Leader of the Nation," from 2010-2022. See: "Nursultan Nazarbayev," Wikipedia. https://en.wikipedia.org/wiki /Nursultan_Nazarbayev

306 He also spent time at Columbia University in New York. See: "Karim Massimov," Wikipedia. https://en.wikipedia.org/wiki/Karim _Massimov

307 Qianying Zhou, "WHU Alumni Karim Masimov Re-appointed Prime Minister of Kazakhstan," Wuhan University, April 4, 2016. https:// en.whu.edu.cn/info/1050/2270.htm

308 "Report on the Biden Laptop," MarcoPolo501c3.org, page 174. https://bidenreport.com/#p=179

309 "Imangali Tasmagambetov," Wikipedia. https://en.wikipedia.org/wiki /Imangali_Tasmagambetov

310 "Kenges Rakishev, Kazakh Investor and Entrepreneur. President of the Fincraft Group," LinkedIn, https://www.linkedin.com/in/kengesrakis hev/?originalSubdomain=kz

311 The foundation recently pledged to contribute 1.2 billion Kazakhstani tenge (or about $2.5 million) to help flood victims in Western Kazakhstan. See: "Kenges Rakishev and Aselle Tasmagambetova Pledge 1.2 billion tenge for Kazakhstan Flood Relief," Global Newswire, April 22, 2024. https://www.globenewswire.com/en/news -release/2024/04/22/2866681/0/en/Kenges-Rakishev-and-Aselle -Tasmagambetova-Pledge-1-2-billion-tenge-for-Kazakhstan-Flood -Relief.html

312 "Aselle Imangalievna Tasmagambetova," Saby Charitable Foundation. https://saby.kz/en/info-pages/founders

313 Kenges Rakishev (@kengesr), X. https://x.com/kengesr?lang=en

314 Serikbek Serikev, "Kenes Rakishev: The President's Man for All Seasons," *Astana Herald*, March 13, 2023. https://astanaherald.com /2023/03/13/kenes-rakishev-the-presidents-man-for-all-seasons/

315 "Kenes Rakishev: The new Kazakhstan, entrepreneur, businessman, philanthropist," *Helsinki Herald*, February 12, 2023. https://helsinkiherald .com/2023/02/kenes-rakishev-the-new-kazakhstan-entrepreneur -businessman-philanthropist/

316 "Kenes Rakishev," *Forbes* Kazakhstan, May, 2024. https://forbes.kz /ranking/object/56

317 "Kazakhstan: Anti-corruption Sanctions," UK Parliament, February 3, 2022. https://hansard.parliament.uk/commons/2022-02-03/debates/41000B02 -86AB-499E-8547-0F5AA84611B0/KazakhstanAnti-Corruption Sanctions

318 Josh Boswell, "EXCLUSIVE: Hunter Biden's Kazakh business partner Kenes Rakishev helped supply armored vehicles to Putin-backed forces that invaded Ukraine alongside Russia, report claims," *Daily Mail*, August 12, 2023. https://www.dailymail.co.uk/news /article-12394729/Hunter-Bidens-Kazakh-business-partner-Kenes

-Rakishev-helped-supply-armored-vehicles-Putin-backed-forces
-invaded-Ukraine-alongside-Russia-report-claims.html

319 Committee on Oversight and Accountability Majority Staff, "Third
Bank Records Memorandum from the Oversight Committee's
Investigation into the Biden Family's Influence Peddling and Business
Schemes," Committee on Oversight and Accountability, August 9, 2023.
https://oversight.house.gov/wp-content/uploads/2023/08/Third-Bank
-Records-Memorandum_Redacted.pdf

320 That "Latvian bank," by the way, is ABLV Bank, according to
Rosemont Seneca's Morgan Stanley statement archived on Hunter's
laptop. See: "Report on the Biden Laptop," MarcoPolo501c3.org, page
169. https://bidenreport.com/#p=173. Once the third largest lender
in Latvia, ABLV shut down in 2018 after receiving a notice from the
US Financial Crimes Enforcement Network (FinCEN) which said it
"has reasonable grounds to believe that ABLV executives, shareholders,
and employees have institutionalized money laundering as a pillar of
the bank's business practices" and that all but a small percentage of its
customers were "primarily high-risk shell companies registered in secrecy
jurisdictions." FinCEN also accused ABLV of doing business with
North Korea even after the bank said it wouldn't. See: Frances Coppola,
"Why The U.S. Treasury Killed A Latvian Bank," *Forbes*, February
28, 2018. https://www.forbes.com/sites/francescoppola/2018/02/28
/why-the-u-s-treasury-killed-a-latvian-bank/?sh=4dc9d7a67adc

321 "Hunter Biden, Burisma, and Corruption: The Impact on U.S.
Government Policy and Related Concerns," U.S. Senate Committee
on Homeland Security and Governmental Affairs and U.S. Senate
Committee on Finance Majority Staff Report, September 18, 2020.
https://www.hsgac.senate.gov/wp-content/uploads/imo/media/doc
/HSGAC_Finance_Report_FINAL.pdf

322 "Report on the Biden Laptop," MarcoPolo501c3.org, page 170.
https://bidenreport.com/#p=175

323 The email was part of that same trove of documents released by the
House Ways and Means Committee in conjunction with evidence
provided by IRS whistleblowers Gary Shapley and Joseph Ziegler
in May, 2024, showing that Hunter Biden did not tell the truth
when he testified before Congress in February, 2024. https://gop-
waysandmeans.house.gov/wp-content/uploads/2024/05/15-Exhibit
-904-RHB-email-re-Porsche-complicated-business-deal-07.16.2014.
pdf. See also: "Ways and Means Committee Releases Evidence
Showing Hunter Biden Lied Under Oath During Recent
Congressional Testimony," US House Committee on Ways and
Means, May 22, 2024. https://waysandmeans.house.gov/2024/05/22

/ways-and-means-committee-releases-evidence-showing-hunter-biden
-lied-under-oath-during-recent-congressional-testimony/

324 Ibid.

325 Café Milano website. https://www.cafemilano.com

326 "Report on the Biden Laptop," MarcoPolo501c3.org, page 174.
https://bidenreport.com/#p=179. See also: This is one of those media
sites: Elizabeth Stauffer, "The Photo That Could Come Back to Haunt
Joe Biden After Hunter's 'Close Friend' Arrested for Treason," *Western
Journal,* January 11, 2022.

327 "Joint Statement of the Third U.S.-Kazakhstan Strategic Partnership
Dialogue," U.S. Department of State, December 10, 2014.
https://2009-2017.state.gov/r/pa/prs/ps/2014/12/234936.htm

328 That's the Burnham Financial Group, the company set up in 2012 by
Archer, Hunter and Jason Galanis. More on that later in this chapter.

329 "Report on the Biden Laptop," MarcoPolo501c3.org, page 167.
https://bidenreport.com/#p=171

330 Not only was his Yale roommate Chris Heinz, Kerry's stepson, Archer
also co-chaired the national finance committee for Kerry's unsuccessful
2004 presidential campaign. "Devon Archer," Wikipedia. https://
en.wikipedia.org/wiki/Devon_Archer

331 "18 U.S. Code § 951 – Agents of foreign governments," Legal
Information Institute, Cornell Law School. https://www.law.cornell
.edu/uscode/text/18/951

332 "Ukraine's gas company Burisma enters Kazakhstan," *Times of Central
Asia,* December 22, 2014.
https://archive.ph/ZkHvT

333 Catherine Putz, "Karim Massimov, Former Kazakh Intelligence Chief,
Sentenced to 18 Years on Treason, Coup Charges," *The Diplomat,* April
24, 2023. https://thediplomat.com/2023/04/karim-massimov-former
-kazakh-intelligence-chief-sentenced-to-18-years-on-treason-coup
-charges/

334 She lost that spot in 2020 to Wildberries founder Tatiana Bakalchuk,
whose fortune of $1.4 billion topped Baturina's mere $1.2 billion,
according to *Forbes* Russia. See: Elena Ganzhur, "The owner of
Wildberries became the richest Russian according to Forbes," *Forbes,*
Russia, February 19, 2020. https://www.forbes.ru/milliardery/393387
-vladelica-wildberries-stala-bogateyshey-rossiyankoy-po-versii-forbes

335 At one point Inteco was "said to control 20 percent of construction"
in Moscow, reportedly thanks to Elena's marriage to Luzhkov. But she
and Victor fell out in 2005, leading to his dismissal; he sued her for
£120 million but insisted he wasn't upset with her. "We celebrate the
holidays and talk on the telephone to each other." See: Tony Halpin,

"Tycoon sues billionaire little sister for £120m," *The Times*, January 22, 2007. https://web.archive.org/web/20110612040519/http://business. timesonline.co.uk/tol/business/markets/europe/article1295112.ece

336 "Interview of Devon Archer," Committee On Oversight And Accountability, U.S. House Of Representatives, July 31, 2023. https:// oversight.house.gov/wp-content/uploads/2023/08/Devon-Archer -Transcript.pdf

337 "Hunter Biden, Burisma, and Corruption: The Impact on U.S. Government Policy and Related Concerns," U.S. Senate Committee on Homeland Security and Governmental Affairs and U.S. Senate Committee on Finance Majority Staff Report, September 18, 2020. https://www.hsgac.senate.gov/wp-content/uploads/imo/media/doc/ HSGAC_Finance_Report_FINAL.pdf. Wikileaks expanded a bit on those corruption allegations. When Luzhkov was fired, the organization leaked a cable written by the US ambassador to Moscow, John Beyrle, claiming that the dismissed Mayor "sat on top of a 'pyramid of corruption'." See: Luke Harding, "WikiLeaks cables: Moscow mayor presided over 'pyramid of corruption'," *The Guardian*, December 1, 2010. https://www.theguardian.com/world/2010/dec/01/wikileaks-cables -moscow-mayor-corruption. Baturina was also highlighted, as her sister, Natalya Yevtushenko, is married to Vladimir Yevtushenko, the head of a company called Sistema, which initially privatized Moscow's real estate and gas. "Sistema's president, Yevgeny Novitsky, controlled the Solntsevo criminal gang...widely regarded by Russian law enforcement as one of the most powerful organized crime groups in Russia." See: "The Luzhov Dilemna," WikiLeaks, February 12, 2010. https:// wikileaks.org/plusd/cables/10MOSCOW317_a.html

338 "Interview of Devon Archer," Committee On Oversight And Accountability, U.S. House Of Representatives, July 31, 2023. https:// oversight.house.gov/wp-content/uploads/2023/08/Devon-Archer -Transcript.pdf

339 Josh Boswell, "EXCLUSIVE: Leaked emails reveal Hunter Biden's real estate company received a $40MILLION investment from Russian oligarch Yelena Baturina, the billionaire widow of corrupt Moscow mayor, who also paid president's son $3.5million consulting fee," *Daily Mail*, October 17, 2022. https://www .dailymail.co.uk/news/article-11250873/Hunter-Bidens-company -received-40MILLION-investment-Russian-oligarch-Yelena-Baturina .html

340 Ibid.

341 Emails between Devon Archer and Hunter Biden. https://justthenews. com/sites/default/files/2023-08/Fwd%20Chelsea%20Deal%20 updated%20version-Redacted.pdf

342 Josh Boswell, "EXCLUSIVE: Leaked emails reveal Hunter Biden's real estate company received a $40MILLION investment from Russian oligarch Yelena Baturina, the billionaire widow of corrupt Moscow mayor, who also paid president's son $3.5million consulting fee," *Daily Mail*, October 17, 2022. https://www.dailymail.co.uk/news /article-11250873/Hunter-Bidens-company-received-40MILLION -investment-Russian-oligarch-Yelena-Baturina.html

343 Note that Archer was also charged. He was convicted, appealed, had his appeal denied and still has not been sentenced. Hunter was never even charged. "Seven Defendants Charged In Manhattan Federal Court With Defrauding A Native American Tribe And Investors Of Over $60 Million," United States Attorney's Office, Southern District of New York, May 11, 2016. https://www.justice.gov/usao-sdny/pr /seven-defendants-charged-manhattan-federal-court-defrauding -native-american-tribe-and. See also: Zach Schonfeld, "Supreme Court lets stand ex-Hunter Biden associate Devon Archer's criminal conviction," *The Hill*, January 22, 2024. https://thehill.com/regulation /court-battles/4421414-supreme-court-hunter-biden-devon-archer -criminal-conviction/; and Victor Nava, "Ex-Hunter Biden business partner Devon Archer to be resentenced, fed judge rules," *New York Post*, May 15, 2024. https://nypost.com/2024/05/15/us-news/ex -hunter-biden-biz-partner-devon-archer-to-be-resentenced-judge/

344 "Interview of Jason Galanis," Committee On Oversight And Accountability Joint With The Committee On The Judiciary, U.S. House Of Representatives, February 23, 2024. https://oversight.house. gov/wp-content/uploads/2024/03/Jason-Galanis-Transcript.pdf

345 Steven Richards and John Solomon, "Dollars to Dining: Bank records show proximity of Joe Biden meetings to son's foreign payments," *Just The News*, August 9, 2023. https://justthenews. com/accountability/political-ethics/dollars-dining-bank-records -expose-proximity-joe-biden-meetings

346 Excerpt from Joe Biden's speech May 21, 2014 at Cotroceni Palace in Bucharest, Romania: "Corruption is a cancer, a cancer that eats away at a citizen's faith in democracy, diminishes the instinct for innovation and creativity; already-tight national budgets, crowding out important national investments. It wastes the talent of entire generations. It scares away investments and jobs. And most importantly it denies the people their dignity. It saps the collective strength and resolve of a nation. Corruption is just another form of tyranny." See: "Remarks

by Vice President Joe Biden to Romanian Civil Society Groups and Students," White House Archives, May 21, 2014.

347 RomaniaCorruptionWatch, "Gabriel 'Puiu' Popoviciu—The businessman with a finger in every pizza pie," *Medium*, August 3, 2017. https://medium.com/romania-corruption-watch/gabriel-puiu-popoviciu -the-businessman-with-a-finger-in-every-pizza-pie-d898673d34a9

348 This is also where the US Embassy to Romania is located. "In 2012, the United States dedicated the new embassy compound with an address from Beau Biden." Jill Biden went there in 2022 to meet with Ukrainian refugees. See: "Embassy of the United States, Bucharest," Wikipedia. https://en.wikipedia.org/wiki/Embassy_of_the _United_States,_Bucharest

349 Laura Strickler and Rich Schapiro, "Hunter Biden's legal work in Romania raises new questions about his overseas dealings," NBC News, October 24, 2019. https://www.nbcnews.com/politics/politics -news/hunter-biden-s-legal-work-romania-raises-new-questions -about-n1071031 One account put the loss to the state at £600 million. See: RomaniaCorruptionWatch, "Gabriel 'Puiu' Popoviciu — The businessman with a finger in every pizza pie," *Medium*, August 3, 2017. https://medium.com/romania-corruption-watch/gabriel-puiu -popoviciu-the-businessman-with-a-finger-in-every-pizza-pie-d898 673d34a9

350 Laura Strickler and Rich Schapiro, "Hunter Biden's legal work in Romania raises new questions about his overseas dealings," NBC News, October 24, 2019. https://www.nbcnews.com/politics/politics -news/hunter-biden-s-legal-work-romania-raises-new-questions -about-n1071031

351 Irina Marica, "Update: Wanted Romanian investor, detained in London," *Romania-Insider*, August 14, 2017. https://www.romania -insider.com/gabriel-popoviciu-detained

352 Jon Levine, "Hunter Biden met with dad immediately after Romanian business meetings," *New York Post*, August 15, 2022. https://nypost .com/2022/08/13/hunter-biden-met-with-dad-immediately-after -romanian-business-meetings/

353 Iulian Ernst, "Romanian businessman Popoviciu wins in court a 224-ha plot of land in northern Bucharest," *Romania-Insider*, April 12, 2024. https://www.romania-insider.com/popoviciu-wins -northern-bucharest-land-court-2024

354 "WATCH: The Biden Impeachment Hearings – Day 1," PBS News, September 28, 2023. https://www.pbs.org/newshour/politics/watch -live-the-biden-impeachment-hearings-day-1

355 James Lynch, "Romanian Oligarch Who Allegedly Paid Hunter Biden For 'Client' Services Wins Extradition Case In British Court," *Daily Caller,* August 28, 2023. https://dailycaller.com/2023/08/28 /romanian-oligarch-paid-hunter-biden-client-services-wins-extradition -case-british-court-gabriel-popoviciu/

356 "WATCH: The Biden Impeachment Hearings – Day 1," PBS News, September 28, 2023. https://www.pbs.org/newshour/politics /watch-live-the-biden-impeachment-hearings-day-1

357 Jon Levine, "Hunter Biden met with dad immediately after Romanian business meetings," *New York Post,* August 15, 2022. https://nypost .com/2022/08/13/hunter-biden-met-with-dad-immediately-after -romanian-business-meetings/

358 Jessica Chasmar, Cameron Cawthorne, "Hunter Biden traveled to at least 15 countries with VP dad: 'I can catch a ride with him'," Fox News, August 23, 2023. https://www.foxnews.com/politics/hunter-biden-traveled-least -13-countries-vp-dad-i-can-catch-ride-him

359 "Miguel Alemán Magnani," Wikipedia. https://en.wikipedia.org/wiki/ Miguel_Alemán_Magnani

360 Miranda Devine, "Laptop shows Joe Biden attended meetings between Hunter and his Mexican business partners," *New York Post,* June 30, 2021. https://nypost.com/2021/06/30/laptop-shows-joe-biden-was-with -hunter-and-his-mexican-biz-meetings/

361 Jesse Emspak, "How Carlos Slim Built His Fortune," *Investopedia,* September 25, 2023. https://www.investopedia.com/articles/investing/103114 /how-carlos-slim-built-his-fortune.asp

362 "The World's Real-Time Billionaires," *Forbes.* https://www.forbes. com/real-time-billionaires/#49d0cb0a3d78 Slim was also the *New York Times'* biggest shareholder at one time. See: "Mexican billionaire becomes largest NY Times shareholder," Associated Press, January 14, 2015. https://apnews.com/article/fe35e07b35f24d3eb752b47213da9f60

363 Chuck Neubauer and Tom Hamburger "Biden family ties pose questions," *LA Times,* August 28, 2008. https://www.latimes.com/archives/la -xpm-2008-aug-28-na-biden28-story.html

364 Miranda Divine, *Laptop From Hell,* (Liberatio Protocol, New York/ Nashville, 2021), Page 82.

365 Frank James, "Obamas Host State Dinner For Mexican President," NPR, May 19, 2010. https://www.npr.org/sections/thetwo-way/2010/05 /white_house_hosts_state_dinner.html

366 Josh Boswell, "EXCLUSIVE: Joe Biden entertained Hunter's Mexican billionaire business associates in the vice president's office in 2014 and even flew with his son to Mexico City on Air Force 2 so Hunter could attend meetings over a 'flippin gigantic' deal," *Daily Mail,* June 30,

2021. https://www.dailymail.co.uk/news/article-9678005/Joe-Biden
-entertained-Hunters-billionaire-business-associates-vice-presidents
-office.html

367 James Burgess, "Carlos Slim Positions Himself to Benefit from the End
to Pemex's Monopoly," Oilprice.com, July 13, 2013. http://oilprice
.com/Latest-Energy-News/World-News/Carlos-Slim-Positions
-Himself-to-Benefit-from-the-End-to-Pemexs-Monopoly.html

368 Josh Boswell, "EXCLUSIVE: Joe Biden entertained Hunter's Mexican
billionaire business associates in the vice president's office in 2014 and even
flew with his son to Mexico City on Air Force 2 so Hunter could attend
meetings over a 'flippin gigantic' deal," *Daily Mail,* June 30, 2021. https://
www.dailymail.co.uk/news/article-9678005/Joe-Biden-entertained
-Hunters-billionaire-business-associates-vice-presidents-office.html

369 Ibid.

370 Sarah Bedford, "Hunter Biden investigation: Joe Biden met with Mexican
business partners amid son's pursuit of deals," *Washington Examiner,*
September 26, 2023. https://www.washingtonexaminer.com/news
/2582372/hunter-biden-investigation-joe-biden-met-with-mexican
-business-partners-amid-sons-pursuit-of-deals/

371 "Report on the Biden Laptop," MarcoPolo501c3.org, page 188.
https://bidenreport.com/#p=193 Typos are all James's.

372 "ePlata Announces Distinguished Global Board of Directors,"
Business Wire, August 26, 2019. https://www.businesswire.com/news
/home/20190826005007/en/ePlata-Announces-Distinguished-Global
-Board-Directors

373 "Arrest warrant issued against Mexican businessman Miguel Alemán
Magnani," *Yucatan Times,* July 9, 2021. https://www.theyucatantimes
.com/2021/07/arrest-warrant-issued-against-mexican-businessman-miguel
-aleman-magnani/. Alemán Magnani was being pursued by
his native country for tax fraud. As this article noted, "Alemán
Magnani has no intention to travel to Mexico for the time being."
See: Andrea Navarro, "Tycoon Takes Refuge in France as Mexico
Seeks Arrest in Tax Case," *Bloomberg,* July 13, 2021. https://www
.bloomberg.com/news/articles/2021-07-13/interjet-founder-is-fighting
-mexico-arrest-warrant-from-france

374 "Interjet," Wikipedia. https://en.wikipedia.org/wiki/Interjet

375 "Report on the Biden Laptop," MarcoPolo501c3.org, page 191.
https://bidenreport.com/#p=195

376 Ben Schreckinger, "Biden Inc.," *Politico,* August 2, 2019. https://www
.politico.com/magazine/story/2019/08/02/joe-biden-investigation
-hunter-brother-hedge-fund-money-2020-campaign-227407/

377 "James B. Biden Joins Hill International Subsidiary as Executive Vice President," Global Newswire, November 23, 2010. https://www.globenewswire.com/news-release/2010/11/23/434923/207583/en/James-B-Biden-Joins-Hill-International-Subsidiary-as-Executive-Vice-President.html#

378 "Hill International," Wikipedia. https://en.wikipedia.org/wiki/Hill_International

379 "Hill International Names Four Executives to Lead New Subsidiary HillStone International," CNN Money, September 24, 2010. https://money.cnn.com/news/newsfeeds/articles/globenewswire/202295.htm

380 "Great Recession," Wikipedia. https://en.wikipedia.org/wiki/Great_Recession

381 Kevin, a Delaware guy, was the son of Kermit Justice, the state's one-time powerful Secretary of Transportation. But Kermit was convicted of bribery and saw prison time. See: "Former Transportation Secretary Kermit Justice dies at 75," *Newark Post*, August 15, 2010. https://www.newarkpostonline.com/news/local/former-transportation-secretary-kermit-justice-dies-at-75/article_b33a3b50-10c5-5eb1-b5a8-be796bfad601.html. And just to underscore how insular the legal and political communities are in Delaware, Justice wanted to hire David Weiss as his defense attorney. Yes, that's the very same special counsel David Weiss that prosecuted and eventually secured a conviction for Hunter Biden for three felony gun charges, then saw him plead guilty to nine federal tax charges. See: Andrew Goudsward, "Who is David Weiss, US prosecutor in Hunter Biden case?," Reuters, August 13, 2023. https://www.reuters.com/legal/who-is-david-weiss-us-prosecutor-hunter-biden-case-2023-06-20/

382 Peter Schweizer, "How five members of Joe Biden's family got rich through his connections," *New York Post*, January 20, 2020. https://nypost.com/2020/01/18/how-five-members-of-joe-bidens-family-got-rich-through-his-connections/

383 Charlie Gasparino, "The Ties that Biden," *Fox Business*, October 22, 2012. https://www.foxbusiness.com/politics/the-ties-that-biden

384 Peter Schweizer, "How five members of Joe Biden's family got rich through his connections," *New York Post*, January 20, 2020. https://nypost.com/2020/01/18/how-five-members-of-joe-bidens-family-got-rich-through-his-connections/

385 Charlie Gasparino, "The Ties that Biden," *Fox Business*, October 22, 2012. https://www.foxbusiness.com/politics/the-ties-that-biden

386 Ibid.

387 Ibid.

388 Annie Linskey and James T. Areddy, "How Joe Biden's Kin Profited Off the Family Name. 'The Big Guy Is Calling Me,'" *Wall Street Journal*, September 28. 2023. https://www.wsj.com/us-news/law/how -joe-bidens-kin-profited-off-the-family-name-the-big-guy-is-calling -me-547220ab

389 Beatrice Thomas, "US construction firm admits mistake over Iraq investment," *Arabian Business*, February 24, 2014. https://www .arabianbusiness.com/americas/us-construction-firm-admits-mistake -over-iraq-investment-540113

390 John Lee, "Biden's Brother to Bag Lucrative Iraq Deal?" *Iraq-Business News*, October 25, 2012. https://www.iraq-businessnews .com/2012/10/25/bidens-brother-to-bag-lucrative-iraq-deal/

391 Nikita Biryukov, "Richter says he has no ties to Biden brother, pushes back on Gibbs allegation," *New Jersey Globe*, March 10, 2020. https:// newjerseyglobe.com/congress/richter-says-he-has-no-ties-to-biden -brother-pushes-back-on-gibbs-allegation/

392 "David Richter (New Jersey)," https://ballotpedia.org/David_Richter _(New_Jersey)#:~:text=He%20lost%20in%20the%20 general,Candidate%20Connection%20survey%20in%202020.

393 John Boswell, "EXCLUSIVE: Jim Biden admitted he was hired to negotiate with Saudis over a secret $140million deal 'because of his position and relationship' to his VP brother Joe -who would be 'instrumental to the deal,' bombshell affidavit claims," *Daily Mail*, February 14, 2023. https://www.dailymail.co.uk/news/article-11731831 /Jim-Biden-negotiated-deal-Saudis-relationship-Joe.html

394 Ibid.

395 Caroline Downey, "Biden's Brother Was Paid to Settle Business Dispute with Saudis during VP Tenure," *National Review*, February 14, 2023. https://www.nationalreview.com/news/bidens-brother-was -paid-to-settle-business-dispute-with-saudis-during-vp-tenure/

396 Ibid.

397 John Boswell, "EXCLUSIVE: Jim Biden admitted he was hired to negotiate with Saudis over a secret $140million deal 'because of his position and relationship' to his VP brother Joe -who would be 'instrumental to the deal,' bombshell affidavit claims," *Daily Mail*, February 14, 2023. https:// www.dailymail.co.uk/news/article-11731831/Jim-Biden-negotiated -deal-Saudis-relationship-Joe.html

398 "Hill International wins $34m of Saudi contracts," *Construction Week*, October 10, 2012. https://www.constructionweekonline.com /projects-tenders/article-18960-hill-international-wins-34m-of-saudi -contracts

399 "Hill International chosen to manage two-thirds of Saudi Arabia's schools," *Global Construction Review,* January 13, 2021. https://www.globalconstructionreview.com/hill-international-chosen-manage-two-thirds-saudi/

400 "Hill International Awarded Contract To Provide Project Management Support For The Dahiyat Al-Fursan Development By The Kingdom Of Saudi Arabia's National Housing Company," Hill International, March 27, 2023. https://www.hillintl.com/press-release/hill-international-awarded-contract-to-provide-project-management-support-for-the-dahiyat-al-fursan-development-by-the-kingdom-of-saudi-arabias-national-housing-company/

401 "Biden and Latin American Leaders in Costa Rica." White House archives, https://obamawhitehouse.archives.gov/photos-and-video/photos/biden-and-latin-american-leaders-costa-rica. See also: "Biden, Central American leaders hold talks in Costa Rica," CNN, March 30, 2009. https://edition.cnn.com/2009/POLITICS/03/30/biden.costa.rica/index.html

402 "New Partnership Seeks to Reform Real Estate in Latin America," *The Costa Rica News,* September 2, 2009. https://thecostaricanews.com/new-partnership-seeks-to-reform-real-estate-in-latin-america/

403 Andrew Conte, "Biden name drives Costa Rican golf dream," *Pittsburgh Tribune,* April 6, 2014. https://archive.triblive.com/local/pittsburgh-allegheny/biden-name-drives-costa-rican-golf-dream/

404 Jaime Lopez, "Major Solar Energy Project Planned in Guanacaste," *The Costa Rica Star,* January 23, 2014. https://news.co.cr/major-solar-energy-project-planned-in-guanacaste/31894/

405 Andrew Conte, "Biden name drives Costa Rican golf dream," *Pittsburgh Tribune,* April 6, 2014. https://archive.triblive.com/local/pittsburgh-allegheny/biden-name-drives-costa-rican-golf-dream/

406 Haris Alic, "Joe Biden's Brother Frank Linked to Projects Receiving $54,000,000 in Taxpayer Loans from the Obama Administration—Despite No Experience," *Breitbart,* January 20, 2020. https://www.breitbart.com/2020-election/2020/01/20/joe-bidens-brother-frank-linked-to-projects-receiving-54000000-in-taxpayer-loans-from-the-obama-administration-despite-no-experience/

407 Ibid.

408 Ibid.

409 Alana Goodman, "Ashley Biden organization received $166K federal grant while father was vice president," *Washington Examiner,* January 29, 2020. https://www.washingtonexaminer.com/news/2639525/ashley-biden-organization-received-166k-federal-grant-while-father-was-vice-president/

410 Ibid.

411 "5 CFR § 2635.702 - Use of public office for private gain," Legal Information Institute, Cornell Law School. https://www.law.cornell.edu/cfr/text/5 /2635.702?ref=themilsource.com Italics are mine. See also: Joseph Lyttleton, "Family Benefits: How politicians' families profit off their connections," *The MilSource*, May 6, 2020. https://themilsource.com/2020 /05/06/family-benefits-how-politicians-families-profit-off-their -connections/

412 "Crony capitalism," Merriam-Webster Dictionary. https://www .merriam-webster.com/dictionary/crony%20capitalism

413 One of the bills – the "Bankruptcy Abuse Prevention and Consumer Protection Act of 2005" – would have made it harder for delinquent credit card holders to declare bankruptcy. Joe supported it, and it passed in 2005. Hunter's $100,000 payments stopped that year too. Coincidence? See: Ben Schreckinger, "Biden Inc.," *Politico*, August 2, 2019. https://www.politico.com/magazine/story/2019 /08/02/joe-biden-investigation-hunter-brother-hedge-fund-money -2020-campaign-227407/ and Eric Umansky, "Biden's Cozy Relations With Bank Industry," *ProPublica*, August 25, 2008. https://www .propublica.org/article/bidens-cozy-relations-with-bank-industry-825

414 Annie Linskey and James T. Areddy, "How Joe Biden's Kin Profited Off the Family Name. 'The Big Guy Is Calling Me,'" *Wall Street Journal*, September 28. 2023. https://www.wsj.com/us-news/law/how -joe-bidens-kin-profited-off-the-family-name-the-big-guy-is-calling -me-547220ab

415 James told the FBI in a 2022 interview that he had "operated in 35 states and was licensed in all 50 states," though none of his licenses were current. He also said he had "done an extensive amount of consulting with unions and municipalities…had been asked to participate and advise several fortune 500 companies…worked in real estate development…had owned restaurants and night clubs…[and was] currently trying to purchase a rugby franchise in Philadelphia." See: "James Biden, Memorandum of Interview," Department of Treasury, September 29, 2022. https://justthenews.com/sites/default/files/2023 -09/T19%20Exhibit%20401-Memo-FINAL%20Memo%20of%20 Interview%20w%20James%20B%20SPORTSMAN-09.29.2022 _KPM%20Unredacted_Redacted.pdf

416 "Statement of James Biden," House Committees on Oversight & Accountability and the Judiciary February 21, 2024. https://www .politico.com/f/?id=0000018d-cc98-dda8-abff-ddbd91900000

417 Mariah Blake, "The Fall of the House of Moon," *The New Republic*,
     November 12, 2013. https://newrepublic.com/article/115512/unification
     -church-profile-fall-house-moon#footnote-115512-3

418 "Anthony V. Lotito, Jr. et al v. R. Hunter Biden et al," Supreme Court
     of the State of New York, January 5, 2007. https://iapps.courts.state
     .ny.us/fbem/DocumentDisplayServlet?documentId=sxEiZam5udb
     /HIp0qCJVAQ==&system=prod

419 Ibid. Americore International Security, according to its business profile,
     was "a security firm dealing with new technology such as retinal scans
     and fingerprint machines, as well as personal body security guards." See:
     "Americore International Security," Better Business Bureau. https://www
     .bbb.org/us/ny/brooklyn/profile/security-system-monitors/americore
     -international-security-0121-87738

420 "Anthony V. Lotito, Jr. et al v. R. Hunter Biden et al," Supreme Court
     of the State of New York, January 5, 2007. https://iapps.courts.state
     .ny.us/fbem/DocumentDisplayServlet?documentId=sxEiZam5udb
     /HIp0qCJVAQ==&system=prod

421 The "group" consisted of several LLCs with similar names – similar to
     what the Biden Crime Family did later with the many Rosemonts and
     Hudson West entities. This batch used several versions of BG Equity for
     the corporate names. Besides the Bidens, there was an outside investor
     involved named Lawrence Rasky, described in the legal papers as "a
     longtime friend of the Biden family." "Anthony V. Lotito, Jr. et al v. R.
     Hunter Biden et al," Supreme Court of the State of New York, January
     5, 2007. https://iapps.courts.state.ny.us/fbem/DocumentDisplayServl
     et?documentId=sxEiZam5udb/HIp0qCJVAQ==&system=prod

422 Ibid.

423 Ben Schreckinger, "New book reveals how Biden's family used his
     position for profit," *New York Post*, September 13, 2021. https://nypost
     .com/2021/09/13/new-book-reveals-how-joe-bidens-family-used-his
     -position-for-profit/

424 Mariah Blake, "The Fall of the House of Moon," *The New Republic*,
     November 12, 2013. https://newrepublic.com/article/115512/unification
     -church-profile-fall-house-moon#footnote-115512-3

425 The managing partner of Simmons Cooper was Jeff Cooper – the same
     Jeff Cooper from Chapter 5 who hoped to cash in on the Mexico/
     Carlos Slim deals with Hunter. The law firm had lobbied Joe on
     asbestos legislation – legislation that he voted in favor of – and worked
     with Beau on cases in Delaware. In addition, they contributed to
     both Joe and Beau's political campaigns. They pledged $2 million to
     the Paradigm venture. But when the deal fell through, James Biden
     claimed the Bidens were then indebted to Simmons Cooper to the

tune of $1 million. See: Chuck Neubauer and Tom Hamburger Biden family ties pose questions, *LA Times*, August 28, 2008. https://www.latimes.com/archives/la-xpm-2008-aug-28-na-biden28-story.html and Stacy-Marie Ishmael, "The politics of Paradigm," *Financial Times*, May 1, 2009. https://www.ft.com/content/b49b9a01-8b4b-3b5f-ae41-713a1e86143d

426 "Anthony V. Lotito, Jr. et al v. R. Hunter Biden et al," Supreme Court of the State of New York, January 5, 2007. https://iapps.courts.state.ny.us/fbem/DocumentDisplayServlet?documentId=sxEiZam5udb/HIp0qCJVAQ==&system=prod

427 Mariah Blake, "The Fall of the House of Moon," *The New Republic*, November 12, 2013. https://newrepublic.com/article/115512/unification-church-profile-fall-house-moon#footnote-115512-3

428 "Anthony V. Lotito, Jr. et al v. R. Hunter Biden et al," Supreme Court of the State of New York, January 5, 2007. https://iapps.courts.state.ny.us/fbem/DocumentDisplayServlet?documentId=sxEiZam5udb/HIp0qCJVAQ==&system=prod

429 Stacy-Marie Ishmael, "The politics of Paradigm," *Financial Times*, May 1, 2009. https://www.ft.com/content/b49b9a01-8b4b-3b5f-ae41-713a1e86143d

430 Ibid.

431 Ibid.

432 "Provini v. Paradigm Global Advisors, LLC," https://archive.org/details/gov.uscourts.njd.214636

433 Ben Schreckinger, "New book reveals how Biden's family used his position for profit," *New York Post,* September 13, 2021. https://nypost.com/2021/09/13/new-book-reveals-how-joe-bidens-family-used-his-position-for-profit/

434 Annie Linskey Follow and James T. Areddy, "How Joe Biden's Kin Profited Off the Family Name. 'The Big Guy Is Calling Me,'" *Wall Street Journal*, September 28, 2023. https://www.wsj.com/us-news/law/how-joe-bidens-kin-profited-off-the-family-name-the-big-guy-is-calling-me-547220ab

435 Provini's Paradigm appointment merited a mention in the prestigious *Financial Times.* "People: Paradigm Global Advisors, Mercer Investment Consulting, Commerzbank," *Financial Times*, January 18, 2007. https://www.ft.com/content/8695c235-e71a-377c-8927-1aad37f4448e Note that Provini's later employment announcements don't mention his Paradigm tenure. "Charles R. Provini, Chief Executive Officer at Natcore Technology, Inc.," *MarketScreener.* https://ca.marketscreener.com/insider/CHARLES-R-PROVINI-A0Q65H/#google_vignette

436 The Stanford Financial Group scheme, run by Allen Stanford, wasn't as big as the one perpetrated by Bernie Madoff, but it was "massive." See: Susan Schmidt et al, "Stanford Had Links to a Fund Run by Bidens," *Wall Streeet Journal*, February 24, 2009. https://www.wsj.com /articles/SB123543815326954907 and "Stanford Financial Group," Wikipedia. https://en.wikipedia.org/wiki/Stanford_Financial_Group

437 Ben Smith, "Biden son's, brothers firm downplays ties to closed hedge fund [UPDATED]," *Politico*, April 29, 2009. https://www.politico .com/blogs/ben-smith/2009/04/biden-sons-brothers-firm-downplays -ties-to-closed-hedge-fund-updated-017947

438 "Statement of James Biden," House Committees on Oversight & Accountability and the Judiciary February 21, 2024. https://www .politico.com/f/?id=0000018d-cc98-dda8-abff-ddbd91900000

439 "Charles Provini, Plaintiff, v. Paradigm Global Advisors, LLC, Defendant," May 13, 2008. https://archive.org/details/gov.uscourts.njd .214636/gov.uscourts.njd.214636.4.0.pdf

440 As long as Joe was in office, James was supposedly tasked with keeping the family in the manner to which it hoped to remain accustomed, according to *The Bidens*. "With his older brother on a government salary, the Bidens' financial fortunes rested disproportionately on his shoulders. 'Jim's job,' one of his former business partners explained to me, 'is to ensure the lifestyle is good for the family.'" Schreckinger, *The Bidens*. Page 91.

441 Michael Kranish, "James Biden's dealmaking caught on FBI tapes in unrelated bribery probe," *Washington Post,* December 17, 2023. https://www.washingtonpost.com/politics/2023/12/17/james-bidens -dealmaking-caught-fbi-tapes-unrelated-bribery-probe/

442 Ibid.

443 In his testimony before the House Oversight Committee on February 21, 2024, James says the entity to be formed was going to be a law firm. Other accounts have called this a consulting firm and a Democratic lobbying firm. "Interview of James Brian Biden," Committee On Oversight And Accountability Joint With The Committee On The Judiciary, U.S. House Of Representatives, February 21, 2024. https://oversight .house.gov/wp-content/uploads/2024/06/James-Biden-Transcript-1 .pdf. See also: Michael Kranish, "James Biden's dealmaking caught on FBI tapes in unrelated bribery probe," *Washington Post,* December 17, 2023. https://www.washingtonpost.com/politics/2023/12/17/james -bidens-dealmaking-caught-fbi-tapes-unrelated-bribery-probe/ and Paul Speery, "Who Is Sara Biden? Joe's In-Law Emerges as Central Figure in Foreign Cash Deals," *RealClearInvestigations*, December 11, 2023. https://www.realclearinvestigations.com/articles/2023/12/11/who_is

_sara_biden_joes_in-law_emerges_as_central_figure_in_foreign
_cash_deals_996942.html

444 They tried to bribe a judge. The feds used wiretaps to make their case against the lawyers. James was also heard speaking on the wiretaps but never charged with wrongdoing. Michael Kranish, "James Biden's dealmaking caught on FBI tapes in unrelated bribery probe," *Washington Post*, December 17, 2023. https://www .washingtonpost.com/politics/2023/12/17/james-bidens-dealmaking -caught-fbi-tapes-unrelated-bribery-probe/

445 Paul Speery, "Who Is Sara Biden? Joe's In-Law Emerges as Central Figure in Foreign Cash Deals," *RealClearInvestigations*, December 11, 2023. https://www.realclearinvestigations.com/articles/2023/12/11/who_is _sara_biden_joes_in-law_emerges_as_central_figure_in_foreign_cash _deals_996942.html

446 Daniel Golden et al, "The Benefits of Being Joe Biden's Brother," *ProPublica*, February 14, 2020. https://www.propublica.org/article /the-profitable-business-of-being-joe-bidens-brother

447 Cheryl Clark, "Hustling Hope: Diabetes clinic founder headed to prison for attempted bribery," *inewsource*, May 28, 2019. https:// inewsource.org/2019/05/28/trina-health-diabetes-gilbert-sentenced -conspiring-bribe-alabama-lawmaker/

448 Not the Americore International Security firm James had owned with Anthony Lotito in the Paradigm days. This is a completely different entity.

449 Ben Schreckinger, "Biden's brother used his name to promote a hospital chain. Then it collapsed," *Politico*, February 18, 2024. https://www .politico.com/news/2024/02/18/the-biden-name-how-the-presidents -brother-became-embroiled-in-a-hospital-fiasco-00141868

450 "Interview of Carol Fox," Committee On Oversight And Accountability Joint With The Committee On The Judiciary, U.S. House Of Representatives, December 18, 2023. https://oversight.house.gov/wp -content/uploads/2024/02/Carol-Fox-Transcript.pdf

451 Keaton Langston has had his own legal run-ins over Fountain Health. In May, 2024, he pled guilty to conspiring to defraud Medicare of $51 million. Also charged as a co-conspirator in the case is Thomas Farese, identified as "a high ranking member of the Colombo organized crime family of La Cosa Nostra." See: Steven Nelson, "James Biden associate Keaton Langston pleads guilty to $51M Medicare fraud," *New York Post*, May 27, 2024. https://nypost.com/2024/05/27/us-news/james -biden-associate-keaton-langston-pleads-guilty-to-51m-medicare -fraud/; Russ Latino, "Family Tradition: Keaton Langston pleads guilty in $51 million Medicare fraud," *Magnolia Tribune*, May 26, 2024.

https://magnoliatribune.com/2024/05/26/family-tradition-keaton -langston-pleads-guilty-in-51-million-medicare-fraud/ and Letter from US Attorney Loretta Lynch to Judge Robert E. Levy in the case of "United States v. Thomas Farese," March 5, 2012. https://www.politico .com/f/?id=0000018e-4e2e-dddf-a19f-ff2ebe5d0000

452 "Interview of Carol Fox," Committee On Oversight And Accountability Joint With The Committee On The Judiciary, U.S. House Of Representatives, December 18, 2023. https://oversight.house.gov/wp -content/uploads/2024/02/Carol-Fox-Transcript.pdf

453 "Statement of James Biden," House Committees on Oversight & Accountability and the Judiciary February 21, 2024. https://www .politico.com/f/?id=0000018d-cc98-dda8-abff-ddbd91900000

454 "Interview of James Brian Biden," Committee On Oversight And Accountability Joint With The Committee On The Judiciary, U.S. House Of Representatives, February 21, 2024. https://oversight.house .gov/wp-content/uploads/2024/06/James-Biden-Transcript-1.pdf

455 One of those presentations was a pitch letter to a Qatari sheikh offering to "provide a wealth of introductions and business opportunities at the highest levels...on behalf of the Biden family." The sheikh didn't contribute. Nor did any other Middle East investors that Biden claimed he could deliver. "Report on the Biden Laptop," MarcoPolo501c3.org, page 525. https://bidenreport.com/#p=529

456 "Statement of James Biden," House Committees on Oversight & Accountability and the Judiciary February 21, 2024. https://www .politico.com/f/?id=0000018d-cc98-dda8-abff-ddbd91900000

457 "Interview of Carol Fox," Committee On Oversight And Accountability Joint With The Committee On The Judiciary, U.S. House Of Representatives, December 18, 2023. https://oversight.house.gov /wp-content/uploads/2024/02/Carol-Fox-Transcript.pdf

458 A 2022 lawsuit in Florida alleged that Lewitt had actually embezzled that $20 million from investors in the Third Friday Total Return Fund. The suit claims "Lewitt's scheme involved the use of 'sham' loans to third parties and to himself and fraudulent misstatements and omissions to cover up his embezzlement of the Fund's capital, self-dealing, and other related malfeasance." See: David A. Rocker, et al, Plaintiffs, v. Michael E. Lewitt, the Third Friday Total Return Fund, L.P, et al, Defendants. December 14, 2022. https://www.politico.com /f/?id=0000018e-6184-dc9c-ab9f-69f44b670000

459 "Statement of James Biden," House Committees on Oversight & Accountability and the Judiciary February 21, 2024. https://www .politico.com/f/?id=0000018d-cc98-dda8-abff-ddbd91900000

460 Ibid.

461 Ben Schreckinger, "Biden's brother used his name to promote a hospital chain. Then it collapsed," *Politico*, February 18, 2024. https://www .politico.com/news/2024/02/18/the-biden-name-how-the-presidents -brother-became-embroiled-in-a-hospital-fiasco-00141868

462 "Interview of James Brian Biden," Committee On Oversight And Accountability Joint With The Committee On The Judiciary, U.S. House Of Representatives, February 21, 2024. https://oversight.house .gov/wp-content/uploads/2024/06/James-Biden-Transcript-1.pdf

463 Ben Schreckinger, "Biden's brother used his name to promote a hospital chain. Then it collapsed," *Politico*, February 18, 2024. https://www .politico.com/news/2024/02/18/the-biden-name-how-the-presidents -brother-became-embroiled-in-a-hospital-fiasco-00141868

464 "Interview of James Brian Biden," Committee On Oversight And Accountability Joint With The Committee On The Judiciary, U.S. House Of Representatives, February 21, 2024. https://oversight.house .gov/wp-content/uploads/2024/06/James-Biden-Transcript-1.pdf

465 Ben Schreckinger, "Biden's brother used his name to promote a hospital chain. Then it collapsed," *Politico*, February 18, 2024. https://www .politico.com/news/2024/02/18/the-biden-name-how-the-presidents -brother-became-embroiled-in-a-hospital-fiasco-00141868

466 Lisa Rab, "Mavericks charter schools don't live up to big promises," *Miami New Times*, December 29, 2011. https://www.miaminewtimes .com/news/mavericks-charter-schools-dont-live-up-to-big-promises -6385627

467 A *Wall Street Journal* article elaborated on Frank's fondness for touting his family ties. "Frank Biden, as the president's youngest brother Francis is known, was hired by the Illinois-based industrial manufacturing firm Federal Signal Corp. to help connect the company with Florida lawmakers. During a weekly call, Frank Biden, 69 years old, would frequently interrupt the meeting and say he had to take a call from 'the Big Guy,' as he put it. The then-vice president's brother would say: 'I've got to put you on hold, the Big Guy is calling me,' recalled Matthew Brady, then working at Federal Signal. 'I thought, 'OK, great, your brother is the vice president.' The same day that Joe Biden was inaugurated as president, the Florida-based law firm that employs Frank Biden as a member of its executive leadership team ran a newspaper ad that included a photo of Frank Biden and quoted him trumpeting his brother." Annie Linskey and James T. Areddy, "How Joe Biden's Kin Profited Off the Family Name. 'The Big Guy Is Calling Me,'" *Wall Street Journal,* September 28. 2023. https://www.wsj.com/us-news/law /how-joe-bidens-kin-profited-off-the-family-name-the-big-guy-is -calling-me-547220ab

468 Lisa Rab, "Mavericks charter schools don't live up to big promises," *Miami New Times*, December 29, 2011. https://www.miaminewtimes .com/news/mavericks-charter-schools-dont-live-up-to-big-promises -6385627

469 Ibid.

470 Valerie Strauss, "Brother of VP Biden promotes charters, invoking family name," *Washington Post*, December 10, 2011. https://www .washingtonpost.com/blogs/answer-sheet/post/brother-of-vp-biden -promotes-charters-invoking-family-name/2011/11/22/gIQAnh LFfO_blog.html

471 Amy Shipley and Karen Yi, "Mavericks in Education: Failing to make the grade," *South Florida Sun-Sentinel*, October 10, 2014. https://www.sun-sentinel.com/2014/10/10/mavericks-in-education -failing-to-make-the-grade/

472 Charlie Gasparino, "The Ties that Biden," *Fox Business*, October 22, 2012. https://www.foxbusiness.com/politics/the-ties-that-biden

473 Barclay Palmer, Are Personal Loans Considered Income? *Investopedia*, August 11, 2024. https://www.investopedia.com/ask/answers/120315 /are-personal-loans-considered-income.asp#:~:text=Personal%20 loans%20can%20be%20made,C%20tax%20form%20for%20filing. The italics are mine.

474 Daniel Golden et al, "The Benefits of Being Joe Biden's Brother," *ProPublica*, February 14, 2020. https://www.propublica.org/article/the -profitable-business-of-being-joe-bidens-brother

475 The actual amount was reportedly $900,000. See: Paul Speery, "Who Is Sara Biden? Joe's In-Law Emerges as Central Figure in Foreign Cash Deals," *RealClearInvestigations*, December 11, 2023. https://www .realclearinvestigations.com/articles/2023/12/11/who_is_sara_biden _joes_in-law_emerges_as_central_figure_in_foreign_cash_deals _996942.html

476 Maureen Milford, "Battle over $5 million Chateau Country estate ends for Tigani," *The News Journal*, April 10, 2015. https://www .delawareonline.com/story/news/local/2015/04/10/battle-million -chateau-country-estate-ends-tigani/25601795/

477 "About Winner," Winner Auto Group. https://www.winnerauto.com /about-winner

478 "Interview: John Hynansky, Owner & CEO Winner Group Ukraine," *Ukraine The Report.com*, 2018. https://www.ukraine.the-report.com /interview/john-hynansky/

479 Leena Kim, "All of Joe Biden's Homes, In Photos," *Town & Country*, July 21, 2024. https://www.townandcountrymag.com/leisure/real-estate/a3380 9100/joe-biden-real-estate-homes/

480 Ben Schreckinger, "Donor with deep Ukraine ties lent $500,000 to Biden's brother," *Politico*, August 15, 2019. https://www.politico.com /story/2019/08/15/james-biden-bungalow-ukraine-donor-1463645

481 Ibid.

482 Paul Sperry, "All About Ukraine Auto Magnate and Joe Biden Megadonor John Hynansky," *RealClearInvestigations*, April 26, 2023. https:// www.realclearinvestigations.com/articles/2023/04/26/war_threatens _ukraine_auto_empire_of_biden_megadonor_urging_greater_us_role _895319.html

483 Ibid.

484 Ibid. That's the same OPIC that loaned Frank Biden $54 million for his Caribbean endeavors. See: Haris Alic, "Joe Biden's Brother Frank Linked to Projects Receiving $54,000,000 in Taxpayer Loans from the Obama Administration—Despite No Experience," *Breitbart*, January 20, 2020. https://www.breitbart.com/2020-election/2020/01/20/joe-bidens -brother-frank-linked-to-projects-receiving-54000000-in-taxpayer -loans-from-the-obama-administration-despite-no-experience/

485 Paul Sperry, "All About Ukraine Auto Magnate and Joe Biden Megadonor John Hynansky," *RealClearInvestigations*, April 26, 2023. https:// www.realclearinvestigations.com/articles/2023/04/26/war_threatens _ukraine_auto_empire_of_biden_megadonor_urging_greater_us_role _895319.html

486 "Keewaydin Island," Wikipedia. https://en.wikipedia.org/wiki /Keewaydin_Island

487 Paul Speery, "Who Is Sara Biden? Joe's In-Law Emerges as Central Figure in Foreign Cash Deals," *RealClearInvestigations*, December 11, 2023. https:// www.realclearinvestigations.com/articles/2023/12/11/who_is_sara _biden_joes_in-law_emerges_as_central_figure_in_foreign_cash_deals _996942.html

488 Ben Schreckinger, "Donor with deep Ukraine ties lent $500,000 to Biden's brother," *Politico*, August 15, 2019. https://www.politico.com /story/2019/08/15/james-biden-bungalow-ukraine-donor-1463645

489 Ibid.

490 Ibid.

491 Paul Sperry, "All About Ukraine Auto Magnate and Joe Biden Megadonor John Hynansky," *RealClearInvestigations*, April 26, 2023. https:// www.realclearinvestigations.com/articles/2023/04/26/war_threatens _ukraine_auto_empire_of_biden_megadonor_urging_greater_us _role_895319.html

492 Ben Schreckinger, "Donor with deep Ukraine ties lent $500,000 to Biden's brother," *Politico*, August 15, 2019. https://www.politico.com /story/2019/08/15/james-biden-bungalow-ukraine-donor-1463645

493 "Interview of James Brian Biden," Committee On Oversight And Accountability Joint With The Committee On The Judiciary, U.S. House Of Representatives, February 21, 2024. https://oversight.house .gov/wp-content/uploads/2024/06/James-Biden-Transcript-1.pdf

494 Ibid.

495 Besides the property mentioned above, in 2005, the James Bidens bought an acre of land in the Virgin Islands for $150,000, divided it into thirds, and sold one of them for nearly the initial investment to a former Joe Biden staffer turned lobbyist. The lobbyist, Scott Green, later gave James and Sara a mortgage on the rest of the property. A few years afterwards, during the Obama administration, Green's firm, the Lafayette Group, got "tens of millions of dollars in contract awards…from federal agencies." See: Ben Schreckinger, "Lobbyist bought tropical land from Biden's brother," *Politico*, January 28, 2020. https://www.politico.com/news/2020/01/28/james -biden-lobbyist-virgin-islands-099318

496 Daniel Golden et al, "The Benefits of Being Joe Biden's Brother," *ProPublica*, February 14, 2020. https://www.propublica.org/article/ the-profitable-business-of-being-joe-bidens-brother. Joe had to abandon that presidential bid when it was discovered that he not only cheated in law school, plagiarizing an article for a paper he wrote, but that in a campaign speech, he essentially copied the life story of British politician Neil Kinnock, re-telling it as if it was his own experience. See: E. J. Dionne, Jr., "Biden Admits Plagiarism in School But Says It Was Not 'Malevolent'," *New York Times*, September 18, 1987. https://www .nytimes.com/1987/09/18/us/biden-admits-plagiarism-in-school-but -says-it-was-not-malevolent.html

497 Daniel Golden et al, "The Benefits of Being Joe Biden's Brother," *ProPublica*, February 14, 2020. https://www.propublica.org/article/the -profitable-business-of-being-joe-bidens-brother

498 Ibid.

499 Ibid.

500 That was the same Third Friday that paid the Bidens $610,000. The day they got that wire transfer, Sara wrote Joe the much-referenced $200,000 check with "loan repayment" on the memo line.

501 David A. Rocker, et al, Plaintiffs, v. Michael E. Lewitt, the Third Friday Total Return Fund, L.P., et al, Defendants. December 14, 2022. https:// www.politico.com/f/?id=0000018e-6184-dc9c-ab9f-69f44b670000

502 "Interview of James Brian Biden," Committee On Oversight And Accountability Joint With The Committee On The Judiciary, U.S. House Of Representatives, February 21, 2024. https://oversight.house .gov/wp-content/uploads/2024/06/James-Biden-Transcript-1.pdf

503 Ben Schreckinger, "DOJ looked at transactions linked to Jim Biden as part of criminal investigation," *Politico*, March 26, 2024. https://www.politico.com/news/2024/03/26/jim-biden-business -feds-investigation-00148909

504 "Interview of James Brian Biden," Committee On Oversight And Accountability Joint With The Committee On The Judiciary, U.S. House Of Representatives, February 21, 2024. https://oversight.house .gov/wp-content/uploads/2024/06/James-Biden-Transcript-1.pdf

505 Steven Nelson, "James Biden associate Keaton Langston pleads guilty to $51M Medicare fraud," *New York Post*, May 27, 2024. https://nypost .com/2024/05/27/us-news/james-biden-associate-keaton-langston -pleads-guilty-to-51m-medicare-fraud/

506 Barclay Palmer, Are Personal Loans Considered Income? *Investopedia*, August 11, 2024. https://www.investopedia.com/ask/answers/120315 /are-personal-loans-considered-income.asp#:~:text=Personal%20 loans%20can%20be%20made,C%20tax%20form%20for%20filing.

507 Ibid.

508 Steven Nelson, "Biden calls on rich to 'step up and pay' 'fair share' in taxes — despite report that he didn't," *New York Post*, September 24, 2021. https://nypost.com/2021/09/24/biden-calls-on-rich-to-step-up -and-pay-fair-share-in-taxes/

509 Louis Casiano, "Hunter Biden trial on tax charges given start date," Fox News, July 22, 2024. https://www.foxnews.com/us/hunter-biden -trial-tax-charges-given-start-date

510 Catherine Herridge, "Hollywood attorney Kevin Morris, who financially backed Hunter Biden, moves closer to the spotlight," CBS News, January 12, 2024. https://www.cbsnews.com/news/hollywood -attorney-kevin-morris-who-financially-backed-hunter-biden-moves -closer-to-the-spotlight/

511 Sarah Fitzpatrick and Rebecca Kaplan, "Here's why Kevin Morris says he paid Hunter Biden's back taxes," NBC News, January 23, 2024. https://www.nbcnews.com/politics/congress/s-kevin-morris-says-paid -hunter-bidens-back-taxes-rcna135277#

512 Ibid.

513 Betsy Woodruff Swan and Brittany Gibson, "Hunter Biden's legal defense has a problem: The patron paying the bills is running out of cash," *Politico*, May 15, 2024. https://www.politico.com/news/2024/05/15 /hunter-biden-legal-defense-kevin-morris-money-00158237

514 Sarah Fitzpatrick and Rebecca Kaplan, "Here's why Kevin Morris says he paid Hunter Biden's back taxes," NBC News, January 23, 2024. https://www.nbcnews.com/politics/congress/s-kevin-morris-says-paid -hunter-bidens-back-taxes-rcna135277#. What doesn't get reported

much is the fact that, through one of his many business entities (Skaneateles, in this case), Hunter held onto his 10 percent equity in the Chinese BHR Partners fund until 2021 when he sold that to Morris. See: "Interview of Robert Hunter Biden," Committee On Oversight And Accountability Joint With The Committee On The Judiciary, U.S. House Of Representatives, February 28, 2024. https:// oversight.house.gov/wp-content/uploads/2024/02/Hunter-Biden -Transcript_Redacted.pdf. See also: "Report Of The Impeachment Inquiry Of Joseph R. Biden Jr., President Of The United States Of America," Committee on Oversight and Accountability Committee on the Judiciary Committee on Ways and Means, August 19, 2024. https://oversight.house.gov/wp-content/uploads/2024/08/2024.08.19 -Report-of-the-Impeachment-Inquiry-of-Joseph-R.-Biden-Jr. -President-of-the-United-States.pdf

515 Priscilla DeGregory, "Hunter Biden says he pleaded guilty in $1.4M tax evasion case to 'spare' family from 'embarrassment', *New York Post*, September 6, 2024. https://nypost.com/2024/09/06/us-news/hunter -bidens-guilty-plea-was-to-spare-embarrassment/

516 Ibid.

517 Ibid.

518 Betsy Woodruff Swan and Brittany Gibson, "Hunter Biden's legal defense has a problem: The patron paying the bills is running out of cash," *Politico*, May 15, 2024. https://www.politico.com/news/2024/05/15 /hunter-biden-legal-defense-kevin-morris-money-00158237

519 Adam Cancryn and Jonathan Lemire, "Hunter Biden's plea avoids a trial, and further pain for his father," *Politico*, September 5, 2024. https://www.politico.com/news/2024/09/05/white-house-biden-wont -pardon-son-00177551

520 "109. RICO Charges," U.S. Department of Justice. https://www.justice .gov/archives/jm/criminal-resource-manual-109-rico-charges#:~:text =All%20that%20must%20be%20shown,United%20States%20v.

521 "It shall be unlawful for any person who has received any income derived, directly or indirectly, from a pattern of racketeering activity or through collection of an unlawful debt in which such person has participated as a principal within the meaning of section 2, title 18, United States Code, to use or invest, directly or indirectly, any part of such income, or the proceeds of such income, in acquisition of any interest in, or the establishment or operation of, any enterprise which is engaged in, or the activities of which affect, interstate or foreign commerce." "18 U.S. Code § 1962 - Prohibited activities," Legal Information Institute, Cornell Law School. https://www.law.cornell .edu/uscode/text/18/1962

522 "109. RICO Charges," U.S. Department of Justice. https://www.justice.gov/archives/jm/criminal-resource-manual-109-rico-charges#:~:text=All%20that%20must%20be%20shown,United%20States%20v.

523 "During five decades in public office, Joe Biden built his political brand on his working-class roots. Over that time, members of his family capitalized on his political success by invoking the Biden name to bolster their business pursuits in deals worth millions of dollars." Annie Linskey and James T. Areddy, "How Joe Biden's Kin Profited Off the Family Name. 'The Big Guy Is Calling Me,'" *Wall Street Journal*, September 28. 2023. https://www.wsj.com/us-news/law/how-joe-bidens-kin-profited-off-the-family-name-the-big-guy-is-calling-me-547220ab

524 When asked by House Oversight Committee member Andy Biggs (R-AZ) if, by the Biden "brand," was he referring to Joe Biden, Archer replied, "Obviously, that brought the most value to the brand." "Interview of Devon Archer," Committee On Oversight And Accountability, U.S. House Of Representatives, July 31, 2023. https://oversight.house.gov/wp-content/uploads/2023/08/Devon-Archer-Transcript.pdf

525 Ibid.

526 "Report on the Biden Laptop," Marco Polo 501c3.org., page 55. https://bidenreport.com/#p=59 The spellings are all MarcoPolo's.

527 Tim Murphy, "House of Cards," *Mother Jones*, November/December 2019. https://www.motherjones.com/politics/2019/11/biden-bankruptcy-president/

528 Ben Schreckinger, "Hunter Biden's prosecutor rejected moves that would have revealed probe earlier," *Politico*, July 16, 2021. https://www.politico.com/news/2021/07/16/hunter-biden-probe-prosecutor-499782

529 "Delaware: The US Corporate Secrecy Haven," *Transparency International*, January 12, 2016. https://www.transparency.org/en/news/delaware-the-us-corporate-secrecy-haven

530 "Joe Biden Lied At Least 16 Times About His Family's Business Schemes," House Committee on Oversight and Accountability, August 28, 2019. https://oversight.house.gov/blog/joe-biden-lied-at-least-15-times-about-his-familys-business-schemes/

531 Tim Haines, "WH Response To Hunter Biden Questions: 'The President Was Never In Business With His Son'," *RealClearPolitics*, July 24, 2023. https://www.realclearpolitics.com/video/2023/07/24/kjp_response_to_hunter_questions_the_answer_remains_the_same_the_president_was_never_in_business_with_his_son.html

532 "Interview of Anthony Bobulinski," Committee On Oversight And Accountability Joint With The Committee On The Judiciary, U.S. House Of Representatives, February 13, 2024. https://oversight.house .gov/wp-content/uploads/2024/02/Bobulinski-Transcript.pdf

533 Ben Schreckinger, "Biden Inc.," *Politico*, August 2, 2019. https://www .politico.com/magazine/story/2019/08/02/joe-biden-investigation -hunter-brother-hedge-fund-money-2020-campaign-227407/

534 Caroline Downey, "Biden's Brother Was Paid to Settle Business Dispute with Saudis during VP Tenure," *National Review*, February 14, 2023. https://www.nationalreview.com/news/bidens-brother-was -paid-to-settle-business-dispute-with-saudis-during-vp-tenure/

535 Natashe Korecki, et al, "'For Christ's sake, watch yourself': Biden warns family over business dealings," *Politico*, January 28, 2021.

536 A screenshot of the text appears on the "Report on the Biden Laptop," MarcoPolo501c3.org, page 205. https://bidenreport.com/#p=209. Typos and misspellings are all Hunter's.

537 "109. RICO Charges," U.S. Department of Justice. https://www.justice .gov/archives/jm/criminal-resource-manual-109-rico-charges#:~:text =All%20that%20must%20be%20shown,United%20States%20v.

538 "Report Of The Impeachment Inquiry Of Joseph R. Biden Jr., President Of The United States Of America," Committee on Oversight and Accountability Committee on the Judiciary Committee on Ways and Means, August 19, 2024. https://oversight.house.gov/wp-content /uploads/2024/08/2024.08.19-Report-of-the-Impeachment-Inquiry -of-Joseph-R.-Biden-Jr.-President-of-the-United-States.pdf

539 "18 U.S. Code § 201 - Bribery of public officials and witnesses," Legal Information Institute, Cornell Law School. https://www.law.cornell .edu/uscode/text/18/201

540 "Joe Biden on Defending Democracy," Council on Foreign Relations, January 23, 2018. https://www.youtube.com/watch?v=Q0 _AqpdwqK4&t=3108s.

541 This could also possibly fall under 18 US Code § 1951, The Hobbs Act, "which prohibits actual or attempted robbery or extortion affecting interstate or foreign commerce." See: "9-131.000 - The Hobbs Act - 18 U.S.C. § 1951," US Department of Justice. https://www.justice.gov/ jm/jm-9-131000-hobbs-act-18-usc-1951. Ironically, that's what the House Democrats used when they impeached Donald Trump the first time. See: "Impeachment of Donald J. Trump President Of The United States," House of Representatives, December 15, 2019. https://www .congress.gov/116/crpt/hrpt346/CRPT-116hrpt346.pdf

542 "Fraud," Merriam-Webster Dictionary. https://www.merriam-webster .com/dictionary/fraud

543 "18 U.S. Code Chapter 63 - Mail Fraud and Other Fraud Offenses," Legal Information Institute, Cornell Law School. https://www.law .cornell.edu/uscode/text/18/part-I/chapter-63

544 "Interview of Anthony Bobulinski," Committee On Oversight And Accountability Joint With The Committee On The Judiciary, U.S. House Of Representatives, February 13, 2024. https://oversight.house .gov/wp-content/uploads/2024/02/Bobulinski-Transcript.pdf

545 Committee on Oversight and Accountability Majority Staff, "Second Bank Records Memorandum from the Oversight Committee's Investigation into the Biden Family's Influence Peddling and Business Schemes," Committee on Oversight and Accountability, May 10, 2023. https://oversight.house.gov/wp-content/uploads/2023/05/Bank -Memorandum-5.10.23.pdf

546 Ibid.

547 Glenn Kessler, "How Republicans overhype the findings of their Hunter Biden probe," *Washington Post*, August 17, 2023. https://www .washingtonpost.com/politics/2023/08/17/how-republicans-overhype -findings-their-hunter-biden-probe/

548 "Racketeering and RICO Violations Under the Law," *Justia*. https:// www.justia.com/criminal/offenses/white-collar-crimes/racketeering -rico/#:~:text=Elements%20of%20Racketeering&text=Efforts%20 to%20conceal%20the%20criminal,money%20laundering%20 and%20tax%20evasion.

549 Josh Christenson, "No sign of $40K loan from Joe Biden to brother James, first family's moneyman says — undercutting White House story," *New York Post*, March 18, 2024. https://nypost.com/2024/03/18 /us-news/no-sign-of-40k-loan-from-joe-biden-to-brother-james-first -familys-moneyman-says-undercutting-white-house-story/

550 Jordain Carney, "House GOP subpoenas Hunter Biden in impeachment inquiry," *Politico*, November 8, 2023. https://www.politico.com/live -updates/2023/11/08/congress/hunter-biden-subpoenaed-00126137

551 "War Room, Episode 3445," War Room.org, March 7, 2024. https:// warroom.org/episode-3445-pre-sotu-coverage/

552 "Pattern-or-practice case," LSD Law. https://www.lsd.law/define/pattern -or-practice-case

553 "FAQ about Pattern or Practice Investigations," US Department of Justice, Civil Rights Division. https://www.justice.gov/d9/2023-10 /pattern_or_practice_investigation_faqs_english.pdf

554 Before the House Oversight Committee issued their comprehensive impeachment report which said Joe was definitively guilty of influence peddling, they put together an Influence Peddling Timeline for the Bidens, which covers 2014-2017. See: "The Bidens' Influence Peddling

Timeline," Committee On Oversight And Accountability. https://oversight.house.gov/the-bidens-influence-peddling-timeline/. Many articles have been written about the Biden Crime Family practices over the years. This is one of the more comprehensive ones. See: Ben Schreckinger, "Biden Inc.," *Politico*, August 2, 2019. https://www.politico.com/magazine/story/2019/08/02/joe-biden-investigation-hunter-brother-hedge-fund-money-2020-campaign-227407/

555 "Influence peddling," Wikipedia. https://en.wikipedia.org/wiki/Influence_peddling#:~:text=Influence%20peddling%20per%20se%20is,corruption%20and%20may%20therefore%20delegitimise

556 Joseph N. Distefano, "Joe Biden's Friends and Backers Come Out on Top—at the Expense of the Middle Class," *The Nation*, November 7, 2019. https://www.thenation.com/article/archive/biden-delaware-way-graft/

557 That associate was Jeff Cooper, who was involved in Hunter's Mexico deal with Carlos Slim and Paradigm. Here's more on Cooper and the Bidens: "[F]rom 2012 to 2014, Hunter listed himself as a manager of Eudora Global, an investment firm that lawyer Jeffrey Cooper set up in Edwardsville [IL].... Jeffrey Cooper first connected his name to the family of Vice President Joe Biden on public record in 2005...through Joe's late son Beau. The asbestos firm that Cooper and John Simmons led, Simmons Cooper, began filing suits in Delaware in association with Beau's firm. At the time, Joe Biden served as U.S. Senator in Delaware. Biden, in his position on the Senate judiciary committee, blocked reform of asbestos litigation. In 2008, the *Los Angeles Times* reported that Simmons Cooper employees had donated about $200,000 to Joe Biden's campaigns since 2001.... [Cooper] created Eudora Global as a limited liability company in 2008.... Hunter Biden appeared as a manager on Eudora Global's annual reports for 2012, 2013, and 2014." Steve Korris, "Hunter Biden was manager of Edwardsville-based investment firm," *Madison-St. Clair Record*, October 19, 2020. https://madisonrecord.com/stories/558121641-hunter-biden-was-manager-of-edwardsville-based-investment-firm

558 Michael Kranish, "James Biden's dealmaking caught on FBI tapes in unrelated bribery probe," *Washington Post*, December 17, 2023. https://www.washingtonpost.com/politics/2023/12/17/james-bidens-dealmaking-caught-fbi-tapes-unrelated-bribery-probe/

559 Byron York, "The Senator From MBNA (From Our January 1998 Issue)," *The American Spectator*, September 4, 2015. https://spectator.org/63981_senator-mbna-our-january-1998-issue/

560 Caitlin Yilek, "Sen. Bob Menendez convicted in bribery trial; New Jersey Democrat found guilty of accepting gold bars and

cash," CBS News, July 16, 2024. https://www.cbsnews.com/news /bob-menendez-trial-bribery-verdict/

561 Mark Prussin et al., "New Jersey Sen. Bob Menendez set to resign on Aug. 20 after being convicted on federal bribery charges," CBS News, July 23, 2024. https://www.cbsnews.com/newyork/news/sen-bob-menendez-resigns -guilty-federal-bribery-charges/#:~:text=Menendez%20was%20 convicted%20on%2016,said%20he%20plans%20to%20appeal.

562 Jonathan Turley, "The Basis for the Impeachment Inquiry of President Joseph R. Biden" United States House of Representatives Committee on Oversight and Accountability, September 28, 2023. https://oversight .house.gov/wp-content/uploads/2023/09/Turley.Testimony.Biden -Inquiry.pdf

563 United States v. Kemp, 500 F.3d 257, 285 (3d Cir. 2007) ("providing a loan to a public official (or his friends or family) that would have otherwise been unavailable...may constitute a bribe"). "United States v. Kemp, 500 F.3d 257 (3rd Cir. 2007)," Court Listener. https:// www.courtlistener.com/opinion/1193559/united-states-v-kemp/? See also: Hope for Families & Cmty. Serv. Inc. v. Warren, 2009 U.S. Dist. LEXIS 5253 (M.D. Ala. 2009) n. 18 ("The parties do not dispute the general proposition that bribes involving benefits to family members or friends can provide the predicate for a criminal bribery conviction.") "Hope for Families & Cmty. Serv., Inc. v. Warren," Casetext. https:// casetext.com/case/hope-for-families-community-service-v-warren-4

564 United States v. Krilich, 159 F.3d 1020, 1024 (7th Cir. 1998). "U.S. v. Krilich," Casetext. https://casetext.com/case/us-v-krilich-2

565 Buchanan County v. Blankenship, 496 F. Supp. 2d 715, 722 (W.D. Va. 2007). "Buchanan County, Virginia v. Blankenship," Casetext. https://casetext.com/case/buchanan-county-3

566 The Impeachment of G. Thomas Porteous, House Report, March 4, 2010, https://www.govinfo.gov/content/pkg/CRPT-111hrpt427/html /CRPT-111hrpt427.htm.

567 Jonathan Turley, "The Basis for the Impeachment Inquiry of President Joseph R. Biden" United States House of Representatives Committee on Oversight and Accountability, September 28, 2023. https://oversight .house.gov/wp-content/uploads/2023/09/Turley.Testimony.Biden -Inquiry.pdf

568 Jonathan Turley, "The grifter defense: The Bidens move to embrace influence peddling with a twist," The Hill, December 21, 2023. https:// thehill.com/opinion/white-house/4369903-the-grifter-defense-the -bidens-move-to-embrace-influence-peddling-with-a-twist/

569 "EU legislation on anti-corruption," European Commission. https:// home-affairs.ec.europa.eu/policies/internal-security/corruption/eu -legislation-anti-corruption_en

570 Sarah Chayes, "Not Illegal, but Clearly Wrong," *The Atlantic*, August 23, 2023. https://www.theatlantic.com/ideas/archive/2023/08/hunter -biden-Burisma-ukraine/675081/

571 "Foreign Agents Registration Act Home, Frequently Asked Questions." U.S. Department of Justice. https://www.justice.gov/nsd-fara/frequently -asked-questions

572 Joseph Simonson and Jerry Dunleavy, "Hunter Biden aimed to avoid violating Foreign Corrupt Practices Act in pursuit of Chinese business deal," *Washington Examiner*, October 27, 2020. https://www .washingtonexaminer.com/news/1519133/hunter-biden-aimed-to -avoid-violating-foreign-corrupt-practices-act-in-pursuit-of-chinese -business-deal/

573 Steven Nelson, "Hunter Biden once again dodges foreign agent charge in new indictment," *New York Post*, December 8, 2023. https://nypost.com/2023/12/08/news/hunter-biden-again-dodges -foreign-agent-charge-in-indictment/

574 "WATCH: The Biden Impeachment Hearings – Day 1," PBS. September 28, 2023. https://www.pbs.org/newshour/politics/watch-live-the-biden -impeachment-hearings-day-1

575 Ankush Khardori, "The Hunter Biden Case Is Solid. There's Something Rotten About It Too," *Politico*, June 7, 2024. https:// www.politico.com/news/magazine/2024/06/07/hunter-biden-trial -truths-column-00162083

576 Ben Schreckinger, "Law firm registers as foreign agent for Hunter Biden-linked company 8 years later," *Politico*. January 8, 2024. https:// www.politico.com/news/2024/01/08/cravath-hunter-biden-foreign -agents-00134307

577 Steven Nelson, "Hunter Biden once again dodges foreign agent charge in new indictment," *New York Post*, December 8, 2023. https://nypost.com/2023/12/08/news/hunter-biden-again-dodges -foreign-agent-charge-in-indictment/

578 "Paul Manafort," Wikipedia. https://en.wikipedia.org/wiki/Paul _Manafort

579 "Joe Biden classified documents incident," Wikipedia.

580 Joe Schoffstall and Cameron Cawthorne, "UPenn, which hosts Biden's think tank, sees Chinese donations soar, including from CCP-linked sources," Fox News, January 18, 2024. https://www.foxnews.com /politics/university-housing-bidens-think-tank-recently-experienced-a -surge-of-chinese-donations-records-show

581 Gabe Kaminsky, "Biden classified documents: UPenn took cash from China donors tied to Hunter Biden deals and Beijing," *Washington Examiner,* May 16, 2023. https://www.washingtonexaminer.com /news/1937178/biden-classified-documents-upenn-took-cash-from -china-donors-tied-to-hunter-biden-deals-and-beijing/

582 Mariah Espada, "President Biden, His Corvette, and the Latest Stash of Classified Documents," *Time,* January 12, 2023. https:// time.com/6246994/biden-classified-documents-delaware-corvette/. See also: Kaelan Deese, "Photos show Biden's classified records in 'mangled' box in his garage," *Washington Examiner,* February 8, 2024. https://www.washingtonexaminer.com/news/2845741/mangled-box -in-biden-garage-held-classified-documents/

583 Robert K. Hur, "Report on the Investigation Into Unauthorized Removal, Retention, and Disclosure of Classified Documents Discovered at Locations Including the Penn Biden Center and the Delaware Private Residence of President Joseph R. Biden, Jr.," U.S. Department of Justice, February, 2024. https://www.justice.gov/storage /report-from-special-counsel-robert-k-hur-february-2024.pdf Biden's documents fall into that classification.

584 "Chapter 37—Espionage and Censorship, §793. Gathering, transmitting or losing defense information (e)," Title 18, Crimes and Criminal Procedure, Gov.info. https://www.govinfo.gov/content/pkg /USCODE-2009-title18/pdf/USCODE-2009-title18-partI-chap37 -sec793.pdf

585 "President Biden on the FBI's search of Mar-a-Lago," "60 Minutes," CBS. September 18, 2022. https://www.youtube.com/watch?v=-Cjzg WJZmtY

586 Glenn Thrush et al, "Garland Appoints Special Counsel to Investigate Handling of Biden Documents," *New York Times,* January 12, 2023. https://www.nytimes.com/2023/01/12/us/politics/biden-documents .html

587 Katherine Faulders et al, "Timeline: Special counsel's investigation into Trump's handling of classified documents," ABC News, August 27, 2024. https://abcnews.go.com/US/timeline-special-counsels-investigation -trumps-handling-classified-documents/story?id=101768329. Trump was charged with violating the same section of the Espionage Act as Biden. See: Quinn Owen, "Trump faces 31 charges under the Espionage Act: The law regulating government secrets explained," ABC News, June 16, 2023. https://abcnews.go.com /Politics/trump-faces-31-charges-espionage-act-law-regulating/story ?id=100129183. Prosecutors ignored Trump's argument that, under the Presidential Records Act, he was allowed to retain his

personal records, which were mixed among the dozens of boxes seized in the Mar-a-Lago raid and had yet to be separated from any official documents. Stefan Becket, Melissa Quinn, "What does the Presidential Records Act say, and how does it apply to Trump?" CBS News, June 13, 2023. https://www.cbsnews.com/news/trump -presidential-records-act-indictment-arraignment/

588 Michelle Shen and Maureen Chowdhury, "Judge dismisses Trump classified documents case," CNN, July 15, 2024. https://www.cnn .com/politics/live-news/trump-classified-documents-case-dismissed -07-15-24/index.html

589 Mat Matza, "Special counsel appeals to resume Trump documents case," BBC News, August 26, 2024. https://www.bbc.com/news /articles/cdd75g4yrpdo

590 Robert K. Hur, "Report on the Investigation Into Unauthorized Removal, Retention, and Disclosure of Classified Documents Discovered at Locations Including the Penn Biden Center and the Delaware Private Residence of President Joseph R. Biden, Jr.," U.S. Department of Justice, February, 2024. https://www.justice.gov/storage /report-from-special-counsel-robert-k-hur-february-2024.pdf

591 Ibid.

592 "Mens rea," Legal Information Institute, Cornell Law School. https:// www.law.cornell.edu/wex/mens_rea

593 Robert K. Hur, "Report on the Investigation Into Unauthorized Removal, Retention, and Disclosure of Classified Documents Discovered at Locations Including the Penn Biden Center and the Delaware Private Residence of President Joseph R. Biden, Jr.," U.S. Department of Justice, February, 2024. https://www.justice.gov/storage /report-from-special-counsel-robert-k-hur-february-2024.pdf

594 Hur testified before the House Judiciary Committee on March 12, 2024 and explicitly stated that he "did not exonerate" Biden, and that he did find Biden "risked serious damage to America's national security." See: Ashley Oliver, "Hur corrects House Democrat: 'I did not exonerate' Joe Biden," *Washington Examiner*, March 12, 2024. https://www.washingtonexaminer.com/news/2916808/hur-corrects -house-democrat-i-did-not-exonerate-joe-biden/ and "Hearing on the Report of Special Counsel Robert K. Hur," House Judiciary GOP, March 12, 2024. https://www.youtube.com/watch?v=iVdN9e6Po24

595 Ben Schreckinger, "Biden Inc.," *Politico*, August 02, 2019. https://www .politico.com/magazine/story/2019/08/02/joe-biden-investigation -hunter-brother-hedge-fund-money-2020-campaign-227407/

596 Charles Lipson, "Biden Inc.: Hunter, Joe, and the Mexican Oligarchs," *RealClearPolitics*, July 7, 2021. https://www.realclearpolitics.com/articles

/2021/07/07/biden_inc_hunter_joe_and_the_mexican_oligarchs
_146043.html

597 "What Is A 'Pattern of Racketeering Activity (PORA)'?" Federal Criminal Practice Group of Price Benowitz LLP. https://whitecollarattorney .net/rico/pattern-racketeering-activity-pora/

598 "Racketeering" definition. Merriam-Webster. https://www.merriam -webster.com/legal/racketeering

599 Christopher Rugaber, "U.S. inflation reached a new 40-year high of 9.1% in June," *LA Times*, July 13, 2022. https://www.latimes.com /business/story/2022-07-13/inflation-june-new-40-year-high

600 Reid J. Epstein et al, "Democrats' Phalanx Around Biden Has an Eric Adams-Size Hole," *New York Times*, May 20, 2023. https://www .nytimes.com/2023/05/20/us/politics/eric-adams-biden-democrats .html

601 "Illegal border crossers total over 10 million since Biden inauguration, *Washington Examiner*, October 30, 2023. https://www .washingtonexaminer.com/news/2455010/illegal-border-crossers-total -over-10-million-since-biden-inauguration/

602 "736 known or suspected terrorists apprehended at U.S. border in fiscal 2023," *Washington Examiner*, October 23, 2023. https://www .washingtonexaminer.com/news/2569957/736-known-or-suspected -terrorists-apprehended-at-u-s-border-in-fiscal-2023/

603 Julia Ainsley and Tom Winter, "DHS identifies over 400 migrants brought to the U.S. by an ISIS-affiliated human smuggling network," NBC News, June 25, 2024. https://www.nbcnews.com/investigations /dhs-identifies-400-migrants-brought-us-isis-linked-human-smuggling -rcna158777

604 Byron York, "The reality of migrant crime," *Washington Examiner*, April 4, 2024. https://www.washingtonexaminer.com/daily-memo /2954997/the-reality-of-migrant-crime/?utm_source=google&utm _medium=cpc&utm_campaign=Pmax_USA_Magazine_21-June -Intent-Audience-Signals&gad_source=1&gbraid=0AAAAAD8dCuyI rnBboKLljEbaGbrIoa4vH&gclid=EAIaIQobChMIuabdqKLQiAMV KkdHAR2J4SmlEAMYASAAEgIRT_D_BwE

605 Ingrid Jacques, "If you like your car, good luck keeping it. Biden's EV mandate drives change people don't want," *USA Today*, April 7, 2024. https://www.usatoday.com/story/opinion/columnist/2024/04/07 /biden-electric-vehicle-mandate-epa-rule-climate-change/73189 241007/

606 Kelly Phillips Erb, "IRS Is Hiring Thousands Of New Workers To Ramp Up Focus On Millionaires And Large Corporations," *Forbes*, September 18, 2023. https://www.forbes.com/sites/kellyphillipserb

/2023/09/18/irs-is-hiring-thousands-of-new-workers-to-ramp-up
-focus-on-millionaires-and-large-corporations/

607 Steven Lee Myers, "Appeals Court Rules White House Overstepped 1st Amendment on Social Media," *New York Times*, September 8, 2023. https://www.nytimes.com/2023/09/08/business/appeals-court -first-amendment-social-media.html

608 Gerard Edic, "Why Is the Biden Administration Completing So Many Regulations?" *The American Prospect*, April 23, 2024. https:// prospect.org/politics/2024-04-23-biden-administration-regulations -congressional-review-act/

609 Alexander Mallin, "3 years later, Jan. 6 by the numbers: More than 1,200 charged, more than 460 imprisoned for role in Capitol attack," ABC News, January 5, 2024. https://abcnews.go.com/Politics /3-years-jan-6-numbers-1200-charged-460/story?id=106140326

610 John Fritze et al, "Supreme Court limits obstruction charges against January 6 rioters," CNN, June 28, 2024. https://www.cnn .com/2024/06/28/politics/supreme-court-limits-obstruction-charges -against-january-6-rioters/index.html

611 "RFK Jr. says Biden is bigger threat to democracy than Trump," CNN, April 1, 2024. https://www.youtube.com/watch?v=KAgQ2sfAjV0

612 Charlie Savage, "Justice Dept. Says It Won't Prosecute Garland for Contempt," *New York Times*, June 14, 2024. https://www.nytimes.com /2024/06/14/us/politics/merrick-garland-contempt-doj.html

613 Meme Defense Fund. https://www.memedefensefund.com

614 "Douglass Mackey," Wikipedia. https://en.wikipedia.org/wiki/Douglass _Mackey

615 Joe Bukuras, "Another Elderly Pro-Life Activist Sentenced to Two Years in Prison," *National Catholic Register*, May 31, 2024. https:// www.ncregister.com/cna/another-elderly-pro-life-activist-sentenced-to -two-years-in-prison

616 Dylan Stableford and Ed Hornick, "Trump criminal charges guidebook: Here are all the felony counts against the former president," Yahoo News, August 27, 2024. https://www.yahoo.com/news/trump-cases -georgia-washington-florida-nyc-charges-key-dates-213951743.html

617 Michael Sisak, "Trump Investigations," Associated Press, September 7, 2024. https://apnews.com/projects/trump-investigations-civil-criminal -tracker/

618 Shayna Jacobs, "Trump owes more than $440 million in fines, damages from civil trials," *Washington Post*, February 1, 2024. https:// www.washingtonpost.com/national-security/2024/02/01/trump -fines-damages-trials/

619 Germania Rodriguez Poleo, "Jill Biden's ex-husband - who claims she cheated on him with Joe - slams 'Biden crime family' for targeting Trump despite Hunter's 'tax crimes' and brands President 'dangerous'," *Daily Mail*, July 27, 2023. https://www.dailymail.co.uk /news/article-12344539/Jill-biden-ex-husband-Bill-Stevenson-Trump .html

620 Katherine Fung, "Hunter Biden's 'Sweetheart' Plea Deal Falls Apart During Hearing," *Newsweek*, July 26, 2023. https://www.newsweek .com/hunter-bidens-sweetheart-plea-deal-falls-apart-during-hearing -1815507

621 Michael Kranish, "Before investigating Hunter Biden, prosecutor worked with brother Beau," *Washington Post*, August 20, 2023. https://www.washingtonpost.com/politics/2023/08/20/hunter-biden -david-weiss-special-prosecutor-delaware/

622 Michael S. Schmidt et al, "Inside the Collapse of Hunter Biden's Plea Deal," *New York Times*, August 19, 2023. https://www.nytimes .com/2023/08/19/us/politics/inside-hunter-biden-plea-deal.html

623 Michael Goodwin, "The media mob's free pass for the Bidens at any sign of scrutiny is no accident – they're all in on it," *New York Post*, March 23, 2024. https://nypost.com/2024/03/23/opinion/when-there-is-scrutiny -among-the-bidens-the-media-gives-them-a-pass/

624 Ibid.

625 Ibid.

626 Susan Shelley, "FBI suppression of the Hunter Biden laptop story," *Los Angeles Daily News*, December 25, 2022. https://www.dailynews .com/2022/12/25/fbi-suppression-of-the-hunter-biden-laptop/

627 Said by, ironically, Vladimir Lenin. "Vladimir Lenin, Quotes," Goodreads. https://www.goodreads.com/quotes/342783-there-are-decades-where -nothing-happens-and-there-are-weeks

628 Emily Crane, "Awkward moment Jill Biden appears to tell Joe not to sit at D-Day ceremony, but he does anyway," *New York Post*, June 6, 2024. https:// nypost.com/2024/06/06/us-news/biden-awkwardly-fumbles-for -seat-during-d-day-ceremony-while-everyone-else-stands/

629 John Christenson, "Biden's condition shocks allies at G7 summit, with one saying it's 'worst he has ever been': report," *New York Post*, June 14, 2024. https://nypost.com/2024/06/14/us-news/bidens-condition -shocks-allies-at-g7-summit-with-one-saying-its-worst-he-has-ever -been-report/

630 "US: President Biden appeared to freeze during Juneteenth celebrations at the White House, and began slurring his words when speaking to the crowd," Sky News, June 11, 2024. https://news.sky.com /video/us-president-biden-appeared-to-freeze-during-juneteenth

-celebrations-at-the-white-house-and-began-slurring-his-words-when
-speaking-to-the-crowd-13151254

631 Conrad Hoyt, "Motionless Biden led offstage by Obama after
    star-studded fundraiser," *Washington Examiner*, June 16, 2024.
    https://www.washingtonexaminer.com/news/campaigns/3047009
    /motionless-biden-led-offstage-by-obama-after-star-studded-fundraiser/

632 Naomi Lim, "White House rips unflattering Biden videos as
    'cheap fakes'," *Washington Examiner*, June 17, 2024. https://www
    .washingtonexaminer.com/news/campaigns/presidential/3048814
    /white-house-rips-unflattering-biden-videos-cheap-fakes/

633 Hadas Gold, "51 million viewers tuned in to CNN's presidential
    debate with Biden and Trump," CNN, June 28, 2024. https://www
    .cnn.com/2024/06/28/media/ratings-debate-trump-biden-cnn/index
    .html

634 Special Counsel Robert K. Hur, "Report on the Investigation Into
    Unauthorized Removal, Retention, and Disclosure of Classified
    Documents Discovered at Locations Including the Penn Biden Center
    and the Delaware Private Residence of President Joseph R. Biden, Jr."
    US Department of Justice, February, 2024. https://www.justice.gov
    /storage/report-from-special-counsel-robert-k-hur-february-2024.pdf

635 Dylan Wells, "Biden offers muddled response on abortion, pivots
    to immigration," *Washington Post*, June 28, 2024. https://www
    .washingtonpost.com/politics/2024/06/28/abortion-presidential
    -debate-trump-biden/

636 "READ: Biden-Trump debate transcript," CNN, June 28, 2024.
    https://www.cnn.com/2024/06/27/politics/read-biden-trump-debate
    -rush-transcript/index.html

637 David Bauder, "How did CNN's moderators do in the Biden-Trump
    debate? It almost didn't matter that they were there," Associated Press,
    June 28, 2024. https://apnews.com/article/cnn-debate-biden-trump
    -tapper-bash-ccff5a67e0dfbbb650b78a087ce268e6

638 Tyler Stone, "Claire McCaskill: Biden Failed At Reassuring America
    At Debate, 'We Are Confronting A Crisis'," *RealClearPolitics*, June
    28, 2024. https://www.realclearpolitics.com/video/2024/06/28/claire
    _mccaskill_biden_failed_at_reassuring_america_at_debate_we_are
    _confronting_a_crisis.html

639 Hadas Gold, "On MSNBC, the mood turns somber following
    Biden's debate performance, CNN, June 28, 2024. https://www.cnn
    .com/2024/06/28/media/msnbc-biden-trump-debate/index.html

640 Alex Griffing, "'You Answered Every Question!' Critics Brutally Roast
    Jill Biden For Praising Husband's Debate Performance," *Mediaite*,
    June 28, 2024. https://www.mediaite.com/politics/you-answered

-every-question-critics-brutally-roast-jill-biden-for-praising-husbands
-debate-performance/

641 See: Editorial Board, "To Serve His Country, President Biden Should
Leave the Race," *New York Times,* June 28, 2024. https://www.nytimes
.com/2024/06/28/opinion/biden-election-debate-trump.html;
Thomas L. Friedman, "Joe Biden Is a Good Man and a Good President. He
Must Bow Out of the Race," *New York Times,* June 28, 2024. https://www
.nytimes.com/2024/06/28/opinion/joe-biden-tom-friedman.html;
and Frank Bruni, "Biden Cannot Go On Like This," *New York
Times*, June 28, 2024. https://www.nytimes.com/2024/06/28/opinion
/presidential-debate-trump-biden-2024.html. One columnist didn't
even wait til the next day to express his opinion. See: Nicholas Kristof,
"President Biden, I've Seen Enough," *New York Times*, June 27, 2024.
https://www.nytimes.com/2024/06/25/opinion/joe-biden-drop-out.html

642 Michelle Stoddart and Ivan Pereira, "Biden addresses poor debate performance,
attacks Trump at Raleigh rally," ABC News, June 28, 2024. https://
abcnews.go.com/Politics/biden-hold-campaign-rally-north-carolina
-hours-after/story?id=111515800

643 Thomas L. Friedman, "Joe Biden Is a Good Man and a Good
President. He Must Bow Out of the Race," *New York Times*, June 28,
2024. https://www.nytimes.com/2024/06/28/opinion/joe-biden-tom
-friedman.html

644 Michael D. Shear and Maya King, "'I Know I'm Not a Young Man':
Biden Confronts Doubts During Forceful Rally," *New York Times*, June
28, 2024. https://www.nytimes.com/2024/06/28/us/politics/biden-rally
-debate.html

645 "Barack Obama, @ BarackObama," X, June 28, 2024. https://twitter
.com/BarackObama/status/1806758633230709017

646 Kevin Dolak, "Newsom Throws Support Behind Biden Amid Calls for
California Governor to Replace President," *Hollywood Reporter,* June 28,
2024. https://www.hollywoodreporter.com/news/politics-news/gavin
-newsom-supports-joe-biden-replacement-2024-1235935152/

647 Marina Watts, "Joe Biden Plans to Stay in the Race and Remains Committed
to Second Presidential Debate in September: Report," *People*, June 28,
2024. https://people.com/joe-biden-staying-in-race-committed-second
-presidential-debate-report-8671073#:~:text=President%20Joe%20
Biden%20does%20not,Donald%20Trump%20again%20in%20
September.

648 "ABC's George Stephanopoulos' exclusive interview with President
Biden: Full transcript," ABC News, July 5, 2024. https://abcnews.go
.com/Politics/abc-news-anchor-george-stephanopoulos-exclusive
-interview-biden/story?id=111695695

649 Ibid.

650 Barkley figures he lost about $30 million during his gambling career. Melanie Porter, "Gamblers Who Lost It All – The Biggest Losses in History," *Gambling News*, August 18, 2020. https://www.gamblingnews.com/blog/gamblers-who-lost-it-all/

651 Sudiksha Kochi, "WURD Radio parts ways with host who interviewed Biden using questions provided by his team," *USA Today*, July 8, 2024. https://www.usatoday.com/story/news/politics/elections/2024/07/08/radio-host-resigns-wurd-questions-biden-team/74326871007/

652 Meg Kinnard, "The Biden campaign drafted questions for the president's interviews on a pair of Black radio shows," Associated Press, July 7, 2024. https://apnews.com/article/biden-black-radio-questions-approval-ff92ebeff33df7ef5a87a59f776c981c

653 Miles J. Herszenhorn, "Biden introduced Zelenskyy. It didn't go well: 'Ladies and gentlemen, President Putin'," *Politico*, July 11, 2024. https://www.politico.com/news/2024/07/11/biden-flub-nato-zelenskyy-putin-00167705

654 "Biden misidentifies Vice President Kamala Harris as Trump," Reuters, July 11, 2024. https://www.reuters.com/world/us/biden-misidentifies-vice-president-kamala-harris-trump-2024-07-11/

655 Sara Dorn, "Donors Withhold $90 Million Promised For Biden In Latest Debate Fallout, Report Says," *Forbes*, July 12, 2024. https://www.forbes.com/sites/saradorn/2024/07/12/donors-withhold-90-million-promised-for-biden-in-latest-debate-fallout-report-says/

656 "In maps: Donald Trump assassination attempt," BBC, July 14, 2024. https://www.bbc.com/news/articles/cevwngjrwzno

657 James LaPorta et al, "Trump rally gunman fired 8 shots in under 6 seconds before he was killed, analysis shows," CBS News, July 25, 2024. https://www.cbsnews.com/news/trump-rally-gunman-fired-eight-shots-under-six-seconds-before-being-killed-by-secret-service-analysis-shows/

658 One of the other shots killed a former firefighter, Corey Comperatore. A retired grandfather, James Copenhaver, and a Marine veteran, David Dutch, were also wounded by Crooks, but survived. Maurice DuBois et al, "Timeline of Trump shooting shows Secret Service was aware of suspicious person 20 minutes before assassination attempt," CBS News, July 18, 2024. https://www.cbsnews.com/news/timeline-trump-rally-shooting/

659 Ibid.

660 Leanne Abraham et al, "A Visual Timeline of the Trump Rally Shooting," *New York Times*, July 14, 2024. https://www.nytimes.com/interactive/2024/07/13/us/trump-rally-shooting-maps-photos.html

661 *New York Times* photographer Doug Mills not only captured the iconic image, but later discovered that he also had a photo of the bullet itself heading towards Trump's head. Ibid.

662 "WATCH: Trump makes emotional entrance at 2024 Republican National Convention," PBS, July 15, 2024. https://www.pbs.org /newshour/politics/watch-former-president-donald-trump-arrives-at -2024-republican-national-convention-2024-rnc-night-1

663 Zolan Kanno-Youngs, "From Buoyant to Frail: Two Days in Las Vegas as Biden Tests Positive," *New York Times*, July 18, 2024. https://www .nytimes.com/2024/07/18/us/politics/biden-covid-democrats.html See also: Alex Gangitano, "Timeline of events leading up to Biden's exit from the race," *The Hill*, July 21, 2024. https://thehill.com/homenews /administration/4784950-timeline-of-events-leading-up-to-bidens -exit-from-the-race/

664 Eli Stokols, "Why Biden finally quit," *Politico*, July 21, 2024. https://www .politico.com/news/2024/07/21/why-biden-dropped-out-00170106

665 Leah Sarnoff, "Read President Joe Biden's full letter announcing he's leaving 2024 race," ABC News, July 21, 2024. https://abcnews.go.com /Politics/read-joe-bidens-full-letter-announcing-leaving-2024-race /story?id=112143543

666 Eli Stokols, "Why Biden finally quit," *Politico*, July 21, 2024. https://www .politico.com/news/2024/07/21/why-biden-dropped-out-00170106

667 As far back as 2012, Ablow claimed that Joe's frequent gaffes were signs of dementia. See: "Fox News' Keith Ablow: Joe Biden Showed Signs Of Dementia At Vice-Presidential Debate," *HuffPost*, October 15, 2012. https://www.huffpost.com/entry/keith-ablow-joe-biden-debate _n_1967272

668 "Report on the Biden Laptop," MarcoPolo501c3.org, page 555. https://bidenreport.com/#p=559. See also: "EXCLUSIVE: Hunter Biden Seemingly Acknowledged Joe Has Dementia in Texts Sent to Psychiatrist," *National File*, November 11, 2021. https://nationalfile.com/exclusive-hunter-biden-seemingly -acknowledged-joe-has-dementia-in-texts-sent-to-psychiatrist/

669 "Report on the Biden Laptop," MarcoPolo501c3.org, page 555. https ://bidenreport.com/#p=559

670 Bojan Pancevski, "One Million Are Now Dead or Injured in the Russia-Ukraine War," *Wall Street Journal*, September 17, 2024. https://www .wsj.com/world/one-million-are-now-dead-or-injured-in-the-russia -ukraine-war-b09d04e5

671 In the wake of Joe's decision to step down, articles about the group surrounding him and how they hid his condition started pouring out. Here are a few. See: Natasha Korecki et al, "'It's Shakespearean':

Long-simmering tensions between Biden's family and aides spill out," NBC News, July 6, 2024. https://www.nbcnews.com/politics/joe -biden/tensions-biden-family-aides-spill-rcna160468; Nancy Cordes, "Biden's brother says president's health played role in decision to end campaign," CBS News, July 21, 2024. https://www.cbsnews.com /video/bidens-brother-on-decision-to-drop-out/; and David Leonhardt and Ian Prasad Philbrick, "Presidential Medical Secrets," *New York Times*, July 11, 2024. https://www.nytimes.com/2024/07/11/briefing /president-biden-age-election.html;

672 Here's a selection of some Biden defenders' declarations: Alexandra Marquez, "Biden allies say president is 'sharp,' special counsel criticism is 'B.S.'," NBC News, February 11, 2024. https://www.nbcnews.com /politics/white-house/mayorkas-defends-biden-sharp-intensely -probing-detail-oriented-rcna138192; Charisma Madarang, "White House on Biden Mental Acuity After Debate Flop: 'He's as Sharp as Ever'," *Rolling Stone*, July 3, 2024. https://www.rollingstone.com /politics/politics-news/biden-white-house-mental-acuity-cognitive-test -1235053064/; Asher Notheis, "Kirby insists 'robust' Biden is 'the president that I see every day'," *Washington Examiner*, July 9, 2024. https://www.washingtonexaminer.com/news/white-house/3074289 /kirby-insists-robust-biden-president-see-every-day/; and Colleen Long et al, "Biden at 81: Often sharp and focused but sometimes confused and forgetful, observers say," *LA Times*, July 4, 2024. https://www .latimes.com/world-nation/story/2024-07-04/biden-at-81-often-sharp -and-focused-but-sometimes-confused-and-forgetful

673 Tamar Lapin, "VP Harris says she was last person in the room before Biden's withdrawal decision," *New York Post*, April 25, 2021.

674 Transcript of CNN Exclusive Interview With Harris & Walz, August 29, 2024. https://transcripts.cnn.com/show/se/date/2024-08-29/segment /01

675 *Boston Herald* opinion columnist Howie Carr summed it up well. See: Howie Carr, "The truth about Biden comes out yet again," *Boston Herald*, June 29, 2024. https://www.bostonherald.com/2024 /06/29/howie-carr-the-truth-about-biden-comes-out-yet-again/. See also: Reagan Reese, "White House Aides Reportedly Confirm Biden Exhibits Classic Dementia Symptom," *Daily Caller*, June 29, 2024. https://dailycaller.com/2024/06/29/white-house-aides-biden -dementia-symptom-debate/

676 In addition to Hunter Biden, in August, 2019, Fox News' Britt Hume said that Biden was showing "the kind of memory loss associated with senility." "Brit Hume, @ brithume," X, August 24, 2024. https://x .com/brithume/status/1165388395629207553